CONVENIENCE

HOW FAR WILL WE GO FOR THE SAKE OF CONVENIENCE?

A LEC M ARCHI

CLAY BRIDGES
P R E S S

Convenience: How Far Will We Go For The Sake Of Convenience?

Copyright © 2023 by Alec Marchi

Published by Clay Bridges Press in Houston, TX
www.ClayBridgesPress.com

All rights reserved. No part of this publication may be reproduced, stored in a retrieval system, or transmitted in any form by any means, electronic, mechanical, photocopy, recording, or otherwise, without the prior permission of the publisher, except as provided for by USA copyright law.

ISBN: 978-1-68488-073-7 Paperback
eISBN: 978-1-68488-074-4

Special Sales: Most Clay Bridges titles are available in special quantity discounts. Custom imprinting or excerpting can also be done to fit special needs. Contact Clay Bridges at Info@ClayBridgesPress.com

For God. And for the well over 60 million unborn Americans who should be here with us today. I can only imagine the doctors, scientists, inventors, leaders, athletes, preachers . . . heroes we lost in those 60 million people.

For the two women who, in one of the most difficult times in their lives, decided to have their babies, which God predestined to be one of our sons and one of our daughters—who have blossomed into wonderful adults.

And for the "B Team" (which is really the "A Team"). I'm so proud of you all.

Chapter One

There they were. Four tall cottonwood trees still welcoming visitors to our old block. There were two on each side of the street, towering over houses and power lines. In the spring, those trees would produce so many white cottony seedlings that it looked like a light dusting of snow had covered the yards surrounding them.

After twelve years, the old neighborhood looked surprisingly similar. I guess things don't change as quickly in a small town in Montana as they do in the constantly expanding suburban neighborhood in Atlanta, where we had lived for the last eight years.

So many memories rushed past my mind's eye as we drove through Franklin. I connected places with specific memories as we passed. And I pictured people's faces as we drove by the old homes. They evoked distinct feelings of fear, anger, love, and childhood carelessness.

As we passed through the cottonwood gateway and into my old block, more thoughts scurried by. Back in days long past, this had been a very close-knit neighborhood, and I'd been in every house on both sides of the block for one reason or another. I remembered the layouts of some of those houses and even some of the smells—like the little gray house where old Mrs. Madison lived. When my childhood friends and I knocked on her door, she would give us a smile and a greeting as though she'd been expecting us.

Her house had a musty sort of smell, probably from the dusty overcrowding of trinkets on all the shelves and the old carpet in the living room. But the musty smell was always overtaken as we approached the kitchen, where the aroma of fresh-baked chocolate chip cookies flooded our senses. We would sit and say very little while we enjoyed several cookies as Mrs. Madison watched with satisfaction.

    She paid as little attention to the conversation as we did. Just having kids around seemed to make her day. Judging by the black and white photos on the cluttered shelf, she had four children and a handsome husband. I didn't know anything about her family except that they weren't with her, and I never remember them visiting. She passed away about a year after I left for college. I couldn't make it back for her funeral.

    As we approached my parents' house, I expected Mom to run out as she usually does, screaming with joy as she reached to hold my daughter. I was focused on the front door, waiting for Mom to run out, when suddenly, out of the corner of my eye, I saw a figure appear in front of my car! I hit the brakes almost by instinct, jolting my wife and daughter against their seatbelts. Sticking my head out the window, I braced myself to pounce on someone for their poor judgment in stepping out in front of my moving vehicle, but two things stopped me. First, I knew that I was probably at fault for not watching the road. More importantly, though, was the fact that I recognized the woman standing in front of the car.

    It was Lynn Bower, a childhood friend. Well, actually, Jim and John Bower, Lynn's younger twin brothers, and I were close friends when I was a kid. We had great times playing ball with the rest of the neighbor kids. We'd spend endless hours playing every sport we could think of and running around the neighborhood. I always felt a bit sorry for the Bower kids, though. Both their parents were alcoholics and abusive. I remember the terror on their faces after we had played all day when they realized they had to go home and face their parents. I remember Jim telling me once that his parents often beat them for no apparent reason. Lynn seemed to try to protect them all, especially when they were younger. Both their parents drank themselves into an early grave and left the kids just as the boys were graduating from high school.

Convenience

Anyway, the twin's older sister, whom I had not seen for over ten years, now stood in front of my car with a furious look on her face. Then Lynn recognized who I was, and a smile came over her face as though she had returned to an earlier, simpler time in life. She came around to my open car window.

"Levi . . . Levi Bell, is that you?"

"It sure is," I said with a smile.

"And Emma" . . . she stopped to try to remember Emma's maiden name. My wife chimed in quickly to help her.

"Williams, but it's been Bell now for six years. And this is our daughter, Katie." Katie mustered a low-volume "Hi" and a polite smile. It seemed like Lynn's thoughts were interrupted for a moment. She gazed at Katie.

Regaining her thoughts, Lynn asked, "What brings you back here to the thriving metropolis of Franklin?"

"Well, it's kind of a long story, but I'll give you the nickel version. After I finished college in Georgia, I got a job as a maintenance manager for Delta Airlines in Atlanta. After I got settled into my job, Emma and I got married and bought a house outside of the city. We had Katie a year later.

"Things were going pretty well. I'd worked my way up to director of flight line operations for the evening shift; then there was the accident. One night I decided to go out on the ramp and get to know some of the new folks servicing some of our jets. Well, one of my tow teams was set up to tow a seven-five-seven into a new spot. As the driver of the tow truck backed up to the jet to connect with the tow bar, for some reason, the throttle stuck wide open while the truck was in reverse."

I am not sure why I plowed headlong into my somewhat personal story, but I guess I felt like I knew Lynn well enough as a friend. I continued, "I remember the look of fright on the driver's face as the truck lunged backward. He tried to swerve out of the way of the aircraft and the tow team. Unfortunately, a young guy who was sitting on the tow bar, waiting to connect the truck, couldn't get out of the way in time. As the truck veered past, its back tires ran over the back of my legs as I tried to get out of the way. I wish I could say that I was the least fortunate person involved. As the truck swerved past, it rolled over and pinned the young man down.

"That young man died before the ambulance arrived. Later, I remembered I had never even met him before the accident. It took me a full year and six surgeries to recover physically. I'm not sure if I've recovered emotionally yet. My right leg couldn't be saved, and I have an artificial one from the knee down. It's amazing how this leg works. I don't even have a limp. Of course, I'm not sure how it will work out when it's fifty below zero this winter. Anyway, after the accident, I didn't feel I could do the same job, at least not for a while. I just wanted to get away from those memories. I had some disability money and a little from the accident settlement, so Emma and Katie, and I decided to move back to Franklin. I'm going to teach history at the high school and might do a little coaching. Enough about me. How about you and your family?"

"Well, it's a lot less exciting than where you've been. After high school, I moved over to Deer Lake, up north by the Canadian border. I got a job as a receptionist at a clinic, and for nearly ten years, that was pretty much my life. I never married. I came close a few times but never quite made it to the altar. A few years back, I decided to do something with my life, so I started going to school here in town, and I had just finished an accounting degree. And in fact, I just landed a job at Mason and Associates. And guess what, I'm buying old lady Madison's house right here in the old neighborhood!"

Suddenly, her excited face gave way to a more concerned look. "Oh yeah, there is one other thing: I'm three months pregnant. Talk about bad timing. I'm finally just getting my life together, and this has to happen."

I didn't know how to respond. There was an uncomfortable silence for a moment.

"Well, anyway, my brothers moved away as quickly as they could. Jim is married and lives in Billings. John owns a motorcycle shop near Portland. He's doing OK . . . other than the fact that he's covered in tattoos!" We all chuckled a bit. "I'll give you their phone numbers some time. I should probably quit standing in the middle of the road and get going."

Convenience

As Lynn walked away from the car, she still had that concerned look on her face. She turned toward us once more and forced a smile, more aimed at Katie than Emma or me.

"I'll see you guys around," she said as she walked away.

Now I was only a few houses away from Mom and Dad's, and still, there was no Mom running out to greet us. As I approached the house, there was no room to park in front. I was so excited to get in that I decided to park, facing the wrong way, on the left side of the road.

Emma looked at me. "Are you going to leave the car parked like this?"

"I think it'll be OK for a minute or two, Emma; I'll come back and fix it later. Where else am I going to park? Besides, it's just more convenient right now. It'll be all right, honey."

As we stopped, Dad came out to greet us. "Hi, Dad. Where's Mom?" My dad, Alexander, is a pretty reserved, quiet man. He came to the United States from Ukraine about forty years ago after marrying my mom, who was from Italy. They met after World War II when my dad, who served in the British Army, ended up in Italy at the end of the war. After they got married, they moved to my dad's home country, Ukraine, which was a republic of the Soviet Union at the time. They lived there for several years before finally making their way to the US.

Dad still has a pretty heavy accent. Mom and Dad went through some hard years in Ukraine. Since he had fought for England in the war, and since they were on the winning side, he thought things would be much better in Ukraine than in earlier years. He thought he and my mom would go to Ukraine and have a great life together there. But as soon as he arrived, he realized that the Soviet-led communist party in power in Ukraine would rule him, his family, and everyone else with an iron fist. He told me that the communist government had a saying, "What's yours is mine, and what's mine is yours." Dad said the locals changed it to a more accurate statement, "What's yours is mine, and what's mine, you don't touch!"

The communist leadership in Ukraine told him that he shouldn't have fought for capitalist England—a harsh scolding for a man who fought on the same side as the Soviets and was a recipient of numerous medals for his efforts in several pivotal battles in North Africa and Italy—not to mention earning a purple heart for being severely wounded. The local governing body in Ukraine gave him a job in a thread factory and told him that unless he joined "the party," he would never progress beyond the factory job.

My mother grew up in a well-to-do family in Italy. She had a unique character. She was a refined lady, gentle and meek, yet determined and almost super-human at times—a survivor. Even after years of struggles, her face retained its softness. She lived through nine years of near starvation, battling dark, cold winters in Ukraine. During that time, she had my two sisters and her first son, Joseph. Joseph was born with a malformed digestive system. He required a special liquid diet and a lot of medical expertise—more than what was available to the common person in a communist country. Mom took it upon herself to try to prepare his meals out of the very minimal amount of food the whole family had each day. When Joe was about five, the government hospital required that he be checked into a room for "observation" for a period of time. Mom watched Joe grow weaker and weaker. They seemed to be starving him to death. Mom took this for about a month, then she barged into the hospital and told them she was taking her son home. She took care of him for another several months, and, at first, he seemed to be responding well. But soon, the family realized he was dying. Four months later, Joe died, at home, with his family.

Eventually, Mom and Dad decided to petition to visit Mom's family in Italy. The Ukraine Secret Service would follow Dad to work every day and tell him that if he joined the Communist Party, he could have his visa the same day. Dad never did join the party. But for some reason, after months of inquiries into obtaining visas to visit Italy, God only knows why they received the visas for the whole family. Once they got to Italy, they never returned to Ukraine. Instead, they stayed in an Italian refugee camp for two years, waiting to come to the States. Mom's family in Italy had lost their fortune during the war and couldn't help much. But once again, almost miraculously, they were granted passage and entrance into the US. After living through all that, they remained appreciative of even the smallest things. They couldn't be prouder to be called Americans and to learn the language and culture.

Anyway, in response to my question about my mom, Dad answered, "She's not feeling too good today."

"What's the problem?"

"Lately she gets . . . uh, dizzy, dizzy, need to lie down."

"Has she been to the doctor?"

"Yes, they checked her over and could not find any problem. She still takes blood pressure pills."

As I entered the house, a familiar clean, soapy smell filled my nose. I couldn't exactly put my finger on it, but whether it was some detergent Mom used or just the old house itself, even after all these years, it smelled like home.

And there was Mom, sitting on the couch. She screamed with joy to see us and especially to see Katie.

"How is my sweet Katie?"

From the time Katie was just a baby, she and my mom seemed to have a special bond, more so than I've ever seen between a grandmother and granddaughter. Their personalities seemed almost identical. Katie quietly walked over to Mom and sat on her lap. At five, Katie looked almost exactly like my mother looked in pictures taken of her when she was Katie's age. They had great admiration for each other, the gracious kindness that unselfishly builds the other person up whenever they're around each other.

"Why don't we go into the kitchen, and you can help me make some supper," Mom tempted her small friend.

"OK, Grandma," Katie replied as she looked back at Emma for approval.

Off they went to the kitchen while we settled on the couch and talked to Dad for a while. "Well, where's Giorgio?" I asked.

George, or Giorgio as I called him, was my younger brother. He was seventeen and would be a senior in high school this year. George and I differed in personality; he was a full twelve years younger than me, and it seemed like we were several generations apart. When I left home, George was just starting kindergarten. From a distance, I'd watched him grow, spending time with him when I came home for visits. I never really felt like I was part of his life as he was growing up. Now, I feared that it might be too late as he was fast approaching manhood. One of my goals for moving back was to get to know my brother.

Dad answered with a troubled look. "George is in Mineville (a few hours west of Franklin) at the mall with his girlfriend, that Johnson girl. She's trouble, but George is too blind to see it."

"Well, Dad, maybe she, or they, will grow up one of these days, and everything will be fine."

"I don't know, Levi. George is different from you."

"Well, I was no saint. Do you remember when my friends and I decided to take Jim's car for a ride in the middle of a winter night—without Jim's dad's permission and without a driver's license? A statewide, all-points bulletin about a stolen car was issued, and we were driving it down Main Street!" We all chuckled.

Dad nodded and said, "Now, you had your times, but you always seemed to care about us and things that were important. You were easy to raise. You went off to college. You make a good life for yourself and your family. I don't know what George cares about—only himself, maybe."

"Dad, he'll grow up."

"I hope so, Levi. I really do." He turned to Emma, who had sat down beside me. "Emma, how are you?"

"I'm doing fine, Dad, and looking forward to settling down."

Emma was comfortable around my family most of the time, but she didn't quite know what to say to Dad, and he was the same way toward her. But they loved each other, and both worked hard to find things to talk about.

Emma was the best thing that had ever happened to me. She is really the reason why I "make a good life for myself," as my dad put it. She came from a Christian home and was, in my mind, the definition of a gracious, loving, and kind person. She was so gracious that overbearing, insecure people would read that as a weakness. At times people seemed to talk to her or treat her in a brash manner, trying to lower her status in some way so as to hide their own shortcomings. When that happened, it would make Emma angry, but she would take it and forget about it. My mother took her in as her own and many times told her that she thought of her as her own daughter, equal to my two sisters (the twins). Anyway, I loved Emma more than I ever thought I could love anyone. When I looked into her big, brown eyes and basked in her smile, it seemed to heal all my ailments and every other problem within miles.

"Dad, did you say there was a house for sale on Broad Street?" Emma asked.

"Yes, there was, but I don't know if it is still for sale. It's an old house, though. It would need some work inside and out, but maybe you can buy cheap," he answered. "Maybe you could fix it the way you want."

With her redecorating instincts peaked, Emma turned to me. "Maybe we should take a look at it."

I smiled and said, "Hey, why don't we get up early tomorrow and go." Just then, a loud scream from the kitchen interrupted my suggestion.

"Grandma! Grandma! Daddy, help!"

We rushed to the kitchen to find Mom on the floor. She was lying on her back. Her face, so soft and wrinkly, looked hot and red. Emma grabbed a wet cloth to tend to her forehead. As I dabbed her with it, her eyelids flickered a little and opened slowly. Then her brows wrinkled further in confusion.

"What . . . what happened?" she asked.

"I don't know, Mom. You must have passed out. Do you feel OK now?" I asked her.

"My eye hurts," she said. "I must have hit my face or something."

The area around her right eye was really red and beginning to swell. "I think you're gonna have a nice shiner. Let's get you up and to the couch," I suggested.

We helped Mom to the couch, and we all sat around her for a while and talked.

"Dad, can you get me the doctor's number?"

That evening, we took Mom to the doctor's office, and he gave her a quick examination. He said he couldn't find any reason for Mom's recent troubles, and he really didn't have much to say beyond that. I thought that he and his staff seemed a little too quick in their work and more eager to get back home than to figure out Mom's problem. Exhausted, we all went home.

Without unpacking or getting dinner, my family and I started getting ready for bed. The bathroom made me smile—that same tiny bathroom with that same soap smell and those same tiny trinket decorations Mom loved were all in place. I brushed my teeth and washed up. Emma and Katie were already asleep when I got to the bedroom.

Tired as I was, I stared at the fake wooden ceiling boards for a long time before falling into a restless sleep. I thought about Mom. What a gruesome feeling—seeing Mom lying so still on the floor. The terrible thought filled my mind: What if she were dead, lying there with all the wonderful, precious life gone out of her? It was the first time I'd thought of Mom that way—that someday, I would probably see her that way, lifeless, no longer here with us. It was a haunting thought that would return from time to time after that day.

Judging from the look on Dad's face when Mom was lying on the kitchen floor, I wondered if he had a similar premonition. He had a distant and worried look on his face whenever the subject of Mom's health came up. I wasn't sure what he would do without her. He had a heart attack a few years back when he was only sixty-seven years old. Now that Mom had reached the same age, I think he somehow felt she was more vulnerable to serious health problems too. He wasn't comfortable with the doctors shrugging off Mom's health problem, and neither was I.

Chapter Two

Mom ignored the fainting episode. To her, it was as if it had never happened. She was up the next morning, dressed in her apron, knee-highs, and black shoes. Her tiny blond-haired friend stayed close by her side in the kitchen as they made breakfast together. Emma came in and had a cup of coffee with Mom. Afterward, Emma helped with the dishes, and then she and Mom watched a game show on Mom's tiny kitchen TV while Katie played in the living room. I was a bit slow to get going after all the travel, but I eventually got into the kitchen for coffee.

I smiled at Katie as I passed by, making a beeline for the kitchen and coffee. "Hey guys, good morning!"

Mom turned and smiled as she responded. "Good morning, son. I have lots of company this morning, and I love it."

Emma was in the middle of a sip of coffee, looking up at me from behind the mug. As she finished her sip, the mug revealed that beautiful smile I am so thankful for. I sat down and chatted with them as we grabbed a little breakfast. Dad wasn't up yet, but I remembered that he had told us about a house nearby for sale.

"Emma, let's drive around and look at houses. On my new teacher's salary, we should be able to get a real mansion," I said with a smile.

Emma smiled back. "Sure, Levi, let's get two."

Emma and I got ourselves together and began the hunt. We checked out the outside of the house Dad had told us about. It was still for sale, according to the sign out front. We jotted the realtor's number down and planned to call later. The house looked like it had been ignored for a long time. It had the old slate-type siding, which was a weathered and faded ocean blue color. It also had an old white picket fence that sagged at certain spots and was crying out for a new paint job. It was a far cry from the suburban house we had in Georgia. But the house had potential and would probably cost a fraction of what we paid for our Georgia place. After talking with the realtor, we were able to get an appointment to see the inside, but we would have to wait until Friday. So, we spent the next few days relaxing and spending time with Mom and Dad. Dad and I ran errands and stopped at the gym to work out each day. Two days passed quietly. We ate home-cooked Italian meals, watched TV, and rested. I was beginning to wonder about George. Dad was pretty reluctant to talk about him.

George had been staying with a friend out of town. It was Thursday night, and I'd just returned from the high school where I was looking at the classroom where I'd be teaching.

As Dad and I were sitting in the living room, George rushed in.

"George! How are you?"

"Hey, brother, you made it home all right," George replied while walking through the room.

I grabbed his arm to slow his rush toward the stairs. "You're already taller than me and still in high school."

"You should have eaten your veggies," he countered.

"So, tell me, stranger, where's this girlfriend I've been hearing about? When do I get to meet her?"

He looked uneasy and glanced back at Dad. "So, you've heard about my girlfriend. What've you heard?" he asked with a snide tone.

We walked to the red velour couch in the other room.

"What did Dad say to you about her? He thinks she's the devil in the flesh."

"George . . ."

"No, really," he interrupted. "He can't stand her."

He stopped walking and faced me directly. "I was pretty young when you left home, but I don't remember Dad ever treating your girlfriends like they were terrorists."

I started to talk, but George interrupted me again, growing more defensive. "Don't even start with me, brother. And don't think you're going to come back here and be my dad too. I don't need to be double-teamed. One wacko dad is enough, thanks."

"Watch your mouth, George. What's wrong with you?" I didn't understand where this tirade was coming from.

"Wrong with me?" He took a deep breath, rolled his eyes, and started for the stairs again.

"Welcome home, brother," he said, flailing both arms and shaking his head. He bounded up the stairs to his room.

I had been with George for only ten minutes, and we were already fighting. I wish I knew how to relate to him. I guess I did feel more like George's dad than his brother, though I knew I'd only turn him away acting like that.

"That went well," Emma said with a smirk as she walked in from the kitchen.

"Did you hear all that?"

"Bits and pieces from the kitchen."

"What'd I do wrong?"

"Ah, he was ready to pounce before you opened your mouth. He seemed really on edge," she said, trying to be comforting.

"I hope I can get to know him one of these days."

"That's a little hard to do when you're a thousand miles away. Maybe now you'll have a chance."

Mom walked in from the kitchen, her little friend in tow.

"Daddy!" Katie squealed. "Grandma, let me make supper."

"That's right," Mom said, grinning down at her.

Mom prided herself in being an excellent cook and was now in heaven to have someone to appreciate and teach.

"Well, I only helped a little," Katie admitted.

"Sweet Katie did a great job. I want us all to have a nice supper together tonight."

Mom could sense the impeding conflict. She knew George, and

I might need a little extra help to get comfortable, especially since we'd be living in the same house until Emma and I could find our own place. I guess I really never got to know George too well. My twin sisters, Melissa and Rebecca, kept me pretty busy when I was growing up; they were five years older than me. It seemed like they couldn't wait to go their separate ways after high school, but surprisingly, after they got married, they ended up living near each other in Minneapolis. They have very busy lives, raising their families and working all the time, so we seldom talk or get together. We simply drifted apart as our lives sped past. It'd been at least six months since I'd talked to either of them. If it wasn't for Mom, I'm not even sure they would have known I was moving back home.

"Giorgio!" Mom yelled. "You will come down and eat with us in a half hour."

She almost sounded like a general giving an unpleasant order. There was no answer. I wanted to chime in and suggest to George that we had a guest chef tonight (he had a soft spot for Katie), but I thought it might sound like I was hounding him again.

Soon, we all sat down for dinner, except, of course, the chefs, who refused to be seated until everything was perfect on the table and everyone was served. I guess Mom thought it was part of her duty to do that, and Katie shadowed Mom's every move.

Just then, George came slowly down the stairs and took a seat. No matter how hard anyone tried to make conversation, the tension between George and me made everything awkward. He turned to Katie.

"This is so good. Did you really make this, Katie?" George asked her.

Katie gave a shy giggle and a nod from her half-filled seat.

"Why yes, she did, with just a little help from me," Mom piped in.

"Well, you did a great job," George said.

Katie gave a high-pitched thank you.

"Maybe you can become a professional chef. You and my mom could open a restaurant."

Things seemed to finally have eased up a bit. What could I say to help? I blew it completely. "George, you should invite your girlfriend over some night and let our chefs . . ."

Convenience

George interrupted again. "Didn't you hear? Dad won't let her set one foot into this house."

"Oh now, George," Dad began but was cut off in mid-sentence by George.

"What do you mean 'Oh, George?' You said those very words a couple of weeks ago, remember?"

Dad said, "I was a little upset at the time. I didn't really mean to...." George cut him off again.

"So, you didn't mean what you said when you slammed the door shut in my face while I was still talking? I see. Don't try to act all nice just because he's here." George was referring to me.

Fear, anger, and confusion passed over Dad's face all at once. He was obviously struggling for something to say but was afraid to say anything else that might make matters worse. So was I. I wasn't sure what to say that wouldn't make George angrier.

We all sat in silence for a few seconds, which seemed like hours.

"Maybe you could invite her over some time," Mom said, trying to add some hope to the situation. "Dad really won't mind."

Her words, like a referee in a ball game, produced some aggravation for both George and Dad, but neither talked back. After that, we all tread carefully, sticking to small talk. George went back to thank Katie for her work. Soon after, he told Mom he was in a hurry and needed to get to work and left quickly.

We all helped clean up and relaxed a bit before bed. I could see on Dad's face that he could not figure out how to handle George. It puzzled him, it worried him, and it almost seemed as though it made him age before my eyes. I knew that he was concerned for George's sake and for the rest of the family's sake as well. The night grew a bit colder and darker as we all turned in.

The next morning, I woke up early and wanted to go over to the house we were looking at to check out the property more closely. The morning paper was already on the porch, so I grabbed it and sat down with a cup of coffee and read for a while, trying to learn what I could about my *new* old hometown. As I sat by the big window on the side of the living room, hoping to soak up some of the early morning sun rays, George came bounding down the stairs. When he noticed me, his eyebrows lowered a bit, and he reset his disposition to being focused, mature, and about his business. I could tell he wasn't about to start a conversation with me as he sped through the room. I tried to slow him down and engage him in at least a quick morning conversation.

"Good morning, George." He didn't respond. "Are you late for work?"

"No, I've still got an hour before I have to be there."

"Sit down and have a cup of coffee with me. I just made a fresh pot."

He seemed surprised that I would consider drinking coffee with him. I think he saw himself as a kid around me, and I wanted him to know that I considered him to be a grown-up young man.

He sat down, and I poured him a cup. I could sense he was trying to think of something to say. Then he stared out the big window into the sunlight, deep in thought for a moment. A half smile came over his face that had an element of arrogance to it. Without turning away from the window, he began to speak.

"Did you see Mom's eye?" George was referring to the black and blue and green color that was beginning to engulf Mom's eye from falling in the kitchen two days ago.

George wore a smirk, and his head shook back and forth as he spoke.

"I mean, I'm glad she's OK and all, but she does look a little silly with her shiner."

"What?" I grimaced. "What do you mean, silly? She's your mom, George."

He crunched a cookie that had been left in a bowl on the table from last night.

"I know who she is. But she's getting older and, I'm just saying, we can probably expect more 'accidents,'" he said, as he gestured air quotes. Then he grabbed another cookie and leaned back in his chair in the sunlight.

"Are you really that callous toward all this? Aren't you worried about her? She's your mom, and she's still a person."

He just stared at me.

"I can't believe you're acting like this," I said. "She's not subhuman because she's getting older. You'll be in her shoes someday."

Convenience

"I doubt it," he said haughtily.

I paused for a moment, scrunching my eyes together and then opening them again. "What do you mean? You don't plan on aging?"

He paused. "I don't want to be a burden on people. I'd give serious thought to ending my life before I got too old. You know, in Europe, most countries allow people to take their own lives with the help of doctors."

"You can't be serious. You really buy into all that?" I blurted out, stunned.

"I'm completely serious. Do you know there are studies showing that the earth may only last another fifty years because of the rate we're destroying our resources? Why would I want to just sit around, take up space, and use up resources when I'm old?"

"George, statistics can say anything the creators want them to. I could find you studies that claim we have plenty of resources, *more* forests than we had fifty years ago, and ingenuity to move to a new level of energy production?"

He shrugged. I grew more irritated with his attitude.

"Do you really think old people just take up space? Some of the greatest contributions to better this world have come from people in their seventies and eighties, not to mention the guidance, encouragement, and wisdom people get every day from older folks. Besides all that, God made us, and he ultimately owns our lives, not us."

I knew he wasn't really listening at all, but I kept on.

"We were 'fearfully and wonderfully made' by God; he decides when life begins and ends."

George quickly interrupted me. "Hey, don't start your religious crap with me."

But I was on a roll and was going to finish. "George, God is the author of life. How can we assume we can end innocent life just because we don't want the burden? You can rationalize all day, but when it comes down to it, God is in charge and has a plan for each life. Each of us is unique and special and holds an eternal soul. How can we presume on God's plan and God's most precious creation—people."

"Get with the program, brother!" George responded. "Europeans have been around a long time and have evolved in their thinking way beyond all that. Step into the twenty-first century!" He threw the rest of his cookie on the table and started to walk out of the room, but he stopped just short of the door, ready to boil over. He turned and looked me in the eyes. He seemed to have no fear or concern, no feeling, no compassion as he said, "Having a bunch of old people around doing nothing but taking up space is not efficient, and it's *inconvenient* for everyone else. They were young once, and they ought to let others have a turn and enjoy what's left of this planet!"

He turned and walked out the door, leaving it wide open. I sat stunned, wondering how he had come to the point where he could think the way he was thinking. How did his heart become so hard and crusted over? I also wondered how we were going to live in the same house, even for a short time, and whether we'd ever be able to talk without enraging each other.

Chapter Three

The next month and a half passed quickly. I was busy concentrating on getting the family settled, buying a house, and getting set for my high school math class teaching debut. I was excited about teaching. It was something I'd always wanted to do later in my life. It seemed to me that growing up, especially during the teen years, was becoming harder and harder. With information and communication at our fingertips, you'd think it might be easier. Yet, teens seemed more confused than ever in trying to figure out who they are and what life is really about. I thought as a teacher; maybe I could help some of those confused kids through some of their challenges.

The house we looked at near Mom and Dad's seemed to be the best deal around, although it wasn't perfect by any means and was going to take some fixing up. But time was getting short, and I wanted to get something definite before school started. We closed on our house three weeks before school was to begin. It had been vacant for a full year and wasn't taken care of for a lot longer than that. The seller had to get a new roof installed, new plumbing in many areas, and some new wiring in the basement. Since her house had been on the market for so long, she seemed eager to do whatever we wanted to get the house sold. I wondered if she thought that she had finally found someone to dump this house on and she wasn't about to lose the opportunity. She was happy, and really, we got the house for a song as compared to what we paid in Atlanta.

And even with the money we planned to put into the house to fix it up the way we wanted, the total investment was certainly reasonable and affordable, even on my much smaller salary. And I thought we could get our money out of the house if we needed to sell it in a few years.

Once we closed the deal, Emma and Katie, and I went to work on it. We painted it inside and out. We also painted that white picket fence. Katie "helped." She would paint a picture on a fence post with her white brush. Then I would "touch it up" with my big broad brush. Although there was still a lot we wanted to do on the house, we moved in two weeks after we closed and only one week before school was to start. We ended up only five blocks from Mom and Dad's house. It was definitely one of the older neighborhoods in town, but very few new houses were built after the old oil boom days back when I was in high school. Most of that boom dried up almost as fast as it appeared, and our little town settled back down into what it had been for the previous hundred years—a Northwestern farming community. Even though our neighborhood was older, it was kept up well and not run down and was certainly a safe place to live.

George and I talked very little the rest of the summer. I was very busy settling in and preparing for school. I probably used my being "busy" as an excuse to stay clear of my brother. It seemed like I grew more confused as to how to approach him and what to say to him. He seemed to make himself busy enough to stay clear of the whole family and me. I was worried about him but felt justified that I had other "priorities," so I didn't do much to change the situation.

Before I knew it, school was beginning. On the morning of the first day of school, I was nervous as a cat—a lot more nervous than I thought I'd be. As funny as it sounds, it almost felt as if I were attending school again instead of teaching. I got those funny feelings like I did when I was a kid, wondering how things would work out, how I'd fit in. Emma thought I was silly and cracked a few jokes to try to lasso my thoughts back to reality. I grabbed a quick bite to eat and took off. I wanted to stop by Mom's on the way over. Mom must have known I'd be by and had some coffee made and sat me down at the kitchen table. She had some laundry to take care of in the basement and disappeared for

Convenience

a moment. Just then, George appeared from the other room. He also sat down to gobble up a piece of toast and a quick cup of coffee. So, George and I ended up seated at the kitchen table together, alone. Maybe Mom planned it that way.

This was the first time George and I were in the same room longer than five minutes since our blow-up supper.

"I almost feel like I'm a student," I confessed to George.

"Don't worry, brother; no one will mistake you for one. You don't exactly look like a student or dress like one either."

"George, I'm not going to wear a coat and tie every day. I just wanted to look sharp my first day."

He took a swig of orange juice and gave up a big sigh.

"You're sharp, all right, for an 'old-school' teacher. You'll fit right in."

I had no idea what that meant, but not wanting to probe more, I downed that last bit of my coffee and bid my brother goodbye.

"Have a great day," I blurted out and left the room. George didn't respond.

The school was bustling with kids updating their friends about their summer adventures. Other kids seemed lost, confused, and reluctant or afraid to join the general stream of kids in the hallway—ah, freshmen. I remember that well. I tried to help a few but felt like I was trying to rescue a swimmer caught in a current. They just drifted away as I yelled out directions. Maybe they drifted away on purpose to get away from the new old guy wearing a suit. Oh, well. They'll survive, just like I did.

I, too, made my way through the flow to my first-period class. As I was getting settled into my room, students started to trickle in. I was teaching freshman algebra, but this class had about ten students who had failed algebra last year. One of the students returning was a young woman who kept staring at me. Maybe the coat and tie were too much, I thought. Then a more plausible thought came to me. I checked the student roster.

There it was, the name Brittany Johnson, George's girlfriend. I'll bet she's the one. She had red hair—cut short—and wore blue jeans that were torn around both knees, a T-shirt, and black shoes. She must have shopped at the same store as the other students. To me, the style seemed like clothes stores couldn't sell for the last ten years but had kept in the basement, waiting to bring them out for the next 75-percent-off sidewalk sale. George was right. My coat and tie certainly didn't put me in any student category.

The students chose their seats, and I began my introductory speech. I told them a little bit about myself, my background, and the fact that I had sat in the very seats they were sitting in years ago. I also told them a little about my accident and how I ended up back in Franklin.

Then I gave them an idea of what I expected. I tried to give them as much information about the structure of the class as I could. When I was a student, I felt like most of my teachers thought part of learning was some sort of mystery clue game where if you were smart enough and worked hard, you'd figure out what was required to do well. I hated that. We needed to learn, not play some sort of game where some lucky ones come out on top. So, I told the students exactly what they needed to do to succeed and learn. That way, I thought, they could concentrate on learning the material.

I may have rambled on a little too long and could see that I was losing some of them already. Next, I went over the roster. I stumbled over a few names and got some good-natured laughs, and sure enough, the red-haired girl raised her hand as Brittany Johnson. I tried to act unfazed and continued. What little time was left of the hour I spent answering questions, trying to be clear about what I expected, and emphasizing that I had several techniques to help those who might have a tough time learning algebra. Brit didn't ask any questions. The hour went by quickly and closed with my giving the students a reading assignment for the next day. Then, that same bell that had annoyed me years ago rang (somehow, it still annoyed me), and the kids filed out.

Brittany was one of the last to leave. She stopped at my desk and asked, "Why would you decide to come back to a place like this?" Her lip curled. I could tell she expected me to return a smart remark to her. Maybe she expected me to allude to her returning back to algebra for a second time or to mention my brother.

"Well, to be honest, the crime rate's pretty low here, as is the cost of living, plus there's plenty of elbow room, space for raising my little girl. And my folks are getting older, and I kind of wanted to be closer to them."

I could tell Brittany didn't know how to react to someone my age, treating her as an adult and answering her question with respect. I broke the silence. "What do you think? Is it a good place to raise kids?"

Shocked, she finally spoke with a confused half-smile. "I . . . I guess it's a good place for kids." She seemed surprised. She began to walk toward the door. Maybe I wasn't exactly the kind of person my brother must have described to her. I told her goodbye as she walked through the door. She turned around and gave me one last confused look, still a bit thrown off by the whole interchange.

"Bye."

In the next few weeks, I began to realize that this teaching stuff was harder than I thought. But I was enjoying it and even established an extra half-hour "basics" class for those who wanted to establish a good math foundation. I had explained to the students that they could do algebra much easier if they had a firm math foundation, and, strangely, five students took me up on the offer for a basics class twice a week at lunch. I wasn't sure how long it would run or what direction I would take, but I thought it would help those who took it. Brit wasn't among the attendees. I asked her a few times, but I'm pretty sure George occupied her lunch hours. Still, she seemed to enjoy my class (as much as any high school student might enjoy algebra class), and, in a strange way, she seemed to trust me. I was a sort of new personality to this small town and had not fit her into one of the town molds that I suspect most others did. There was a certain way people (teachers) treated you, whether they or anyone else realized it or not. If you were not from a few well-to-do families, or if you're folks didn't hold an "important position" in town, you never quite measured up. It was easy to talk yourself into feeling that way, anyway.

I got that sense from a few teachers of mine when I was a kid. I didn't like the feeling. In fact, I hated it. I guess because of that, I made it a point to be impartial with all my students and to reflect on what I had come to know as God's unconditional love.

Two more weeks passed, and the dinner engagement that Mom had promised would happen was nearly upon us. Tonight, Brit was coming over for dinner with the whole family. George had hardly mentioned it, but I knew she was coming because Brit mentioned it to me after class one day. Mom was preparing a great feast when I stopped by on my way home from school. She made her own recipe for lasagna. It was divine, with a number of special cheeses and spices that you just couldn't duplicate anywhere else! Having grown up in Italy, Mom would scoff at other people's feeble attempts at lasagna, using what she called "fake" cheeses and runny, store-bought sauces.

"Mmm. That smells heavenly," I said and gave her a kiss on the cheek. "Where's Dad?"

"He's out back getting ready to mow the grass."

I looked out the window and noticed that, even from a distance, Dad had a nervous look, the same troubled look he had whenever he mentioned Brittany or "that girl."

I stared at Dad for a moment, wishing he and George might get along better. Dad had conquered a lot of challenges in his life, but he didn't know how to even approach George anymore. I snapped out of my momentary trance and realized that I needed to get home. So, I bid Mom farewell.

"We'll come over a little early because I know Katie will want to help you with the dinner, Mom."

"OK, Levi. Don't be late." She commanded, stressing the importance of the night.

I headed home to see what Emma and Katie were up to. Emma had decided to home-school Katie through kindergarten to try to give her a head start prior to first grade. Having gotten a late start that day, they were just finishing up a reading lesson when I got home.

I guess I was nervous about dinner, too—not the kind of nervous you feel when someone new is visiting. I was more concerned about not blowing it with George again.

"Emma, what should I wear tonight?" Nothing I reached for seemed right.

"What about the same thing you always wear?" she said with a chuckle. "A pair of jeans and a T-shirt seem to work for every other occasion. It's not the Queen of England we're entertaining tonight. Why are you so uptight?"

"I'm not so worried about Brit. I'm worried about saying the wrong thing to George and getting into another argument."

"Levi," Emma replied calmly, with a smile, "you'll be fine. Just don't say anything all night." She laughed. But I knew she meant that I couldn't let fear get in the way of establishing a relationship with George. She was right. She's right, most of the time.

"OK, thanks." I smiled as I reached over and gave her a kiss. "I'll throw on my trusty T and . . ."

"And we'll have fun tonight," she finished.

Emma, Katie, and I got to Mom and Dad's really early, but Katie was glad to "get a jump on things" in the kitchen, and I didn't see her again until dinner. Emma and Dad, and I sat out on the big porch that spanned the length of one side and the front of the house. It drooped a little now that it was getting very old. I wondered how much longer that old porch would last. We talked for a while and enjoyed the cool late summer evening. It was the time of the evening when it cools off but isn't yet dark, and the mosquitoes haven't yet staged their nightly attack. There was no sign of George and Brit yet. As dinnertime approached, we filed back into the house. We were all milling around the table, ready to sit, but George and Brit still hadn't shown up. I was beginning to wonder if I would even have a chance to mess things up with George again. Maybe they were making a statement by not showing up at all.

Just as we were about to give up, George's car screeched to a stop outside, and the two quickly came inside.

"Hi, George. Hi, Brittany," I said.

"Hi, Mr. B," Brit replied with a shy politeness I'd never seen from her before.

"Brit, this is my mom and dad," George said quickly and a bit awkwardly.

They gave a kind hello. They always seemed humbled by guests and were not out to boost their egos. They almost took on a spirit of servitude. I admired their hospitality.

"Supper is ready if you would like to sit down now to eat," Mom offered.

We all found our seats. Brit and George sat together on one side, and Emma and I sat opposite them on the other side of the table. Katie sat next to Brit, and Mom and Dad were on the ends. That seemed to be the least threatening spot for Brit, and she seemed as comfortable as could be expected. We all stared at the wonderful-looking food and prepared to dig in.

Katie piped in, "Daddy, we have to pray."

"You're right, Katie. I was so hungry I almost forgot." We all bowed our heads intently as I began. "Dear Lord, we thank you for providing this wonderful food and for the hands that made it. Thank you for a beautiful day. And we thank you for this time we have together with family and friends. Please bless our time together and our conversation tonight."

George let out a sigh of annoyance over the long prayer. "And Lord, we pray that everything we do will bring you, our creator, honor and glory tonight. Amen."

The second I finished, George reached for the pan of lasagna nearest him. I could tell he was already uncomfortable with all of us being together and even more uncomfortable with us praying together. Brit remained nervously polite. I tried to make her relax a little with some small talk. "So, Brit, how's your family doing?"

"My mom's been pretty tired lately. She's been working double shifts for three months now. We thought it was just for the summer, but the store kept her on the same schedule even after school started."

"That's got to be tough," Emma remarked.

"Yeah, I get home from school and clean up a little and make dinner, and Mom gets in around nine o'clock. My dad doesn't live with us, so it's just the two of us."

Trying to be funny, I asked, "I guess you do all the math homework I give you before dinner, then?"

Brit was too nervous to laugh or even search for humor. "Well, sometimes," she said in a serious tone.

"I usually do it for her," George added, taking a break from his assault on the lasagna.

Convenience

Brit finally smiled.

Mom finally sat down and said with a smile, "We're glad you came over, and I hope you like the food."

"Oh," Brit quickly responded, with a little more confidence, "This is really good, thanks."

"Well, Katie was my helper, and she really helped make it turn out nice." Katie beamed.

"Maybe you two should open a restaurant. Katie could be the head chef," George commented.

Taking advantage of a quiet moment, I asked Brit a question. "Well, I don't mean to bring up work or school stuff, but I wanted to ask you, Brit, what do you think about math class? Since I've never taught at this level, I wanted to hear what the students think so far?"

George rolled his eyes.

"Well, I think I'm learning a lot, a lot more than last year. I think the teacher I had last year had some personal problems—maybe a divorce or something. He would come into class and assign us to read some pages and do the questions. Then he would sit down and read or stare out the window. He never really taught us stuff. I didn't do too well. This year you are actually teaching us something. So, it's going a lot better."

"Well, that's good to hear. And I think you're doing very well so far. After all, you need math to go on to be a nuclear physicist or doctor or something like that!"

George rolled his eyes again and took a deep breath. "Look, brother, Brit's got her hands full at home right now if you didn't pick up on what she's told you already. I think she's concentrating on the *next day*—not grad school at the moment."

"Well, I don't think it hurts to at least think about the future and school. I didn't think about college until the last half of my senior year, so I got a slower start on all the college stuff."

"Oh please," George pressed, "slow start? You finished college right on time and were in the top ten percent of your class, as I heard every day from Mom and Dad. Give me a break. Your humility is making me nauseated, and I'd like to finish my lasagna."

George dove back into his plate. I didn't know how to respond to that, and I could tell he had Mom and Dad wondering, also. George had a way of doing that to us all.

Emma saved us this time. "I'd like to get back to college when we get settled in and try to get an accounting degree. I wonder if I could finish it here at the branch college."

Relieved, I gladly jumped in. "I think you may have to go to the main campus to finish, but we can check on that. You are almost done with your two-year requirements, right?"

"I think so, Levi. That's if all my credits transfer over. Maybe I'll give them a call next week."

Brit was still a bit shocked and embarrassed by George's verbal stab at his brother. But surprisingly, she spoke up. "I think George would be great at something like accounting. He's really smart with money and budgets and all that, and he's really good with numbers." She looked deep into George's eyes and smiled.

I could sense George "melt" at Brit's words; it was obvious that he really cared for Brit and that she cared for him. No one else seemed to be able to get to George quite that way. Of course, he wasn't about to let any of us see any vulnerabilities. He broke the stare with Brit and responded, "Ha, yeah, right!"

Through that conversation, I could see that George and Brit were very close. She seemed to be the only person who could penetrate what seemed to be a crusted-over, cold heart that George had developed for whatever reason. At the same time, it seemed that George was the only person Brit felt understood her, and he seemed to be the only person in the world she really trusted. They made a unique but logical couple.

Throughout the rest of the dinner, we struggled to stick to small talk. Mom worked hard to keep our focus on easier subjects, and Dad worked hard to just get through the rest of the evening.

Chapter Four

The next morning was a bright sunny Saturday, and I was up early. Emma and I still had a lot of things to do around our new old house. We both knew that we only had a few months before late fall and winter would hit, and it would be too cold to take care of the outside stuff that needed to be done. My mission for the morning was to caulk all the basement windows and lay some more insulation in the basement walls and ceiling. The walls down there were open, but someone had begun to frame them and had most of them framed up and insulated. My goal was to add more insulation to the open walls and in the ceiling, which was also open. Then sometime down the road, I'd finish the walls and ceiling and work on creating a spare bedroom, a laundry room, and a family room. That would take some years, but I thought I'd do a little at a time. Since I didn't really know what I was doing, I'd research, ask friends, and then do the work, and then do it over if I messed it up. That's sort of how I remodeled a few rooms in our house in Georgia.

After a hot cup of coffee, I took a quick walk around the house. As I was coming around the side from the back, I noticed, of all things, George's beat-up old car coming down the road. Even though he had the windows up, I could hear the radio in his car when he got about half a block away. I tried not to pay too much attention to his car as he slowed near my house. When he stopped in front of the house, his brakes squeaked a little, and I used that as a reason to finally look up and pretend I had just noticed him. Acting a little surprised, I waved at him.

He got out of his car and started over to me. He had no expression, it seemed, whatsoever. He was also carrying a very fashionable purse! It was Emma's.

"Good morning, George; your purse doesn't exactly match your outfit." He didn't even crack a smile.

"Mom told me to bring this over since Emma forgot it last night." He quickly handed it to me and began to turn toward his car.

"Hey, I'm sorry if I talk too much sometimes, like last night. I was just trying to make conversation. I didn't mean to mess up the night."

George stopped and turned to me and had a bit of a puzzled look on his face.

"Huh, I think it went pretty well—considering . . ." George added sarcastically.

"Considering what?" I responded.

"Well, considering you're the golden boy of this family, and I'm the black sheep, I think the night went pretty well for all."

Confusion again began to set in. I paused for a moment and probably should have kept my mouth shut, but I didn't. George didn't move, seemingly almost hoping for a return shot across the bow from me.

I thought for a moment and, after a deep sigh, responded, "All I did was try my best at some things I thought were important in life. You have the same opportunities and ability to make the same choices."

Then, I really should have shut my mouth. "Why have you chosen to rebel? Why are you so self-focused, so negative toward those who love you, so angry and restless!"

George paused and rubbed this hand around his chin, which had begun to grow a little fuzz on it.

He looked at me, "Rebel?" He squinted and looked more intently at me, straight in the eye. "You really don't get it. I'm not rebelling. You just don't understand my generation. We've got some things figured out—some things that your generation and Mom and Dad's, and probably theirs before them, didn't figure out. We view things with a

Convenience

little more reality and common sense. We don't need to fit into some mold of society and can be ourselves."

"Oh, come on, George. Yours is just another generation like all the rest. I went through the same struggles and challenges, and so did the generation before me. It's just being played out all over again."

"Yeah, right," George interrupted me. "You don't have a clue about me and my generation—yours was as simple-minded as ever."

"What are you talking about? You'll grow up someday—I hope and see how wrong you are about all this. Things were just as tough for me as they might be for you now."

George paused again and looked down for a few seconds, which seemed like minutes. Then he again looked me right in the eye. But surprisingly, this time, his eyes were kind of steamy and moist. He was still determined and angry, but this time there was an element of fear in his demeanor as he struggled to speak.

"Easy for you to say, but what if you were in a situation . . . oh, say, for example, your girlfriend was pregnant and still in high school? It might be a little tougher to be so pious."

Why was he telling me of all people? He started off toward his car. I had to try to talk to him again, so I ran after him and caught him before he got into his beater car. I grabbed his arm, and he turned around.

"George? Is she?"

"Yeah, maybe. Why should you care?"

"Have you told Mom and Dad?"

"I told Mom. She knows. And if I had told Dad, do you think I'd still be allowed under his roof?"

"You've got to tell him somehow. George, I want to help you. Please talk to me."

"That's funny; a minute ago, you wanted to straighten me out. I'm not telling Dad anything yet. Maybe it's a fluke. She's almost a month late, but maybe it was for some other reason. And, yeah, you can help me out, dear brother. You can keep your mouth shut."

"Have you thought about what you're going to do?"

"I, well . . . we . . . have, but that's none of your business, is it?"

"George, please, this is a big deal; take some time to think about this."

"What, you think we should have the baby? And what, hire a babysitter while we're in school? Once again, brother, easy for you to say!"

He got in his car and sped off through the cottonwood trees before I could get another word in. I leaned back and sat on the side of the hill in front of our house, dumbfounded, wondering what could be next.

I couldn't believe what I'd heard. What would they do if Brit really is pregnant? They're both still in high school. How could they manage a baby?

The sun dipped behind a cloud, and a cold breeze blew a shower of leaves across my yard. A cold chill came over me, like the kind you sometimes get in Montana in the fall when you're not wearing a jacket outside, reminding you that dark, cold days are ahead. What if they decided to abort the baby? Lord, please help us through this. I prayed and walked back to the house.

Emma was up, sitting in the living room with a hot cup of coffee warming her hands. She was sitting on the couch with her feet tucked under herself and was trying to soak up some sun rays through the big picture window. But the sky had quickly clouded over. She looked at me as I walked back in.

"What's up, Levi?"

She knew me all too well and could tell I had something more than just crab grass in the front yard on my mind. "Let me grab a cup of coffee, and I'll tell you."

I quickly dashed into the kitchen, poured a nice hot cup of coffee, added some half-and-half from the fridge, and quickly went back into the living room. I sat down next to Emma and took a deep breath.

"Well, George stopped by and brought your purse . . . I forgot to bring your purse in. It's on the porch." I ran out to get it really quickly. "Here you go, Emma."

She was looking at me intently, "So, quit leaving me hanging! What's the big deal with you and George now?"

"OK, OK. But it really is a big deal this time, not for me really but for George and Brit."

"Brit?"

Convenience

"Yeah, Brit too—and possibly a little someone inside Brit."

Emma's eyes opened wide as she stared at me. "You're kidding—pregnant, are they sure?"

"No, but the possibility is real enough to scare the pants off both of them. I guess she is almost a month late. I doubt she's been to a doctor or anything like that. In fact, I'm not sure that she and her mom even have insurance."

"Well, she is going to need to see a doctor soon. What in the world would they do if she really is pregnant? You know what kind of counseling she'll get in school and at the hospital."

"Yeah, I know. They'll be letting out all the stops to convince her to get rid of the 'growth' inside her."

Just then, Katie came down the stairs. "Mom . . . Mom," she yelled.

"We're out here, sweet girl," Emma answered from the living room.

We both tried to quickly change the subject, but I could read Emma's face. She was carrying on a cheerful conversation with Katie but thinking about George and Brit at the same time. We pressed on with the concerns of the day.

Chapter Five

Emma and I both tried to talk to George and Brit about their situation from time to time over the next few weeks. But neither of them wanted to think about it much; they preferred to focus on the possibility of not being pregnant and this being a false alarm. Emma and Brit's mother finally talked Brit into going to the doctor. I think Brit was not only hesitant to go because of the answer she might hear but because her mother didn't have a lot of money to pay for the visit, and it really had to be a significant event before they would spend that kind of money. Emma assured Brit that they could apply for state aid if she was pregnant; that might pay for some of the cost.

Well, almost a month to the day had passed since George told us about the possibility of a pregnancy, and Brit was finally headed to the doctor for an appointment. At about five-thirty that evening, the phone rang. We had just finished dinner, and I was playing with Katie and her toy ponies.

Emma answered, "Hi, Brit." I looked over at Emma. She listened intently for what seemed several minutes. Her eyes focused more as she listened and kept saying. "Right . . . right . . . aah." She looked over at me with the same focus. Still looking at me, she spoke, "All right then; you and George have a lot to think about and a lot to consider. We'll help in any way we can, and we will be praying about the whole situation. Have you told your mom yet? What about George's mom? Please let us help in any way we can."

Emma listened intently once again, paused, and answered, "You're welcome, bye."

Emma hung up the phone and looked at me. She didn't have to tell me what the answer was. Brit is pregnant.

We all began to get the word over the next few days—well, most of us. George still didn't tell Dad. None of us dared to tell him either. George also didn't talk to me or anyone else much about it. I had tried to talk to George about options several times. His goal was clearly to have an abortion, but Brit didn't seem quite ready to make that decision yet.

One night a few weeks later, I remember eating supper at Mom's. We ate an old Italian dish called cappelletti, which means "little hats." It's basically dough wrapped around a spicy meat mixture and served in homemade chicken broth. It is one of my favorites. After dinner, George and I ended up alone at the table for a few moments. George, trying to avoid the subject of the baby, made a comment about our supper. "This stuff just doesn't taste like it usually does."

"What do you mean; it's the same good ole cappelletti."

"No, it doesn't taste right. I think she forgot to add something to it."

"George, give Mom a break. You know she's been a little sick lately."

"She's been sick since last spring. Here, have the rest of mine. I'm gonna get something from the drive-through at The Hangout. I think Brit's working tonight."

"How's she doing?" I dared ask.

"You see her every day in class. Don't you know how she's doing?"

"Well, I haven't really gotten to talk to her in a while. She seems busier than normal."

"Well, like Mom, she's been a little sick lately," George responded sarcastically. "And no, we haven't talked about our little 'problem' lately. Guess she's too sick to talk about it."

With that comment, I lost control. I grabbed his forearm. "You mean a little life."

He jerked back. "Brother, it's a little growth in her stomach, like a tumor. Anyway, we still have time to worry about it."

Convenience

I cringed inside at his comment and thought, society has made it sound like something gross, undesirable, even sickening—a "tumor?" In reality, it is a life God established and created.

George could see my blood begin to boil: an invitation. "You know," he said, "I read about a new procedure or policy. I think it's called the Euro-US Family Management policy that's coming out about abortion. Pretty soon, you'll be able to conduct abortions up to three weeks after birth. So, we *do* still have time to make a decision."

If I had cringed inside before, now my stomach was performing somersaults inside my body. "Three weeks after birth?"

He smirked. I knew he'd said all that to get under my skin, so maybe I'd back away, but his thinking nearly made me jump out of my skin and certainly made me open my big mouth again.

"What's that for? So, you can see if the baby's pretty or not? Then you can just kill it if it's not? Or maybe if the child's born handicapped, you'll still have time to change your mind," I said. "That way, we can all rid ourselves of those little 'problems.' That's the most ridiculous thing I've ever heard!" I was furious now. I bit my lip and, breathing heavily, I physically turned away from George, trying to control myself. I couldn't talk to him anymore right then. It's probably just what he was hoping for.

He smirked and shook his head as he stood up.

I remembered a verse from the Bible about a "soft word," and I tried to calm down before I spoke. He was putting his coat on. I didn't want our conversation to end like most of the others we'd had since I moved back, which ended in anger, rage, and harsh words.

I took a deep breath, "Wait, George. Don't you understand that God is the creator of all? He purposed for those babies to be born. He gave each baby an eternal soul, long before they were formed in their mother's womb."

He looked at me for a moment, almost in disbelief that I would continue on with him. Then he rolled his eyes and shook his head again while he wrapped his wool scarf around his neck.

"The Bible says God 'knew them.' He is the creator of life, and he owns the right to end it if he sees fit—not us." Maybe my calmer tone helped us both catch our breath.

"Calm down, preacher," he said, pulling on his gloves. He walked to the door and turned around. "You might as well quit trying to save this little growth . . . and me for that matter. Oh, and about that Euro-US Family Management thing, relax; the report said that even *if* the newborn may be able to feel some pain at that stage, it really has no self-concept yet, so the pain doesn't mean anything to it. So, aborting it is really not that big of a deal." He ignited my fire again.

"Great! They're less than human. How long before we stretch the three weeks into three months, three years?!"

He shut the door and walked toward his car. I ran to the door and threw it wide open, yelling at George as he walked.

"Who knows, maybe if a kid isn't performing well in school, we could kill him then! You better pull you're grades up, George!"

He gave me a cold look from inside his car. His heart just seemed crusted over so thick from the continuous propaganda in school and other media that it seemed impenetrable. He rolled down the window and yelled, "You're a fanatic. You're crazy! I'm out of here." He turned up the music and sped off in his car.

I stood outside a moment, huffing in the new silence. It had gotten colder outside. I could see my breath. I thought, *Am I a fanatic? How can I connect with him? What's wrong with me? He's my brother, one of the main reasons I moved here. I wanted to be part of his life, but all I could do was push him farther and farther away. I'm not sure he'll ever talk to me again.*

Chapter Six

It was nearly a month before George would even look my way. Even Brit seemed to be distancing herself from me in class. They still hadn't made a decision about the baby. I think George was ready for an abortion as soon as possible, but Brit hadn't decided yet. Maybe she just hadn't decided *when*.

Fall had fully set in now, and the days began to compress. It seemed to get grayer during the days and, of course, darker earlier in the evenings and colder all the time. A certain loneliness seemed to creep in, too—a feeling I remember I felt as a kid this time of year. Yet with the leaves blowing all around, there was also a certain beauty to this abrupt change of scenery that we hadn't experienced living in the South for the last several years.

Well, I had set my sights on using Thanksgiving to try to reconnect with George and Brit. Thanksgiving was a little less than a month away. I also wanted to take the opportunity to invite Lynn Bower over for our Thanksgiving meal. I had talked to her several times since the day we rolled into town—when I almost ran her over. When we talked, I would always invite her to church, but she never accepted. I think she was afraid it might make her think more about the baby she was carrying if she listened too long to the pastor preach. She seemed to not want to think too hard about the baby she was carrying for fear that she might develop some feelings for it. I was sure that she didn't want a baby in her life right now, at what she said herself was the most inconvenient time. I was almost surprised that she hadn't had an abortion yet. I had also tried to talk to her about the Lord, and she would usually steer the conversation to something more benign. But I know she still considered me to be a friend, someone she could talk to. I didn't think she had many friends, especially ones that would listen to her and show concern.

Mom was inviting the whole family over for Thanksgiving dinner. That was where I hoped to talk to George and Brit. So, Emma invited Lynn over for Thanksgiving lunch. We planned to go over to Mom's for dinner afterward. Not only would I end up more stuffed than the turkey, but I'd be running around like one with its head cut off all day. I had high hopes, though. It would be a hectic day, but one of fellowship and hopefully reconciliation with George and a time for my own family to get to know Lynn a little better.

Mom was excited to get everyone together. I knew she'd be busy trying to make the start of the hectic holiday season turn out just right. Even though the event was a few weeks off, she already began planning and preparing— and worrying that everything would work out nicely. Of course, she knew how George and I were getting along and saw the perfect chance to help us build some kind of relationship. She was always the one with insight into how things and people were getting along, and she always, sort of from the background, did her best to help. Many times, I wished I had her wisdom in handling people.

But Mom still didn't seem totally herself since we moved back. Her usual lovely energy seemed to have faded a bit. If I asked her about it, she'd insist it was just the weather.

As the days grew still shorter and colder and Thanksgiving approached, I had school keeping me occupied more than ever. The school had proven to be more work than I originally guessed. It wasn't just the kids that were a challenge, either. Knowing I had played several sports in college and had taken a number of physical education classes, Ed Stone, the physical education teacher, had asked if I wanted to assist him in several large classes. The principal followed up on the request and thought it would be an excellent idea. Even though it would be chewing up some of my free time during the day, I decided to make a career-wise decision.

Convenience

It would broaden my experience and maybe give me more options for other teaching positions, so I accepted the principal's offer.

Ed was a hard old man. I could tell he had spent some time in the Marines by the somewhat faded and now wrinkled tattoo on his forearm. He'd been "released" from the football coaching staff a few years ago for hitting one of the boys. I guess he lost his temper during a big game. In my estimation, Ed seemed to equate every bit of manhood with how physically and mentally tough you were. In Ed's eyes, if you weren't tough enough, you weren't man enough. But to him, being "tough" meant being cold, hard, and mean. Compassion was a red flag for weakness. I didn't know anything about his family or whether he even had one. Even though he didn't show much emotion and I didn't know him very well, he somehow seemed lonely to me. Of course, questions about his personal life were out-of-bounds, so I didn't ask about his family. But I did make it one of my personal goals to try to be his friend.

After a few weeks of being his assistant in the physical education class, Ed got to know me a little better too. The only trouble was the more he got to know me, the more he realized that I didn't exactly agree with his view of manliness. I could tell he was getting less patient with me all the time.

One day, we had just finished a game of what the kids affectionately called "kill ball." It was one of Ed's favorite games for the kids to play, and we usually played it on Fridays. It was a sort of floor hockey, where you tried to throw a ball in between two points on the bleachers that had been rolled back on each side of the gym. If you had the ball, you could only run three steps and then have to pass or shoot if you were close enough. Also, if you had the ball, anyone from the other team could do virtually anything they wanted to you to stop you and take the ball away. Frequently, students would get floored, blindsided, or hurt. Ed said it built character in the boys. Anyway, after the game, all the kids sat on the bleachers for a minute to catch their breath and listen to Ed ramble for a minute or two.

One Friday, Ed was giving the boys their "safety" briefing for the weekend. "So, boys, remember that even a scalding shower can't make you sterile for the next twenty-four hours," Ed said with a snicker. "Be careful and remember to be safe." Ed followed this advice with a big grin on his face.

Some guys rolled their eyes. Most weren't listening. A few chuckled with Ed and mimicked the big grin that lingered on his face. He looked at me for an approving nod, but I just stared at him. After another minute or two of Ed's rambling, the boys were dismissed and headed to the locker room. I sat there for a moment, thinking about how to deal with Ed. Amid the smell of sweat and the sound of sneakers squeaking across the gym floor, I finally got up off the bleacher and headed for the locker room myself. Ed stayed out on the floor for a while longer, so I didn't even talk to him before heading for the showers.

After that, I just waited for him to let me know much he didn't like my outlook. I was spoiling his fun. I think he knew I was a Christian. Maybe he would attack me from that standpoint.

In the few times we talked after that, he seemed to treat me the same, which sort of puzzled me. Didn't he recognize my distaste for his comment that day? Did he forget about it? I couldn't tell and wasn't about to ask him any time soon.

Chapter Seven

A week passed, and Thanksgiving was upon us. Emma was busy in the kitchen when I got home from school the night before the grand evening was to take place. We'd gotten a dusting of snow during the day, and it was probably twenty degrees outside. Winter was definitely setting in.

"Hi, hon," I blurted out as I entered the kitchen.

"Hi, Levi," Emma answered quickly as she continued stirring some delicious strawberry glaze substance that filled the kitchen with a wonderful, warm, sweet smell.

"Making strawberry pie?" I asked in a sort of loud voice, feeling like I almost had to yell through the candied air in the kitchen.

"Trying to," Emma returned. "But it's so hard to stir at first, and I think I made enough for five pies in this big old pot. Interested in giving Chef Emma a hand?"

I snuck up behind her, put my arms around her, buried my head into her brownish-blond hair, and gave her a kiss as I grabbed her stirring hand. "You mean like this?" She smiled at me.

"Not exactly—I thought I might be able to do something else while you did the stirring . . . alone."

"Oh, OK." With a smile, I grabbed the large spoon and began to stir. "How's the rest of the stuff coming? And where's my girl?" I raised my voice a little hoping Katie would hear me.

"Shhh, Dad, I'm trying to make some cookies over here."

I looked around the corner of the center island of our kitchen and saw Katie working diligently on her small table. She was rolling dough around and around.

"Aren't you going to flatten the dough out and cut it into cookies pretty soon?"

"Shhh," she responded again, concentrating closely on her delicate operation.

"Sorry," I said, looking at Emma and not being able to hold back a smile.

"Daddy, who is coming over for Thanksgiving?"

"Well, do you remember the lady we saw the first day we got here? She was crossing the road, and we stopped to talk to her. I remember she gave you a big smile when she met you."

"Oh, I remember that lady. We almost hit her with our car!"

"Well, yeah, that's the lady. I guess that's one way to remember her."

Emma had been wrestling with some cans of food in our large cupboard and pulled her head out for a moment. "What time is she coming over?"

"I don't know yet. I told her that we needed to start kind of early so we would have time to visit and also get over to Mom's. I told her I'd call today and give her the exact time."

We all worked together for another several hours. Emma made enough of all the good stuff for us and our guest, Lynn, with enough left over to bring to Mom's later. After everything was ready and we had cleaned up the kitchen and the rest of the house, I played ponies with Katie for a little while. Then we read a small book and a few verses from the Bible. Katie barely made it through our nightly prayers before falling asleep. She had worked pretty hard and was exhausted. Her cookies turned out great.

Emma and I sat down for a moment to wind down before bed.

I had called Lynn's earlier but got no answer. Although it was a little late, I tried one more time.

"Hello, Lynn? This is Levi. Yes, well, we need to start a little early tomorrow because we have to go over to Mom and Dad's later in the afternoon. I hope that's OK. Let's say around noon?. . OK, and no, you don't need to bring anything. Emma and Katie and I—well mostly, Emma and Katie, have made a ton of food. . . . That's fine. How's the new job? Right, yeah, I know that can be a lot of work, especially just starting out. All right then. . . . We'll see you tomorrow around noon. Bye."

"How did Lynn sound?" Emma asked. "I wonder what she is going to do with her baby now that she is working in her new job at the law firm?"

"Emma, this sounds terrible, but I'm sort of surprised that she hasn't had an abortion yet. In the four or five times I've talked to her, she always mentions how having a baby right now would be the most inconvenient thing in the world. It seems like she keeps saying that, hoping to get someone like me to agree with her. I just don't comment each time she brings that up. You know," I thought for a moment, "she seemed a bit out of focus on the phone tonight."

"What does that mean?" Emma looked at me with a raised eyebrow.

"Well, I'm not sure. Her speech was a bit slurred . . . and she seemed to be thinking about something else, something disturbing. Anyway, I think she understood what I was saying, and I hope she'll enjoy coming over. I wonder if she has anyone to really talk to around here."

"Well, I'm sure she won't bring up those issues tomorrow. We all need to concentrate on being thankful and enjoying the holiday."

"Yeah," I replied, taking a deep breath and pausing for a moment. "You're right, honey. Good night."

"Good night, Levi."

By the time my eyes popped open in the morning, I could hear Emma singing to herself in the kitchen, and I could already smell a fresh, homemade cherry pie. How late was it? Fear rushed over my not-quite-awake body. I jumped out of bed and took a closer look at the clock. It was only six thirty, so I slowed my pace down a bit, got washed up, and followed the wonderful scents to the kitchen.

"Good morning, Emma."

"Good morning, Levi."

"Did you stay up all night cooking," I jokingly asked?

"Yeah, I did," Emma jokingly replied. "I made some coffee a few minutes ago. Do you want some?"

"Oh yes, now you're talking. I slept like a rock, but then I also remember lying there with my eyes wide open, staring at the ceiling, wondering about Lynn and that baby."

"Well, your eyes weren't open too long 'cause you were snoring like crazy!! You sounded like an old Mack truck trying to slow down on a steep hill! I'm the one who could claim no sleep—thanks to your serenade all night."

"Really? I didn't hear a thing, but I hear something now."

Katie was quietly sneaking her way down the stairs. She was rubbing the sleep out of her eyes and had a big smile. I knew what her first question would be.

"Daddy, when is our friend coming over?" she asked.

"Good morning, sweet girl. Our friend, Miss Lynn, will be over in about four more hours. So, you have time to take a nice bath and get dressed, and have a little breakfast. But not much; we are going to be eating all day today!"

We finished our final preparations, made a little breakfast for Katie, and sat down at about eleven-thirty with a second cup of coffee.

"Well, everything is ready," Emma said in an already tired-sounding voice. "The lunch turkey should be ready at about twelve-thirty, so we'll have a little time after Lynn arrives before we can eat."

"Sounds good. You really have worked hard on all this."

"I just want Lynn to feel at home and special. I don't think she has many friends around here. I've only talked to her a few times, but she seems kind of lonely."

"I think you're right about that. Most of her high school friends got married or left town or both. Plus, she lived in Deer Lake for seven years. Now, most of the folks her age are busy with their own families or just aren't around much anymore."

"I'd like her to know that we are friends she can count on—especially if she needs to talk about her pregnancy issue," Emma responded with a concerned look on her face.

Lynn arrived around twelve o'clock, wearing a dress suit. She looked like she was ready for an interview and just about as nervous. I could tell she had gone to great pains not to give away the fact that she was pregnant. She had landed the job she wanted as an accountant and seemed to enjoy it a lot. It seemed like she didn't even want to remember that she was pregnant, but within a month or so, she certainly wouldn't be able to hide it.

"Hi, Levi and Emma. How are you? Thank you for inviting me over. That was really nice. Here's a pie we can devour after lunch."

"Pumpkin," I replied. "Looks great. I can tell I'm gonna be one full guy by the end of this day."

"Let me take your coat, Lynn," Emma said warmly. "It must really be chilly out there."

"It is downright freezing if you ask me, and I've been in this area all my life."

"The pie does look great. Thanks for bringing it, but you really didn't have to go to all the trouble," Emma continued.

"Oh, no trouble at all. Really . . . I wish I could say I made it myself, but I just didn't have much time with the new job."

We all stood at the door, kind of awkwardly. Emma finally broke in. "Please, come in. We need to get away from that drafty door. Katie will be down in a second once she knows you're here. She is so excited."

I could tell that Lynn had been through a few sleepless nights. A slight sinking and darkness around the eyes and a slight dullness of her skin shone through the makeup Lynn had on. I wondered for a moment if it might be from the worry about this pregnancy. Maybe it wasn't so much worry as simply coping with the physical toll of being by herself and pregnant and handling the new job at the same time. In any case, it was good to see her.

My thoughts were abruptly interrupted by Katie bouncing down the stairs. "Hi, Miss Lynn," Katie said with a smile.

Lynn's wide smile stretched even wider, and her tired eyes beamed when she saw Katie coming down the stairs.

Katie could tell from the last time that they met that Lynn liked her and asked if she wanted to go to her room and play. The food wasn't quite ready yet, and we had exchanged a bit of small talk already. So,

Katie and I took Lynn up to see her room. Katie had set out a number of colorful toy ponies.

"Those are really neat ponies you have there," Lynn said in such a kind and loving voice.

Katie gave a polite "thank you" and picked one up for Lynn to hold. "Did you have ponies or horses when you were little?"

Lynn paused for a moment thinking back to the days when she was young. "I didn't have a lot of toys," she answered and shifted her eyes toward the window. She seemed distant for a moment, full of a strange mixture of longing and sadness. "My mom was sick most of the time," she explained. She kept the fact that her mother was an alcoholic from her young friend.

"Dad was too busy working hard to take care of us to worry about a lot of toys," Lynn continued. "He worked so hard that he got sick too." Again, Lynn spared Katie the details of how her father probably drank himself to death. He died when she was twenty-one.

Trying to bend the subject back to a more pleasant topic, I interrupted. "Well, I'm gonna go down and check on the food. Be right back. Lynn, would you like something to drink before lunch—soda or tea or something?"

Lynn focused again on me and answered, "No thanks, Levi. Not right now."

Even at six years old, Katie sensed Lynn's pain in her explanation. She wanted to be comforting. "Daddy told me that he might get me a real horse someday. I think if I ask him, he might get you one too."

Lynn smiled and chuckled slightly, "You're very nice, and you're lucky to have such a nice mom and dad. I'm sure they would do anything to make you happy, and they try pretty hard to help me, too," Lynn said, kneeling down to Katie's level. "Well, what's this pony's name?"

"April," Katie responded. The two played for a while, lost in the world of ponies and enjoying a brief moment together.

After about twenty minutes, Lynn and Katie popped down the stairs like two best buddies. Except for the professional-looking outfit, Lynn seemed almost like a kid herself. She looked as carefree as Katie as the two of them, smiles dominating their faces, continued down the stairs.

Convenience

Then it happened. Lynn's heel caught on the carpet on the stairs. Her foot closest to the railing stuck in place and caused her body to swing down and toward the rail. She immediately grabbed the rail with one hand, squeezing it tightly, and wrapped her other hand around her belly as her whole body swung toward the rail, and her shoulder bounced into it, giving her a slight jolt. She stopped there, breathing a little heavily. We all held our breath, unable to do anything but watch. She took another deep breath and looked at us. Then she quickly said, "I'm fine," so as to allow us all to breathe again.

"Really, I'm fine," Lynn reiterated as she looked down at her belly, noticing her hand still wrapped around it as though instinctively protecting what was inside. As she looked down, her face turned serious, then sad, apparently remembering the realities of her life.

Katie broke Lynn's concentration by asking if she was all right.

"Yes, sweety, I'm fine." She smiled at her concerned little friend. "I guess I need to be more careful. I probably should have taken my shoes off when I came in, huh?" The two continued down the stairs a little more slowly and quietly.

By then, Emma and I had set the table and put the food out so it would cool a bit. We all calmed down and then sat down to deep-fried turkey, a specialty Emma picked up from our neighbors in Atlanta. Lynn had never heard of deep frying an entire turkey before, as I'm sure that few people in Franklin did that. Lynn hadn't had a lot of experience with Southern-style food. She was a little hesitant about the banana pudding and sweet potato pie, but she was sold after the first bite. We had a good conversation over the first feast of the day, although Lynn never really got over her near-fall and reminder of the responsibilities of her life. I was really hoping Lynn could get a little break from the concerns in her life and relax. In any case, Emma and I were glad to have seen a big smile on her face when she played with Katie.

After sampling various pies, I started a pot of coffee for all of us and put on a video for Katie.

"Wow, I don't know if I'll be able to eat again tonight, Emma," I said, leaning back.

"I think you'll find a way. I've seen you in action at the kitchen table a few times," she said. Lynn laughed as she moved to the living room to sit for a moment while the coffee brewed.

"Lynn, would you like decaf coffee," Emma called from the kitchen.

Lynn got that sober look on her face again, perhaps remembering that she was pregnant and probably shouldn't have regular coffee. "Only if it's no trouble, Emma. Thanks."

After a hot cup of coffee, Lynn popped up out of her chair and brought her cup into the kitchen.

"Well, you all have another get-together to go to, so I should be going. Thanks so much for having me over. I really enjoyed myself."

"You're very welcome, Lynn," I responded, feeling rather proud of myself, having made a special effort not to insert foot in my mouth the entire visit.

Emma chimed in, "Yes, you certainly are very welcome, and we hope you can come over again soon. Maybe you could come over for tea sometime."

"Oh, you're very kind," Lynn responded. "Thank you. I'd like to come to visit Katie and all of you again soon."

Feeling a little bolder and wondering if my family could be of any help, I asked Lynn how she's been feeling. She was putting her suit jacket back on. Suddenly, she snapped back.

"What do you mean?" she asked, most definitely offended.

I didn't understand the sudden change when we'd been talking so freely before. "I . . . I guess I was just wondering how you're feeling, physically, with all that's going on with you," I said, stumbling over the words, trying to smooth things back over, but failing miserably.

"I'm fine." She paused for a moment and looked behind me to make sure no one else was around.

"You're still wondering what I'm going to do with this pregnancy, aren't you?" She didn't give me a chance to respond.

"Listen," Lynn paused for a moment, then looked me right in the eye, "I'm glad we're friends, but I'm starting to feel like your latest charity case, and I don't appreciate it. I don't want to hear anyone's opinion about this pregnancy and what I should do—not from you or anyone else. You have a perfect family. You have a perfect life . . ."

Convenience

"Perfect life?" I interrupted and then pulled up my pant leg. I knocked on the plastic shin that replaced my real one after my accident. My knuckles made a dull, lifeless, cold thump-like sound off my artificial leg. "What do you mean?"

Lynn sighed, lowering her head and gathering her thoughts. "I . . . I mean, your parents loved you, and you got to go off to college and build a career. You've got a great life, a wonderful wife . . . and a precious, precious little daughter. It's easy for you to believe in God. If you were in my shoes, it wouldn't be so easy to feel like there's a God who cares."

Lynn began to really get riled up now. "I'm getting tired of pumping up your piety as you keep showing 'concern' for my so-called 'baby and me.'" She breathed out deeply. "I know you're trying to make me feel guilty, trying to guilt me into having this child at the most stressful, difficult, and inconvenient time in my life! And for what? So you can chalk up another good deed under your belt. For your information, I don't plan on having a child at this point in my life. So maybe you should find another charity case to befriend."

By now, she was on the brink of tears and breathing heavily.

I looked away, confused. Was what she said true? Maybe I was just being condescending. "Lynn, I'm sorry. I really don't want you to think . . ."

Lynn again looked down at her shoes for a moment. "I'm sorry too. I have to get home now anyway. Thanks for the meal and tell Emma and Katie goodbye for me. I'll let myself out."

Just then, I could hear Katie coming down the stairs as her video finished. Katie yelled, "Goodbye, Miss Lynn."

Lynn quickly put on a smile and returned a goodbye to Katie. Then she grabbed the front door and opened it. A gust of cold wintry air rushed in. It made Lynn shudder a little. She turned and looked at me, not saying a word, then dashed out into the cold.

I shut the door and stood dumbfounded as I watched Lynn leave. "Katie, did you hear what we were talking about?"

"Yes," Emma replied, "I think we both did."

Katie looked at me with a very serious expression on her face. "Daddy, I'm going to be really good from now on."

"Sweety, you're pretty good all the time. What are you getting at?"

Katie had a half-hearted smile on her face, but I could tell that she was trying to cover up a deep concern. Finally, she said, "I don't want you to be stressed and incon . . . , inconv . . . , inconveeny—and want to get rid of me."

Emma's eyes glazed over as she looked at me. Then she bent down to Katie. "We would never even think about that, honey. You don't ever have to worry about that."

The three of us sat together in the middle of the floor and hugged each other for a while.

I thought that I should have done a better job of keeping my mouth shut. *"You really blew that one, Levi,"* I thought as I scolded myself.

Chapter Eight

I looked again at Emma. "Well, this holiday started off with a bang. I hope the rest of the day will be a little less eventful."

We gradually got back on track with our day and started to get ready to go to Mom's. The thought of going to Mom's got us excited again, especially Katie. When we got to Mom and Dad's, we knew we'd find Mom busy in the kitchen. We let ourselves in, and the smell of onions, turkey, and other great foods filled our nostrils. Katie immediately sprang into action, putting on her apron and assisting Mom in the kitchen.

Dad met us as he came down the stairs. He had that concerned, nervous, almost worried look on his face. He was probably worried about how things would turn out with George and Brit, and me coming over for dinner. He seemed like he spent most of his days lately trying to figure out George and how to handle him . . . and help him.

"Hey, Dad. Happy Thanksgiving," I said with a smile.

"Same to you and your family, son. How did your first meal go with your friend?"

Emma and I looked at each other for a moment. "Ah, not too bad. We . . . we got to know each other a little better," I responded. Emma nodded her head in agreement, eyebrows raised a bit more than normal, slightly giving away our secret. Dad didn't notice, though; he was still thinking a bit too hard about George.

"I'll be right back," Dad exclaimed as he headed for the back door and the garage.

I looked at Emma and asked, "Do you think she's OK?"

"Who?" asked Emma, "Katie or Lynn?"

"Well," I responded, "I was thinking about Katie, but now that you mention it, I guess we should be concerned for both after the day we had. I think Katie is OK. At this point, I'm not sure what to do about Lynn except to pray."

Emma responded, "Let's call her in a few days."

"All right, but let's enjoy our time with family the rest of this day."

Emma joined Katie in the kitchen to help with the meal while I adjourned to the living room, where Dad had circled back. We turned on the TV and began watching a football game.

"Where's George?" I asked.

"He went to pick up Brit. He should be back soon."

It still seemed somehow a bit awkward whenever Dad and I were alone. Neither of us is really talkative.

"Looks like he might be 'fashionably late,' as they say."

Dad didn't answer. I don't think he wanted to, so he focused on the football game.

Shortly after, I could hear Mom and the others busy setting the table, talking, and enjoying each other's company. Katie seemed to have forgotten the morning's episode, at least for now. She had a mission, the Thanksgiving Day feast! And just like her grandma, she was determined to make it a special time for us all.

Thirty more minutes rolled by—still, there was no sign of George and Brit. It was beginning to look like I wouldn't even get a chance to make up with my brother—not on this day, anyway. After another thirty minutes, we decided to sit down and eat without George and Brit. I was starting to feel like this evening was going to be a disappointment, similar to this afternoon. As we began to pass around the scrumptious food, I thought it was really a shame that George and Brit hadn't gotten a chance to see how hard Mom and Katie, and Emma worked on making this meal really nice. We thanked the Lord for all His blessings and for the wonderful meal and began the great culinary adventure!

Convenience

Just as I was passing the honey ham, the phone rang. Emma was nearby, so she got up and answered it. A few seconds after answering with a polite hello, her face grew intense as she listened to the voice on the other end. I knew my wife well. I could tell something was wrong.

"When?" she asked. "OK. . . . Where?" she continued.

With every word, we all seemed to slide closer to the edge of our chairs.

"Right now? OK." was her final word as she hung up the phone and looked at us.

Unable to decode the conversation, I stared at her, honey ham still in my grasp. She looked back at me. "Brit has had an emergency. George found her doubled over on the floor in her living room when he stopped by to pick her up. He took her to Jackson Baptist Hospital. He was calling from the emergency room and wants us to come over right away!"

I sprang into action, almost feeling like I was back on the flight line in Atlanta, handling some aircraft emergency. A chill came over me as, for a split second, I remembered the last emergency I had out there on the line. I remembered the shock on everyone's faces as the tragedy unfolded, and I still wondered if there was something I could have done differently that night, something that might have saved that boy's life. I took a deep breath and regained my thoughts, "Emma, you and I can go over. Mom, will you take care of Katie?"

Mom immediately responded, "I want to go over too."

"You do?" I asked, kind of surprised.

"Yes, I do. I like Brit, and she's carrying George's baby . . . remember?"

"OK, Mom, why don't we all go? But let's hurry."

As we all got into the car, a calm, light snow began to fall silently from the bright night sky. The earlier biting cold wind subsided as night fell, and the lights of the town reflected off of the low-hanging clouds.

"Emma, is Brit's mom going?" I asked.

She looked at me as we got into the car. "George said he couldn't reach her, so he left a message on her cell."

Emma continued to explain what she knew as we all settled into the car. "He said he knocked on Brit's door. When there was no answer, he peeked in and saw Brit, on all fours, on the floor in the middle of the living room. He helped her up and drove her over to the hospital. She wouldn't let George call an ambulance because she didn't know whether their insurance would cover it."

I wondered whether it was wise to bring Katie, but Dad wanted to come too, so there was no time to think beyond getting there to help. I guess, in spite of George's rude behavior at times, we had all grown closer to Brit without even realizing it. Even with the mile-wide distance George and I had constructed between us over the last month, I found myself very worried about Brit, George, and, as Mom reminded me, the baby she was carrying.

We all crammed into my car and sped off for the hospital. It only took about five to ten minutes to get anywhere in our little town, so we got there quickly. I found a spot and parked, and told everyone I was going to run ahead. I ran into the emergency entrance and saw George standing in the hallway.

"George," I called out.

"Levi," George called back, using my real first name for the first time since I moved back.

"What's going on?" I asked. George explained the story that Emma had already told us in the car.

"I got here, and they immediately put her in a bed and wheeled her into that room over there," he explained, pointing to a room across the hall.

Just then, Mom and the rest of the crew walked into ER. George seemed surprised to see all of us there.

"I guess the turkey's getting cold at home, huh," George said, trying to think of something to say.

Mom and Emma looked at George. He could tell what they wanted without a word.

"She's in there," he said as he pointed to the room across the hall. Mom and Emma both went right into the room.

George was especially surprised to see Dad there. Instead of his usual biting wit and sarcasm toward Dad, the best that George could come up with now was, "Hi, Dad."

"Hi, George. How is she?" Dad asked in response.

Convenience

Still surprised at Dad's concern for him and even more surprised at his concern for Brit, George turned away from us and stood speechless for a moment. He turned back toward us and finally responded to Dad's inquiry. "I'm not sure. They wouldn't let me in," George answered, still with a puzzled look on his face.

Then they both just stood and stared at each other. Dad finally broke the staring contest as he looked over to Katie.

"Katie, come here. Let's see what toys they have here. Maybe they have some ponies."

As Dad left for the waiting room, George and I stood looking at each other. Neither of us wanted to maintain silence for too long for fear of remembering why we had been so mad at each other.

"I hope we can find out if she's OK pretty soon," I said awkwardly.

"Uh yeah," George said even more awkwardly. He then looked at me, took a deep breath, and started in.

"Look," he said, "I'm here for Brit. Don't get any big ideas. I saw her on the floor, and it really hit me that I do . . . well . . . care for her a lot. Seeing her in trouble scared me."

He stopped for a moment, thinking of how to proceed with his conversation. He took another deep breath and looked me straight in the eye.

"I'm glad you came so quickly, but I haven't changed my mind about her 'problem,'" referring to her pregnancy.

The word *problem* hit me right between the eyes. How could he refer to a human life, which God himself created, as though it was a little insignificant "problem?" Somehow, I held my tongue (maybe for the first time in my life) and thought of what I should say.

I paused for a moment, "All right, I think you know how I feel about it. But right now, I'm concerned about Brit too. And honestly, how about you? How are you holding up? You are my brother, ya know." I patted him on the upper arm as I spoke. "Have you had anything to eat?"

George had no response. He was a bit shocked at my concern, and I was a bit shocked that those words were coming out of my mouth. So, we both just stood there for a moment awkwardly.

George turned away, seemingly very deep in thought. For a minute, he looked as though he might expose a bit of his heavily guarded heart. Then his eyebrows lowered, and he regained the stern facade he usually maintained and said, "You know, it's been twenty minutes, and they haven't told me anything. I need to find out what's going on."

He spoke loud enough for a nurse who was passing by to hear. She stopped and came over to us and said, "I'll go in and check on the patient for you, sir."

"Thanks," we both exclaimed at the same time; our mannerisms and even our voice were so similar.

I looked at George and said, "Brother, let me go over and get you a cup of coffee out of the machine while you're waiting."

"OK, Levi," George replied.

As I walked over to the machine, it occurred to me that since I had moved back to town, George had called me "brother," usually steeped in sarcasm. And I, in turn, had called him George. Today, for the first time, George called me by my first name, and I called him brother! God has a way of turning things upside down sometimes.

As it turned out, the nurse didn't check on Brit for us. She was called to another emergency. And George and I sat across the hall and drank our coffee. We knew Mom and Emma were in the room with Brit, so we sat a little longer and tried to be patient.

In Brit's room, Mom and Emma tried to provide some comfort.

"How are you feeling?" Emma asked as she moved a little closer to Brit's bedside.

"I'm feeling pretty good at the moment, but I don't really want to talk about it right now if you don't mind."

Emma and Mom were a little taken aback by her comment. They weren't sure whether she didn't like them being there or she just didn't want to talk to anyone. They stood in silence for a moment. Emma finally broke the silence.

"OK, Brit, is there anything else you'd like to talk about?"

"How about," Brit stared at the ceiling while she talked, "well . . . tell me about your . . . your religion, you know, your beliefs or faith, or whatever you call it."

Convenience

Emma was totally surprised at Brit's request from out of the blue. She looked at my mom and silently said a quick prayer, asking God to guide her words, and then she began.

"OK, well, we believe . . . well, let me start from the beginning." Emma went on to explain how God had created us to fellowship with him and to glorify him. But he also loved us so much that he gave us free will to choose and make our own decisions. He didn't make us robots that would be his subjects and be forced to praise him. He wanted a real relationship with us. Back in the beginning, when he gave Adam and Eve free will, they could fellowship with him freely. All they had to do was not choose to eat the fruit of one tree. Well, they were tempted by the devil, who was one of God's fallen angels and wanted to rule over all creation himself. Eve ate from the tree, and that was the first sin of man. But with that sin, Adam and Eve and all of the rest of humanity that followed them were unable to fellowship directly with God because of their sin nature. God, being completely fair and just and holy, proclaimed that "the wages of sin is death," meaning that true justice requires that we all be punished for our sins. Well, you know that we all die sooner or later. But God was also talking about spiritual death and separation from him.

"You see, Brit, we are all spiritual beings, and the Bible tells us that our spirit is eternal. Rather than having eternal separation from God, in his wonderful love and grace, God made a way for us to be forgiven and to be cleansed from our sins forever and to be able to fellowship with him forever. But again, it's our choice."

Emma took a deep breath as she paused to gather her thoughts again. "God sent his son Jesus to step down from his Holy place and take on flesh, and the Bible says that he became a man, but he was a sinless man. I know it seems hard to understand, but God made himself a man like George and Levi, yet he didn't sin because he was to be the perfect offering for our sins. Through his great love and obedience, he endured death on the cross to pay for all the sins of mankind—past, present, and future. All we have to do is accept his free gift of forgiveness, and we can be saved eternally. We are still living in this flesh and are susceptible to being tempted, and we still mess up every day, but we are forgiven and have become, the Bible says, adopted into the fellowship of God and will spend eternity in heaven with him if we accept his gift. When we do, we still have our sinful nature, but we have different motivations and want to serve and worship and love our great God."

Emma stopped and took another deep breath. She hadn't even noticed the roll she was on in explaining her beliefs. Since no one was coming in yet, Emma continued. "God created everything, and he created us, nothing else, in his very own image. I think that makes us very special."

Looking directly into Emma's eyes, Brit blinked a few times and said, "I've never heard that before."

Emma and Mom both realized what Brit was really saying. She didn't just mean that no one had ever told her that before. But based on Emma's explanation of how special a man was, Brit meant that no one had ever told her how special *she* was. Brit smiled at Mom, who smiled back at her in silence.

Just then, breaking the silence, a nurse barged into the room, looking as though she had ten things going on at the same time.

"Brit," she said, looking at Brit for confirmation that she was in the right room.

"That's me," Brit responded.

"The doctor will be in here in a few minutes to explain everything to you," the nurse blurted out. "But basically, you're fine. There was nothing abnormal in any of the tests we ran. He thinks you may have had a big buildup of gas. And that, combined with the pregnancy, caused the pain. Once he talks to you, you'll be able to check out."

"Thanks," Brit responded.

Without another word, the nurse rushed out of the room as quickly as she came in.

"Well," Emma said, "sounds like good news to me."

"I knew I should never have come," Brit replied with a worried look on her face.

"We'll send you over some turkey for when you're feeling better," Mom replied, trying to comfort Brit and change the subject.

Just then, George stormed in almost as quickly as the nurse did shortly before. Brit's eyes brightened up, and she focused solely on George. She reached her hand out to him, and he reached for her. Then their foreheads touched together as George explained, "The nurse said you're OK."

"Yeah, sounds like it," Brit replied. Their eyes still locked on to each other; they hovered in their own private world for a moment, then recalled that Mom and Emma were in the room. George, now a little embarrassed for revealing so much emotion in front of Emma and his mom, looked over at them, trying his best not to reveal too much emotion as he said, "Thanks for coming. You were both a big help."

"You're welcome, George," Emma replied. "We're going to go check on the guys out here," she continued as she and Mom walked out of the room.

Brit, almost in a shout so as not to lose the opportunity, called out to Emma: "Mrs. Bell." Both Emma and Mom turned, and both realized that they had responded to the same name; they gave a little chuckle, then turned back to Brit.

"Thanks," said Brit as she smiled at both of them. They smiled back and left the room.

Emma, walking ahead of Mom, asked, "Well, do you think Brit understood my attempt at sharing the gospel?"

Mom didn't answer. "Mom," Emma called out, still walking. After a moment of silence and no response from Mom, Emma turned and looked back. Mom had stopped walking and was standing there with one hand outstretched as though she was dizzy or couldn't see in front of her.

"Mom," Emma called out again. Then, as Emma quickly moved closer to Mom, she realized that Mom's eyes had rolled back from their normal position.

"Mom!" Emma yelled louder.

Just then, Mom's knees buckled as she started to fall to the floor. Emma caught her before she hit the floor and yelled still louder, "Mom, are you OK!"

I had just rounded the corner when I heard Emma's last call.

"What's wrong?" I yelled.

"We were just walking out of the room, and Mom passed out as I was talking to her. I know it was a long day for her, but I didn't think she was feeling bad."

Just then, two nurses rounded the corner and saw us on the floor. They quickly sprang into action, and before we knew it, they were putting Mom into a hospital bed. They wheeled her into a room across from Brit. Emma and I stood on either side of the bed. I think we were both wondering, what more could happen today?

Mom came to after a few more minutes and immediately began to tell everyone that she was fine, just like the last two times when she had passed out in the last two months. By then, Dad had made his way into the room and had brought Katie with him. Of course, Mom insisted that she didn't need to be in a hospital bed and wanted to leave as soon as she could. The doctor eventually came into the room and checked the newly made chart at the foot of Mom's bed.

Now late into the evening, the doctor looked as though he had put in a long day. He looked to be in his early thirties and had very hairy arms. Once again, the attending physician didn't have a good answer for Mom's problem. He casually stated that she probably just had too hectic of a day and perhaps she simply needed to get more rest. Mom agreed with the doctor and asked if she could be released so she could go home and get proper rest. The doctor responded with an impersonal demeanor, saying that he would let the nurses know to release her in a few minutes. I could see he was already thinking about something else while he answered and began to walk out of the room. My blood began to boil, and I began to feel that I might be the next one to need a room; I caught the doctor outside the room. He was making a speedy getaway, so I grabbed him by one arm. He turned, somewhat impatiently, and asked, "Yes sir, what can I do for you?"

I responded, "Doctor, do you have any thoughts on why Mom keeps passing out? This is the third time she has passed out in the last few months."

The doctor raised his voice slightly, tilted his head, and raised an eyebrow as he spoke to me. "As I said earlier, it could be a number of

Convenience

things. I don't think it's anything serious; it could just be caused by a lack of sleep."

"That's what we were told last time, and since then, she has gotten plenty of sleep. Are there any other tests that can be run?"

"We could give her an MRI and some in-depth chest X-rays, but I'm not sure we are at that stage yet."

Getting more irritated, I asked, "Well, when would we be at that stage? She has passed out several times already."

The doctor calmly, almost mechanically, responded, "I know that, Mr. Bell, but at her age, we don't ask for those extensive kinds of tests this soon in the process. We are not even sure older folks can afford or even want to take the tests."

"Afford! Since when is health a matter of affordability? Is public healthcare just another business? And why would age have an effect on whether Mom gets tests or not?" My eyebrows dropped to the attack position. "Do you have a mom?" I asked.

The doctor chuckled a little and turned and walked away, shaking his head as though he had just spoken to a child who couldn't understand what he was trying to say. He left me standing there, mouth wide open, wondering how life got so crazy. Was the doctor really that callous toward older people? Was society nowadays, as a whole, that uncaring toward older people? Were they now just another inconvenience? I would have pursued him down the hall, but I needed to get back to the rest of the family.

Well, we brought Mom home, and of course, she again insisted that she was fine. I was still worried about her, but there wasn't much I could do about it at that point. I pondered the whole event as we dropped Mom and Dad off at the house. It seemed like the more we humans learn, the more we doubt our creator, and the more we think we control life and death. It almost felt like the doctor had determined that Mom wasn't worth the "extensive testing" and that it was more convenient for all of us if we saved those tests for younger people. I would have pursued getting the tests, but Mom insisted that she was OK and wouldn't let me make a fuss about it.

George had taken Brit home and stayed at her house for a while.

Brit's mom was home, and they had to calm her down and explain all that had happened. Emma and Katie, and I finally made our way home.

What a day, I thought to myself as I sat in my favorite cushy chair in the living room. I had blown it with Lynn, and then just when I thought I wasn't going to even get a chance with George, the Lord, through circumstances I would never have imagined, brought our whole family closer than any turkey dinner would have. I felt like both George and Brit had come to trust us more and that we had made great strides toward a real relationship. So, the day went from a low with Lynn to a high with George and Brit. And just when I thought things were humming right along, Mom goes down in the hospital. Talk about a roller coaster.

Katie had fallen asleep as soon as we got home, and we put her right into bed. At last, we had a few minutes to talk more about the day's events. Emma finally got to tell me about her talk with Brit. She explained how she got to present not a religion but the truth from the Bible and God's message of creation and salvation. I was thrilled to hear about the great opportunity God had given to Emma. She went on to tell me how in the confusion with Mom, she had a chance to talk more with Brit.

"It was just the two of us for a while," Emma explained. "I could tell there was something Brit wanted . . . needed to tell me, woman to woman. Something a man wouldn't understand. She told me that when she was in pain on the floor there at her house, that was the first time she was worried about . . . then she stopped for about thirty seconds and began again. She finally got it out. She said she was worried about the baby! Levi, she called it a baby. I was almost speechless, Emma continued. "We hugged each other and cried together for a moment. No one else even noticed."

Just then, I brushed back a tear of my own and said, "Honey, God is good; God is good." We finally came to the end of a crazy day.

Chapter Nine

I didn't see George for the rest of the holiday weekend. And I only had time to call Mom once on Saturday to see how she was feeling. The answer was "fine," of course. The first time I got to talk to George was the following Saturday morning when I came over to work on Dad's garage door opener. It had stopped working a few months ago, and I didn't want Dad to have to worry about that problem during the ever-closer freezing winter. In Montana, you quickly learn to fix everything before it gets too cold to do the work, or you'll have to wait till spring. I was taking the opener down from the ceiling when George walked by.

"Hey, Levi." He called me Levi again! It was medicine for my soul.

"Hi, George," I responded. I noticed that he had a stern look on his face. I should say that he had an even more stern look on his face than usual. "What's up?" I asked.

He stopped, looked out across the yard, and seemed to be deep in thought. He appeared to be searching, or I guess, reasoning through something. It seemed like he wanted to talk to me about something but wasn't sure whether he wanted to engage in a deep conversation with me. As I thought about it, I realized that he really had no one to talk to around here except Brit.

Finally, he turned to me, "You want to hear something really stupid?" He continued, "Brit wouldn't call an ambulance the other day when she had her emergency because she knew their very lame insurance wouldn't cover it."

"That's not stupid on her part," I cut in.

"I know, but it still makes me mad that she could have really hurt herself. That's bad enough, but listen to this. Now, the insurance company says they aren't going to cover the whole emergency room visit."

"What?" I replied, cutting into George's explanation again.

"Yeah, they found some reason, some stupid loophole, and now Brit owes a thousand bucks! And there is no government aid either that covers an underage, single pregnant girl. Social Support will pay for every little thing we need for an abortion . . . everything. But no one wants to pay for a pregnant girl's health."

"That's not right," I chimed in.

"We should have gotten rid of this 'problem' long ago. And spare me the lecture about abortions."

I bit my lip but held my peace, not wanting to ruin my chance to talk to my brother.

George continued, "We have had so many chances to lose this inconvenience once and for all, but Brit keeps saying that she doesn't have time or that she wants to wait a little longer because we still have plenty of time. I know she wants to get rid of it, but the longer she waits, the more complicated it gets. It's starting to make her sick, and now it's going to cost a thousand bucks! It's just trouble, a pain, no matter how you look at it."

I listened and tried frantically not to look upset about what George was saying. Finally, giving in, I asked, "George, are you sure Brit thinks the same way you do about this?"

George quickly answered, "Of course, Levi; we're kids! She's in high school—remember? How else could she feel!" George was now yelling at me.

I took a long, deep breath to try to calm us both down. Then I spoke, "George, I'm not sure we can know exactly how women feel in this . . . well . . . situation."

George tensed up as he had in our past bad encounters. I waited for the direct shot right between the eyes, figuring I had probably, again, said too much.

Then, surprisingly, George looked down at his feet for a moment and took a deep breath. He looked back at me and began to talk to me in a normal tone of voice.

"We got into a big fight, Levi."

"What? Who?" I asked.

"Brit, yeah, Brit," George replied. "I've never fought with her ever before. I told her she needed to get the abortion right away, so we could get back to normal. She told me she wasn't ready to do it yet. I blew up. Levi, I yelled at her and told her not to be so dumb."

George looked down again. He continued, "When . . . when I said that, she just froze in place. Tears welled up in her eyes. She didn't move a muscle and stared off into space with this puzzled look in her eye. Levi, you may not understand this, but I think I was the only person she ever felt special around. Ya know what I mean? Even her mom and, for sure most everyone else in this town never thought much of her. Then, I go and say those things."

Tears welled up in George's eyes. He continued, "Levi, I can't believe how much I must have hurt her! She trusted me, but now maybe she thinks I'm just like the rest. But I do think she is special. I feel like I've got this huge ship anchor tied up around my insides that I'm dragging around."

I finally interrupted, "George, you've got to talk to her."

"I'm not sure she will talk to me. But she is one in a million, and she makes me feel special too—ya know?"

I stopped and thought for a moment. "Yeah, I know.

George perked up a little and looked at me again, listening attentively.

I continued, "I know exactly what you mean. Emma makes me feel the same way. If you want, I can try to talk to Brit. I can tell her how much you . . . well . . . how much you really care for her."

George interrupted me. "I love her, Levi."

"OK, OK. I knew that," I answered with a smile. "I can talk to her a let her know how you feel if I get a chance."

George, for the first time probably ever, looked at me with some admiration and approval.

I looked him in the eye and responded. "George, will you listen to me on this point? I know how you feel about abortion, but what if Brit feels differently about it and might be afraid to tell you?"

He didn't look angry right away this time like he usually did when I tried to reason with him. He just looked at me with little expression. Then he said, "I don't know, brother; I just don't know. Why is life so stinking complicated?"

Then he sorta shook his head and looked down as he said, "If she got the abortion, life would be a lot simpler."

I bit my lip at that comment. We looked at each other for a moment. Then I took a deep breath and said, "I think you need to give this whole argument thing a day or two and just . . . well . . . sleep on it. You and Brit will feel better in the morning. I'll help in any way I can. Would you mind if . . . well . . . if I pray for you guys?"

George rolled his eyes a bit and replied, "Sure, whatever. But that won't do us any good. We need action right away. Levi, I don't want to lose her. I'd do anything not to lose her."

I felt like I could be straight with him again. "Would you be willing to keep this . . . pregnancy?"

"Don't start that crap with me again," George quickly responded. "And don't 'guide' her into any conclusion like that—promise me. You know that we could never make that work. Remember how old we are? The teacher would be issuing those fake babies in health class that you have to practice with, and we could bring in our own real one!! Give me a break!! Promise me."

I hesitated for a moment and responded, "OK, George. I'm sorry. We'll help in any way we can. I'll just listen and try to let her know your feelings. There is another way we could help. Emma and I could help cover that thousand bucks the hospital wants to charge."

For some reason, George got that very angry look again. I waited for the tongue-lashing. But George stopped midstream and took a deep breath, and replied, "No thanks, Levi. We'll manage that ourselves. I don't want to take your money. I just need to talk to someone. And, of course, Dad won't listen to me. He'd just give me a lecture on being responsible for my actions, blah, blah, blah, and get mad."

Convenience

I took another risk and said, "George, have you ever considered that Brit might not . . . " I struggled for the right words to say, but there just weren't any substitutes for the ones I had in mind, "that Brit might not want an abortion at all?"

George replied immediately. "There's no way, brother. She's smarter than that."

I interrupted, "But I'm telling you, it's hard to figure out a woman sometimes. What if she insisted on not getting an abortion?"

"I wouldn't let her," George replied quickly.

I fired back, "What do you mean you wouldn't let her? I guess the phrase 'possession is nine-tenths of the law' sort of applies here. Don't you think? The baby is in her, remember?"

"But part of me is in there too."

I couldn't help but think that whether he knew it or not, at the same time, George acknowledged the wonderful miracle that part of him was in Brit; he also buys the story that it's just a mass of flesh growing like a limb or something on Brit's body? The two thoughts aren't compatible.

George went on, "There's no way I could let her keep this. First, I refuse to be part of the overpopulation problem this world has, which is destroying the earth. Second, I don't want to ruin the start we have on a possible life together."

I pushed back again, "You know, George, those overpopulation stats can be made to look any way people want them to look to serve whatever purpose they have in mind."

"Brother, don't start all that with me. Let's quit talking population and religion stuff." George paused for a second, looked out into space, and said, "I just don't get why life has to be so complicated."

George seemed almost a little scared as he spoke, certainly confused and yet a little angry.

I reaffirmed, "I'm here to help you in any way I can."

George looked at me. His eyes still seemed distant, and he looked even more confused with my offer of help—something for nothing.

My hope was that he saw my offer of help as a gesture of love for my brother—even though he's not been all that lovable most of the time. I continued, "Listen, George. Today's Saturday; I think you should just lay low for a while. If I get a chance, I'll try to let Brit know how you feel about her and that you're sorry. Maybe I can catch her Monday in class."

George, again with a concerned look on his face, answered, "Monday is light-years away." Then he looked out at the yard again and paused and let out a deep, long exhale before he continued. "But I guess that will have to do—not like you're gonna go hang out with her this weekend or something."

George turned to me, and I could tell he struggled a bit but managed to say thanks.

As he began to walk toward the house, I called out to him to ask again: "George, can I . . . uh . . . can I pray for you and Brit?"

"George turned back to me with a scowl on his face. Then he sarcastically answered, "I already said sure, whatever."

Chapter Ten

The weekend passed all too quickly, as usual. I was back in school teaching before I knew it. Brit hadn't spoken or even looked at me all class period. After class, she was the last one out of the room. As she passed by my desk, I called out to her. "Brit, how are you doing?" She was quiet and reserved. She again wouldn't look at me. I think she was pretending to be looking at or reading her math book as she passed.

I took a quick deep breath and called out again. "Look, Brit, I talked to George this weekend, and he told me what happened."

Brit didn't lift her eyes from the book, but one eyebrow perked upward slightly, and I knew I had her attention. So, I took advantage and continued. "Brit, I have to tell you that George feels terrible about your argument and the things he said."

Her facial expression perked up again, but still, she didn't look up at me. I continued. "He told me that he felt like he had an anchor tied around his insides, and it was pulling at his heart. He also told me how much he cares for you."

She finally looked up at me as she spoke. "He said some pretty mean things to me, not that I'm not used to that sort of thing," she said sarcastically.

I pressed. "I know he didn't mean them. I think he thinks you're the only one on the planet who understands him, and he's afraid he might lose you. Hey, he came to me to talk—that's how desperate he is," I said jokingly.

Brit was now talking into her math book again as she spoke with a touch of embarrassment. "Ya know, that's the way I feel about him. I mean that he seems like the only one on the planet who understands me." She paused for a moment and then spoke into her book again. "I . . . I sorta feel, well, like I'm real when I'm around him; I'm not invisible. I feel . . . ," she paused again. And I, as I, unfortunately, try to do often, tried to finish her sentence. "You feel complete?"

Brit thought for a moment and then looked up from her book and at me and answered, "Yeah, that's a good word for it."

I continued. "The Bible talks about a husband and wife becoming one, complete in each other. I . . . I don't mean to imply that you guys are close to becoming husband and wife, but I can see you both care a lot for each other. And in a way, maybe you complete each other."

Brit responded, "I think you're . . ." a cough interrupted her response; another cough, and yet another.

"You OK?" I asked.

"I'm just feeling a little sick today. Anyway, I was gonna say that I think you're right about us sorta being a good match, completing each other."

I thought for a moment and responded, "Brit, we men are kind of funny sometimes. I think George was just a little worried about his little family . . ."

"What?" Brit interrupted.

"What do you mean 'little family'? It's just George and me. There's no family. I'm in high school, remember?" she asked sarcastically.

Brit's mood went from melancholy to monster in seconds. I tried to clarify. "I didn't mean to imply anything else," but she cut me off again.

"Do you think I'm stupid? We can't be strapped with a kid right now! That's got to be pretty obvious! Don't think for a minute I don't want to get an abortion." Brit's eyes began to well up with tears. "I'm . . . I'm just waiting for a good time to go get it done. Social Support tells me I still have plenty of time and that it's a really simple procedure."

Convenience

I was in shock by the whole exchange. "Sorry, Brit" was all I could come up with.

We both stood there for a moment, puzzled and trying to digest what had just happened. Talking into her book again and forcing a half smile, Brit finally spoke up. "I've got to go."

I could tell she wasn't feeling very well physically, and she probably just had an emotional swing from the hormonal imbalance of the pregnancy. I could also tell she felt bad about the outburst too. Brit walked out without another word.

I wondered to myself: *Did I do it again—that is, open my big mouth a little too much?* Seems like I always end up doing that. I also wondered if she really meant what she said about having an abortion. Lord only knows. I knew that Social Support practically comes to your doorstep these days if you're even slightly inclined to have an abortion. If I didn't know any better, I'd guess that somehow, they find out who's pregnant and recruit candidates to have abortions just to keep their number up to justify government funding. What a crazy world. *Lord, please help us in this abortion mess that this country and the world have gotten into.*

When I dragged myself home after school, Emma and Katie met me with smiles. It was like a cool drink of water in the middle of the desert. I needed a "session" with my favorite counselor, my wife, but I figured I'd better wait a while and play with Katie and then schedule an appointment for after Katie fell asleep. After supper and about an hour of playing ponies with Katie, she took her bath and quickly fell asleep before I could even finish our story and Bible reading.

Now I had a few minutes where I could rewind the events of the day with Emma and get her take on things. Emma was sitting on the couch with her legs tucked under herself, engrossed in a home improvement show. I sat down beside her and watched for a minute. Feeling almost as though I needed permission to interrupt, "tips for making a room less cluttered," I asked, "Can I tell you about this weird day I had?"

"Sure," Emma responded as she turned to me, a sign she really didn't care about the show and wanted to give me the attention I was hoping for.

"I talked to Brit today. I wanted to try to help her and George through this big fight that I told you about. Brit wouldn't look at me all during class. As she was walking out the door, I asked her about things. She responded but still didn't look at me. She kept her head down, looking into her math book. I tried to tell her how sorry George was and how he felt about her. I was really getting through to her, and she confided that she felt real strongly about George. I guess maybe I should have stopped there, but . . ."

Emma perked up and sighed as she rolled her eyes in disappointment. "What did you say now, you smooth-tongued matchmaker."

I cut in quickly. "Emma, I'm trying to be serious here. I said some things about George being worried about, well, about his little 'family.'" Emma rolled her eyes again. "But I didn't mean anything by it, and really, I was just thinking about George and her. Anyway, she blew up after I said that. She said she never intended not to have an abortion and that it would be stupid to think otherwise. Brit went from courteous to downright ugly in seconds. She also started coughing and could hardly stop. I think she was a little sick—as in morning sickness."

I stopped for a moment and looked out into the darkness of the kitchen next to where we were talking. "Emma, at first, Brit really seemed to be interested in and searching for the right thing to do. It was almost like a bright sunny morning breaking through. Then after I said what I said, the nuclear bomb hit right smack in the middle of the place. Suddenly, she was like a different person altogether. She said she was just waiting for the right time to have the abortion and that Social Support is going to 'help' her."

I stopped to gather my thoughts again. "Emma, I tried to help her, and now I wonder if she might be more prone to go through with the abortion just because of what I said?"

"Calm down, Levi," Emma cut in. "You were just trying to help." Emma peered into her coffee cup as she took a long slow sip. "I think you're right in that her emotions are probably all messed up. She's eighteen, lives in a broken home, had a fight with her best friend and boyfriend, and she is pregnant and sick. Yeah, she's probably not got it all together right now. But here's the real tough part. I think she sees no alternative but to have to choose between George and this baby. What

Convenience

a terrible position to be in. She doesn't want to lose the best and maybe only real friend, who happens to be the boy she is in love with. I know how she feels about him. I saw how she looked at him in the hospital. Yet, I also saw her expression when she talked about her pregnancy. Levi, I think she'd like to have this baby too! But she thinks she can't have both, and she may be right. If I'm right and she really does want to have this baby and goes ahead with the abortion anyway, she is going to be miserable the rest of her life. Levi, what in the world can we do?"

"Pray, I guess . . . we can pray, honey."

Chapter Eleven

The next week was especially tough at school. I could tell that Brit felt a bit awkward in class. She had confided in me—personal thoughts—probably because she, just like George, couldn't talk to anyone else. But at the same time, I was her teacher. She also looked a little pale. I think the cold, shorter days, along with her being pregnant, weighed heavy on her physically. I wondered if she was eating right, getting the rest she needed, and taking the vitamins she should be taking. I really doubted that any of that was happening. Well, the class came and went, and we didn't talk to each other directly.

I went from my math class to PE class with jolly old Ed Stone. He liked me less every time we worked together teaching PE. He was in a particularly bad mood on Monday. After class, he grumped at me continually for about ten minutes. Finally, I'd had enough.

I turned to him and asked, "Ed, are you feeling all right today?"

He looked at me a bit surprised, thought to himself for what seemed like a long time to me, then answered. "Yeah, I'm fine, I guess."

I looked him right in the eye again, "You guess?"

He looked away quickly and paused even longer to answer me. Then he looked back at me, eye to eye again. He had anger in his look and his tone as he spoke. "You know what those kids call me behind my back—'the old man'?! And they think my hearing is going, so I can't hear them anymore either."

"Well," I responded slowly, feeling like I was about to jump into a fenced-in yard with a couple of unfriendly Dobermans. "You are about sixty-four, right? I . . . I mean, from their perspective, you probably seem older, don't you think?"

"Levi, it's not my age. I know I'm sixty-four. But those stupid little kids think I'm . . . you know 'old,' like I'm expired, don't know anything. Like I'm . . . ," Ed gritted his teeth, "like I'm not . . . not even a person anymore! I feel like I've got one of those 'use before' expiration dates on my forehead, and the date has already passed. I feel like people think I'm more and more useless. And to have those snotty little boys look down at me or even right through me like I don't even exist, it makes me want to grab them by the collar and pop their little heads off!" Ed took another long pause and caught his breath. "I feel like I'm disappearing more and more every day—like I'm on a boat drifting out to sea with no control, no oars!"

I thought for a while, wondering why Ed had suddenly decided to download on me, and responded. "Yeah, I sort of know how you feel, I think. I felt pretty out of touch when I started here this year. I thought I'd fit right in with these kids, but I learned pretty quickly that I am definitely not part of their generation."

There was silence again, and I finally broke in with a thought that was rolling around in my head. "Ed," I asked, "do you go to church anywhere? Maybe you could come with us some Sunday. I think you'd feel better after that."

"Church?" Ed chuckled. "No, Levi. I said I needed oars, not crutches!" In raising his voice, Ed stirred up some phlegm and began to cough loudly.

I decided to change the subject. "I would think these guys would want to hear some of your war stories and experiences in life. Kids just don't recognize the wisdom and knowledge you carry around. They could learn a lot from you."

Ed acknowledged my comment but, at the same time, looked off into space, thinking for a moment. "Do you know, Levi, I was watching TV the other day and heard that in Europe last year, a Dutch doctor came up with what he called a 'usefulness test.' It was a test that people over sixty-five could take to tell them how useful they were to society! Is that crazy, or what? But it gets better. On the show, they said that the doctors are offering to 'help' people take the test. What are they gonna do next year? Run the 'old' checklist on people themselves! I can just see some doctor telling me the results of how much he thinks I'm **not** useful—or maybe it will be a useless test!"

Ed was really getting riled up now. "How about the year after that? Are they gonna use the results of their little 'evaluation' to tell us we should—or have to—end our useless lives for the sake of the rest of society? Give me a break! The next thing ya know, the undertaker will be giving me the eye, sizing me up for a good fit!"

"That's ridiculous, Ed," I chimed in. Ed was a little taken aback by the fact that I so passionately agreed with him. I added, "I can't believe people don't see where this is all headed. I wonder how old the Dutch guy is. Of course, he might consider himself useful since he made up the stupid test!" My voice had escalated to that of a shout, matching Ed's.

Ed looked at me in surprise, almost as though he thought that no one gets to raise their voice to an annoying level except him. I shut my mouth and just shook my head in disgust. We looked at each other for a moment, and then Ed began to pick up around the area and prepare to leave.

"Ed," I said, "as a Christian, I can handle all this a lot easier. Can I explain to you why?"

"No," Ed quickly responded with just one word—then more silence.

A minute after Ed and I cleaned up, he headed for the door, talking to himself. "I got to get home. Don't need an hour sermon right now." As he walked toward the door, he stopped for a second. Then he turned back to me and said in a very annoyed tone of voice, "I'll give you one minute."

"Fine, I said. I started right in. "You see, I believe God created everything in the universe. He made us in His own image. Not only that, but He gave us each a soul, an eternal soul. We're only here on earth for a short time, but our souls will live on forever. That's what makes us special, unique, and not just a lump of flesh that evolved from a piece of slime!"

Ed's rough and wrinkled face smiled, and he chuckled a little.

I continued, "So, our age shouldn't matter; even our usefulness shouldn't matter. What matters is that each of us is one of God's most special creations, and that's what makes us important." Now, for part two.

"Because God loved us and gave Adam and Eve their own free will, and because of the bad choices they made, we are all justifiably condemned. The Bible says, 'the wages of sin is death.' This death is not only physical death, but the separation of our souls eternally from God in a place of torment called hell."

"I thought you were supposed to be making me feel better," Ed sarcastically piped in.

"It gets better," I responded. "Give me thirty more seconds. But God loves us and sent His son to die on the cross and pay the debt for all of us. All we have to do is accept His free gift of love for us, and we can be redeemed from debt and have eternal life with God in a place where there's no more sin, pain, deterioration—and no disrespect for people. So, if you've accepted Christ, this world is really just a rest stop on the way to heaven. Makes the eighty or ninety years we have here a lot less of an issue, doesn't it?"

Ed didn't answer. He looked at me for a minute with a puzzled sort of look, then cursed and said I was three minutes over. Then he turned, grumbling under his breath, and walked out the door.

As I watched him go, I began to feel like I just wasted a lot of time and maybe even drove Ed further from Christ. Then I remembered God's Word. He said his Word would "never return void," meaning that any time his Word is spoken, it brings some sort of result and blessing. I still felt drained from the whole incident. I slowly got ready to get to my next class. The week dragged on from there.

As Friday morning finally materialized, I was gulping down my last bit of cereal when the phone rang. It was the principal asking me to cover Ed's classes all day. "Why?" I asked. "Did Ed decide to head for the hills for the weekend?"

"No," a stern voice replied, obviously not interested in my light-hearted humor. The now purposefully professional voice addressed me, "No, Ed had a heart attack last night."

Convenience

"A heart attack? Is he OK?"

The principal seemed a little surprised that I wanted to know more details about Ed Stone, of all people. He responded, "Well . . . well, yes, he seems to be OK from what the hospital informed me."

"How long will he be in, and what hospital is he in?" I asked.

Another pause, and I could hear what sounded almost like an annoyed sigh. "I'm not sure which hospital called. It could be Jackson or Grace Medical. I think it is probably Grace, though."

I was the one now pausing, thinking to myself, *Ed has no close family here and really has no one who cares much nearby, and he doesn't even know which hospital Ed's in.*

I finally reconnected with reality. "Well, no problem as far as covering for Ed. Don't worry about that at all, sir."

Sounding chipper, the principal responded like he was moving on to more important things. "Well, thanks, Levi. I'm glad we have you on our staff!"

I worked through my day as best I could and called Emma during lunch to tell her what happened and to ask her to pray for Ed, and also to let her know that I planned to go visit him after school. At the end of the day, I finally finished my paperwork and scooted off to the hospital. As it turned out, Ed wasn't at Grace but was over at Jackson.

Chapter Twelve

I finally made my way to the nurses' station on what I thought might be the right floor. As I approached the desk, I asked one of the nurses where I might find Ed Stone. She wasn't sure and fumbled her way through a hand-written list of patients.

Whatever happened to the high-tech hospital Jackson claims to be in its commercial? I thought to myself as I smiled at the nurse and waited. She finally found Ed's name and directed me to his room.

When I got to the room, I peeked in and found Ed staring at the ceiling.

"Are you counting the little holes in the tiles up there?" I asked.

Ed sternly turned to see who was bothering him. Then, realizing who I was, he raised his eyebrows from their stern, low position. "What in the world are you doing here?" he asked.

"I just wanted to see how you're doing," I responded.

"Doing?" he said. "How do you think I'm doing? Look at all these gadgets! These wires and hoses feel like big ropes tying me down!"

"Come on now. You've got pretty nurses waiting on you hand and foot. You don't need to move around."

"Ha, these nurses are afraid to come in here," Ed responded loud enough for anyone in the hallway to hear. "And you know," Ed continued with a softer voice, "they're not exactly over-qualified in the 'pretty' department, if ya know what I mean."

I shook my head and smiled. After a pause, I asked Ed, "So tell me what happened."

"Well," Ed responded, "I was in the hallway by the old locker room right by that old water fountain when I felt a sharp pain in my side. All I remember is grabbing my side. Next thing ya know, I was waking up in an ambulance. I guess I just passed out. Then, apparently, one of the kids—one of those annoying kids I told you about that normally treat me like an old worn-out shoe—saw me lying there and called 911. It's funny. Ya know how these kids treat me normally. Then, just when I feel like I could easily pass the 'uselessness test,' one of those snotty-nosed punks goes out of his way to help me—maybe even save my life. It all just confuses me, Levi. You remember what I said about feeling like I'm drifting away from shore with no oars?"

"Yeah," I replied.

"I just feel more and more like that all the time. Maybe that's why I had this stupid heart attack."

"Ed, you know my answer already."

"Yeah, yeah, you're going to tell me about being valuable in God's eyes, right? I said I need oars, not a crutch."

I decided to change the subject quickly so Ed wouldn't get too excited. "I've got a question for you, Ed. How did you feel prior to the attack? Did you pass out, have dizzy spells, or anything like that?"

"No. In fact, I was feeling pretty good. Why?"

"My mom has passed out five times in the last several months, and the doctors won't even hardly take a minute to check her out. It really burns me up, Ed!"

"I guess you have to have a heart attack to get any attention around here. What hospital does she go to?"

"Grace, I replied."

"Oh, they are worse than here."

"Oh, thanks, Ed."

"It's the truth, though, Levi. You need to stay with those doctors. Something must be wrong, and they need to check it out!"

"OK, Ed. Don't get over-excited now. You'll make all those gadgets light up, and the doctor will be in here before you know it. Anyway, has anyone else been by to visit?"

"No. Are you kidding? There isn't anyone I can think of who would show up."

Ed tried to look like his comment was comical, yet there was a sort of sadness under a layer or two of his facial expression. I thought to myself, *No one to visit him . . . at his age . . . how sad . . . how lonely.*

"Ed, is there anything I can get you? I should probably get going."

"Yeah, a pizza!"

"What? You're in a hospital, not a bowling alley."

Ed looked at me with his angry and annoyed look he uses a lot. "They have a pizza place on the first floor! Just go get it and bring it up here, but just don't let the nurses see you."

I looked at him with an equally annoyed look and paused for a moment. "You're going to get me into trouble, but I'll do it, and it's on me."

Ed's eyes lit up a little, but he didn't want to show his delight too much. As I walked out, Ed called to me.

"Hey, Levi." I turned around. "Thanks for coming out," he said with a sort of fake stern look. Then he shocked me. His voice got a little quieter, as though he didn't want anyone to hear what he was saying.

"You've been kind of an oar for me." I looked at him, puzzled for a second, then figured it out.

"Really, Levi. I don't know what I would have done on a few of those bad days this year. Some days I just felt useless, expired . . . hopeless." He turned his head away from me for a moment as he continued, "You seemed to generate some hope for me."

I didn't know exactly how to respond to that, so I just said, "I'm glad, Ed." As I left his room on my mission to get a pizza, I thought it was neat to think that I may have somehow helped Ed. God is good!

I told Ed I was going to get him a pizza, and I guess that is what I was determined to do. But . . . I didn't think it would hurt to run the idea by the nurses, so I stopped by the nurses' desk. The nurse at the desk was busy working on something on her computer. I stood for a while and then finally interrupted her. "Excuse me, can I ask you a question?"

"Yes, sir. How can I help you?" came the reply.

"I was visiting in Ed Stone's room, and I wonder if I could bring him up . . . a . . . pizza?" She looked at me in a puzzled way. I began to wonder if asking for a pizza might not have been the greatest idea.

After a pause, the nurse replied. "Oh, you mean the guy in B-5; let me check his chart."

The "guy" in B-5, I thought to myself. Doesn't he even have a name around here? As disturbing as that seemed to me, I held my tongue in hopes of getting the OK for the pizza. After checking a chart, the nurse came back over to me.

"He can have a pizza, but make it cheese only."

"Thanks," I replied. "Mr. Ed Stone will really appreciate that. He hasn't had any visitors besides me, and I think the pizza will make him feel a little more comfortable."

Before I had finished my sentence, the young nurse was back at the computer again, not noticing my emphasis on Ed's name or any of my comments. She did manage to give me an almost mechanical "You're welcome" without lifting her eyes from the computer. I really began to wonder if she had any concern for Ed whatsoever. I bit my lip and headed for the elevator. At the restaurant, I ordered Ed a large cheese pizza. It didn't take long at all to get it, and I was soon back upstairs with the precious cargo.

As I walked into Ed's room, I noticed him again, looking up at the ceiling. "Double-checking the number of holes you counted earlier?"

Ed looked at me. "It's always good to double-check your work," he replied with a smile. He continued, "You actually brought back the pizza. How'd you get it past the evil nurse?" he asked with a chuckle.

"I have my ways—I asked them. They said it would be no problem."

Ed looked at me in a funny way and responded, "Yeah, right."

Ed didn't believe my very truthful response. I just left it at that and handed over the goods.

"Do you want a piece—but just one slice? It's only a large, you know," Ed said with a smile.

"No thanks, Ed. I need to take off; enjoy the food."

Convenience

Ed replied with a pizza slice already in hand, "OK. Thanks, Levi. Give those kids in PE a hard time for me."

"No problem," I responded as I turned and left. I wasn't sure whether my visit or the pizza was a bigger hit, but I think Ed's spirits were lifted a lot.

Chapter Thirteen

The next few weeks before the Christmas break was busy and seemed to fly by. I took care of Ed's classes and kept the kids up to date on Ed's recovery, which was actually very quick. Even though we asked him to take it easy through the upcoming Christmas break, Ed decided to come back to work the last week before the break. It had only been thirteen days since he had his attack, but Ed seemed to want to be around us at school instead of being alone in his quiet house. He seemed a little bit louder and even sterner with the boys when he returned. I think he wanted them to know he was fine. Through it all, Ed and I seemed to have really improved our relationship. He was still a bit blunt with me but seemed to respect me and my position on things. And I think he considered me a good friend.

We talked a number of times that week, and I even got the courage to ask Ed to join us for Sunday service. Ed dug deep for a good reason to turn me down. But since things were winding down toward Christmas break, there wasn't even a school-related reason he could use to decline. He waited two days to respond to me, but on Friday afternoon, he said he would come. I was thrilled but didn't want to let on too much with Ed. But inside, I was already praying that the Holy Spirit would begin working on his heart and prepare him for what might be the first time Ed would hear the gospel preached. The afternoon flew by as everyone seemed to already be in holiday vacation mode and not concentrating much on anything else. I couldn't wait to get home and give Emma the news about Ed.

I woke up extra early on Sunday. I wanted to dress up in a suit but didn't know what Ed might wear. So, I thought I'd just bring a jacket and not wear it. The whole family got up a little earlier, and I had a chance to plan out the day with Emma.

"How 'bout we take Ed out to eat after church?" I asked Emma.

"How 'bout McDonald's?" Katie quickly chimed in.

Emma responded, "Let's wait and ask our guest, Mr. Stone if he likes McD's, and we can stop there on the way home."

"Sounds like a plan," I chimed in, and we all began to gather our Bibles and other things and headed to the car. I turned to Emma on the way out. "I hope he makes it. Do you think we should have called him earlier?"

"Calm down, Levi," Emma responded, quickly bringing me back to reality. "We don't need to be calling people early Sunday mornings. Let's just get to the church and hope for the best. God's in charge, not you—remember?"

"OK, Emma, I got ya. But let's hurry up and get there, so we can get a good seat and be ready for Ed." We piled into the car, juggling Bibles, notebooks, pencils, and coffee. By the time we finished the ten-minute ride, I had managed to choke down my coffee and not spill a drop on my shirt or pants. That usually meant it was going to be a good day.

After we got to church and got seated, I went out to the front entryway and waited for Ed, thinking about all the times I had invited people, and they didn't show up. I prayed that wouldn't be the case with Ed. I knew this might be the only chance for Ed to really hear the gospel up close and personal. We would do our job, get him here, make him feel comfortable and welcome, and hope he isn't distracted and really hears God's Word. But the rest was up to Ed to respond to the draw of the Holy Spirit.

Well, the church filled up, and folks were ready to start. I had already said all my hellos and talked to the pastor, for a few minutes. Still no sign of Ed. Just as I was deciding whether I should just go sit down with Emma and Katie, Ed's car pulled up. I went out and directed him into a visitor's parking spot. He poked his head out the window of the car and asked, "Are you the valet?"

I just smiled and pointed to the spot. Ed quickly parked and met me at the door. He was wearing a nicely kept but somewhat dated suit. He seemed excited to be there, as though he was going to watch a football game or something. Maybe it was the novelty of attending a Baptist church service, which I assumed he had never attended before. That may have been part of it, and it also was probably the fact that he was just out doing something with friends. I'm not sure that happened too often with him anymore. We got seated just before the service started.

Although Ed may have been feeling a little out of place at first, I think he enjoyed the first part of the service. Most of all, I think he enjoyed the portion of the service where we all walked around shaking hands and greeting one another. I'm sure that the friendliness and warmth of the people made Ed feel good. However, Ed seemed to get a little more nervous when Emma's dad began to preach. He was looking down as if reading the bulletin he received from the usher when we first came in, but I could tell he was listening.

As I looked over Ed's head, I couldn't believe what I saw! George and Brit had snuck in and seated themselves in the back row. George saw me notice him and looked even more uncomfortable, and his fair-skinned face seemed to glow hot and red as the pastor began to preach. I quickly turned around so as not to further his stress, but I was so thrilled to see them both attending the service.

Since Christmas would be here soon, Emma's dad preached a Christmas-related message, but as I knew he would, he related it to the salvation that Jesus Christ brings to all who accept him as Savior. He shared the gospel clearly as he spoke of the Christmas story. Through it, he explained how God created us and loved us so much that he also gave us a free will to choose to obey him on our own. Unfortunately, Adam and Eve, prompted by the selfish fallen angel Lucifer, chose to disobey—to sin. Once sin entered the world, God, who is completely just, required punishment for that sin. The Bible says, "the wages of sin is death." So, we were born into this world as sinners, and our just penalty is death—not just physical death, but eternal spiritual death and separation from God. The pastor went on to say those two little wonderful words I had heard many years ago, and that helped lead me to Christ: *But God.* But God so loved us that he sent his only begotten son; he made way for us as only he could do. He made way for our sin debt to be paid by sending his own son into the world as a man and allowing his son to obey and choose to die in our place! It was a perfect solution. God would preserve His perfect justice, and the penalty for our sin would be paid, while we if we choose to accept it, could embrace the free gift of salvation and be with the Lord for eternity as he had wanted from the beginning of creation! The Christmas story was just the beginning of God's plan to send his own son, who would live a sinless life, teach, heal, show us real love, and show us the way to heaven.

The pastor explained everything in detail but didn't overstay his welcome into our attention space. He gave us the simple truth of the gospel, the only real truth that this world will ever experience. I was so glad that of all days to visit, Ed got to hear this particular message. And George and Brit were there as well. God is good!

Ed did look up occasionally, and I could tell he made eye contact with the pastor now and then. It seemed to me that the truth of the gospel might be sinking into this old boy; at least, it seemed like he was listening. As the pastor finished, he paused for a minute and then explained that making a decision to accept Christ's free gift was a choice God allowed each of us to make on our own. But this was a choice that would affect us eternally.

As the pastor offered an invitation to anyone interested in accepting Christ, I sat expectantly, hoping Ed would make a move. I didn't want to look over his way, though, and seem as if I were pressuring him. The pastor waited a moment . . . no one came forward. And I began to lose hope that Ed would act on the invitation. I defaulted to thanking God that Ed even showed up and asking that the seed of the gospel might take root in him. The pastor waited another moment . . . then closed in prayer.

My heart sank a little as we sang the closing song. I looked at Ed with a smile, trying to hide any disappointment and show him kindness. As I smiled at him, Ed just kind of stared at me. It was weird. I wasn't sure whether he was happy or sad or wanted to punch me in the face. I turned and looked at Emma with the same forced smile I had preset for Ed. She had sort of perceived all that had gone on and what I was thinking and gave me a reassuring look. As we began to file out, I started scooting my way to the aisle. Ed was already in the aisle, and I suspected he wanted to leave quickly, so I hurried to him. As I got close, I reached out my hand, expecting to shake his hand and ask him if he enjoyed the message. Ed didn't extend his hand to me . . . and there was the stare again. And it was weird again.

Before I could ask him anything, he looked me in the eye with a very serious stare. "I need to talk to the pastor right now."

Still shocked and a bit confused, I responded. "Ah, sure, Ed . . . lemme see if you can get a word with him." Again, I wasn't sure whether Ed was going to thank him, ask him a question, or punch him in the face. I made my way to the pastor and pulled him aside. "My friend Ed would like to speak with you. Do you have a moment?"

"Of course," the pastor responded. So, I let Emma know what was going on and asked her to please wait around for a little while. Then I made my way to Ed and brought him into the hallway behind the sanctuary and into the pastor's office. After I introduced Ed, we sat down, and he and the pastor engaged in a little small talk ending with Ed joking about being in church and surprisingly not having a lightning bolt zap him as he entered. We all laughed a bit.

Then Ed turned serious, "Pastor, I want to hear a little more about accepting Christ." Ed seemed a little embarrassed and even looked around to make sure no one was passing by the office. I was trying to stay calm but was doing flips on the inside.

The pastor just smiled, took a deep breath, and began to explain again, but in more detail, what he had talked about earlier. Ed listened intently.

After a few minutes, Ed spoke up, "So, even a guy like me," he chuckled, "with a not-so-great past," his smile disappeared, "can be saved?"

With a nod from the pastor, Ed looked at me, paused for a moment, and looked back at the pastor. Then he looked out the office window with a distant stare and then back to the pastor. "I want to get saved," he said as his face lit up with a huge smile.

"Awesome!" I shouted out without even realizing what I'd said. They both looked at me, chuckled a bit, and turned to each other again.

Ed knelt down in that office that wonderful day and accepted Christ as his Savior.

Chapter Fourteen

After Ed accepted Christ as his Savior, he seemed like a totally different person. And . . . I guess he was. He seemed to understand his purpose for being here now. It all made sense, and after sixty-plus years of bounding around in this world and being made to feel less and less valuable as he got older, I could understand how wonderful he must have felt. He finally knew his value. He understood that God had given his only son to die on the cross for our sins—that's how valuable Ed was! He really had pep in his step, and you couldn't wipe the smile off his face if you tried. Then, applying his "loud and proud" Marine Corps personality to his newfound faith, you had quite a sight. He was telling everyone about his salvation and how they could and should follow suit. I got a real kick out of watching Ed in action. As an evangelist, he was like a bull in a china shop. If the kids thought he was a little off before, they were sure that he had finally fallen off the deep end and was getting senile once he became a Christian. But actually, he was thinking more clearly than he ever had before. It was so fun and entertaining to watch the new Ed in action. The Lord really had done a great work in Ed.

Winter's frigid cold and darkness and loneliness were in full season now. But Ed's newfound fire in his soul seemed to be in full bloom to warm things a bit for us all. He was certainly a bright spot in my worries about George and Brit, and Mom and her fainting spells . . . and Lynn.

Through it all, Ed and I became fast friends, and he stopped over to our place often. One Friday night, Ed had eaten at our house while we watched a basketball game on TV.

"Levi," Ed called out, poking his way into my intense concentration on the basketball game. "Levi," he poked harder.

"What, Ed?" I finally responded, trying to act interested in what he had to say, while my eyes shifted quickly from Ed to the TV and back.

"I went to see an old buddy of mine this afternoon."

A bit annoyed with Ed's interruption for what seemed like a conversation we could have later, I responded. "Is that why I had to take care of those fine boys in PE all afternoon, on a Friday, all by myself today?" I jokingly responded while not taking my eyes off the TV. But Ed stayed unusually serious.

"It was an old friend of mine. We were Marines together on the West Coast for a lot of years. He had a stroke this week."

Realizing the seriousness of the issue and Ed's unusually serious voice, I stopped watching the game and turned to look at Ed, giving him my full attention. "Really, that's a shame. Is he OK?"

Ed explained, "I don't know, Levi. Brock, my pal for a lot of years, looked so pitiful in that hospital bed today. In the past, he seemed to me to be so . . . I don't know . . . indestructible for so many years. He was tough as nails, Levi! He survived his wife dying of cancer eight years ago and his son, a highway patrolman, getting shot and nearly dying about three years ago. He was hurt by those things but always maintained that focused look and even-keeled temperament, even in those terribly difficult times. It was like nothing could shake him. Now he is helpless and alone. The people at the hospital are treating him so poorly. It's almost as though they want him to . . . well, die so the inconvenience of having him in their hospital will go away."

I looked at Ed with a questioning expression, and he responded. "Really, Levi, no one at that hospital cared a bit about me, and they don't give a rip about Brock either! You should have seen his face when I came—his reaction was like a climber stranded on Mount Everest when someone comes to rescue him. Brock was so thrilled to see me. Levi, I hate seeing him so pitiful. So anyway, we talked for a while, and I had his attention for sure, so I thought I'd tell him about the Lord. He listened but immediately got this grin on his face and told me he didn't need a crutch and he could handle everything. Can you imagine that Levi, a crutch?!" Ed continued with a half grin at the thought of Christ being just a crutch.

I got a little grin as well, but it was because I recognized that saying right away. It was exactly what Ed told me the first time I told *him* about the Lord! "A crutch, huh?" I responded with a touch of sarcasm.

Halfway through his next statement, the crutch thing hit him, too, as he remembered he had said the same thing. He stopped talking and looked at me, waiting for my next sarcastic comment. But I just looked back at him, now intently trying to get back to the serious story of his friend, Brock.

Ed continued, "Well, anyway, he wouldn't listen to me and even seemed a little annoyed that I brought it up. So, I realized I needed to get going back to school, and I left it at that. I did leave him a little gospel tract that laid out the plan of salvation probably better than I ever could anyway. I put it right in his hand. Brock didn't even look at it before tossing it on his nightstand. I don't get it. It's so simple—so simple." Ed kind of dipped his head and ran his hand through his hair.

"Calm down, Ed," I finally jumped in. "You're right—it's simple, but look how long it took you to finally realize your choice of Christ. I'm sure you planted a seed, at least. He may have been listening and watching without letting on."

"Maybe," Ed responded. "But he sure didn't seem like it."

"You planted a great seed. Let the Lord work on him."

Ed didn't seem hopeful. He turned back to the ball game, but he still had that concerned look on his face. We both went back to watching the game. Afterward, Ed made a bologna sandwich for the road. Before he left, I tried to encourage him again and asked him not to worry about Brock and to pray and leave it in the Lord's hands for now. I continued as he walked toward the door, "Ed, you did your part, and now it's up to Brock to decide." Then, hoping for Ed to leave on a brighter note, I half-jokingly added, "and Ed, you need to lay off the bologna sandwiches at night! I'm sure they aren't on your post-heart attack diet."

Opening the front door, Ed gave me a smile, bit into his sandwich, and proceeded to his car. The days were getting dark much earlier, and it was so cold. I watched Ed struggle to keep his jacket closed and juggle his sandwich while he got his keys out of his pocket as quickly as he could. The ground was covered with a new dusting of snow, which made it feel colder yet. Ed finally got situated and started his car and quickly sped away with a cloud of exhaust and snow kicking up from his car.

I stopped for a moment, looking up at the quiet, cold night sky. *"Lord, please bless Ed and be with him tonight. Please reassure him that you are in charge. You are so amazing, God. It's certainly a miracle that you've taken someone so centered on himself and so distant from you and changed him into someone who's now so concerned about another soul. Wow, Lord, you amaze me every day!"* Coming back to earth, I again looked up into the sky and closed my conversation. *"Good night, Lord, and thank you."* I scurried back into the house.

Chapter Fifteen

I woke up early the next morning. It was Saturday, and I liked getting up early, so I could get a jump on things around the house. The sun was beaming through the front window, warming me a bit, but I knew it was really getting cold outside. There was only one week left before the Christmas break, and I needed to get some papers graded and come up with a plan for how to keep my students focused through the week. I got my cup of coffee and started plowing through a stack of papers.

The school week whipped by, it seemed, in a moment. I was busy with something every night. Katie had a Christmas program on Wednesday night; our church had a get-together on Thursday, and we went caroling afterward. On Friday, the school was a complete waste, with the principal holding an assembly in the gym to wish everyone well and warn everyone to be careful over the long holiday. After he finished his speech, the school offered a Christmas movie in the gym, which no one watched except those kids who were waiting to get a ride home from their parents later in the afternoon. I sat staring at the movie but not seeing a thing. I was recapping what I needed to get done to wrap up my classroom and what to do to finish preparing for the holiday at home.

Then my mind wandered off for some reason to thinking about Lynn. I hadn't heard from her since Thanksgiving. I thought maybe I'd give her a call later in the afternoon and invite her to stop by our house over the holiday. Then I decided to skip the rest of the movie and get right to my room to clean it up and get home. My classroom was a mess with gift wraps, candy wrappers, and other assorted items all over the floor. Even though these kids are in high school and think they are adults most of the time, I knew they would still enjoy a good old-fashioned Christmas party. In addition to handing out their mid-term test results, I served cupcakes, chips, sodas, and candy while we discussed the test results. It was all I could do to keep the kids focused enough to get their grades and turn their papers back in—that and eat a bunch of sugar.

Anyway, I was stuck with the mess. I didn't really mind, though. With all the pressures and self-imposed stress kids had to deal with these days, I was glad to see them cut loose a little and enjoy themselves—all without alcohol, drugs, and fake adult relationships they normally thought they needed to be cool and have fun. So, there I was, stuck cleaning all by myself, or so I thought. I heard a noise across the room and looked over to see Brit quietly picking up wrappers from the floor. Her belly had started to show a little, and that embarrassed her and probably lowered her self-esteem a little. So, she had seemed quieter than her usual self the last few weeks.

"Hi, Brit," I yelled from across the room. "You don't have to help me. I've got all afternoon to get this straightened out. It's kind of therapeutic doing this instead of yelling at kids," I said jokingly with a smile.

Brit looked at me and grinned. Then she went back to picking up wrappers under a chair. "I'm sure you need to get home to Emma and Katie. They are probably excited to have you off work for a few days."

Brit seemed to have matured so much in the last few months and had become a close friend of the family.

"How's your mom doing?" I asked, trying to make conversation as we worked.

"She's busy as ever and working extra hours over the holidays. I wish she would take a break, but she won't slow down. It's tough for her, keeping up our little house, taking care of me, and trying to save a little for Christmas all by herself."

"Yep, I can imagine it would be tough having to do all that, and I suppose she doesn't have much time."

Convenience

I paused for a moment and wasn't exactly sure why I was asking my next question, but it came out before I gave it much thought. "Brit, do you ever see your dad? Does he live around here?"

Brit's face lost what little expression it had. She thought for a moment, let out a deep breath, and responded. "I have no idea who my dad is, and neither does my mom." Brit was comfortable enough with me to open up about her family's past.

"Mom only told me that she had had too much to drink one Christmas eve night at a party that she went to with a couple of friends. She said she doesn't remember much but that she woke up the next day alone, in one of the bedrooms of the house where the party was held. She said that she knew she had made some bad decisions. So, she wound up getting pregnant with me and not even knowing who the father was." Brit forced a smile as she tried to inject a little sarcasm as she lowered her head slightly. Then she slowly looked up with that forced smile. "Pretty crazy, huh?"

Wanting to encourage me that she was over all the pain, Brit added, "He must have been a redhead, though!" She smiled again, and I smiled back. Then she turned and began picking up trash from the floor again.

I now felt like a heel for bringing the subject up and was desperately struggling for something positive to say. "Well, I wonder if he has any idea what a fine young lady you grew up to be."

"Yeah, sure," Brit responded while she continued to pick up trash. She still was uncomfortable with compliments and didn't know how to respond. Then she looked at the clock on the wall, and her eyes lit up, and a real smile came across her face.

"George is meeting me out front in a couple of minutes. Gotta go! See you later, Mr. B!" And off she went, making a quick exit.

"You're coming to our house for Christmas Eve, right?" I yelled as Brit was bolting out the door.

"Yep," she yelled back without breaking her stride.

Alone, I quickly finished straightening up the mess in my room and got ready to leave. As I was getting my coat on, I remembered that I wanted to call Lynn and maybe invite her over sometime during the holidays. I got my cell phone out of my coat pocket and dialed her number. I sat on one of the desks and waited for her answer, but instead, all I got was her voicemail message. Her voice message sounded purposefully professional as she proclaimed, "You've reached 324-5659. I'm unavailable to take your call right now, but please leave a detailed message, and I'll return your call as soon as practical. Thank you, and have a great day."

I left a message for her to please call back and asked if she could come over sometime during the holiday season for dinner. Then I wished her a Merry Christmas and hung up. I grabbed my briefcase and headed home. As I stepped out into the parking lot, the frigid winter day hit me square in the face. I pulled my jacket together with one hand and quickened my step a bit. The parking lot was a mess of cars heading in every direction. People were waving and wishing each other a Merry Christmas and a happy holiday, cars were honking, and everyone was happily departing for the holiday vacation. With the very cold weather, white vapor rose from the exhaust of every car, creating a misty fog throughout the parking lot. It actually became hard to see much past your next step, and I'm surprised no one was run over. A fresh layer of light snow covered everything, and the ground crackled with every step as I crunched the old snow base underneath.

Amid all this commotion, I recognized a familiar voice yelling at me.

"Levi, Levi," Ed Stone yelled as he ran toward me.

I responded by yelling back, "It'd be a shame if you breezed through your heart attack recovery just to get run over in the high school parking lot by one of your favorite teenagers!" I smiled, finally seeing Ed's face.

But Ed didn't even flinch. It was as if he didn't even hear me. I could tell something was wrong. "What's up?" I asked, attempting again to get a response from Ed.

Chapter Sixteen

Ed was nearly out of breath as he caught up with me in the parking lot, still not saying a word as he tried to catch his breath. White vapor bellowed out of Ed's mouth as he exhaled in the frigid air. Finally, he managed a few words.

"Levi, my friend, Brock, who was in the hospital." Ed paused for a moment as we walked. "He died, Levi. Sometime during the night last night, he just gave it up." I was silent as Ed continued. "I'm sure there were no nurses around or at least none who cared about Brock. He was all alone in that dark, cold room and just slipped out of this world without anyone even noticing. I wouldn't have even known if I didn't stop by today to see how he was doing. Levi, what about him accepting Christ? I felt so sure the Lord gave me that opportunity the other day to tell him about salvation." Ed walked a bit further. "He just blew me off in a second. It seemed like he thought it was a big joke, and now he's gone."

As I got to my car, I turned to Ed. "I'm so sorry, Ed," I said, sighing. "I don't know what to say." Then I remembered what I had told Ed before. "Do you remember what I told you a couple of days ago? You planted the seed when you shared the gospel with Brock. You did what God wanted you to do. The Lord even provided just the right moment if I remember what you told me. But it was Brock's choice."

Ed responded, "I know, Levi, but I just thought —" He ran out of words and just looked at me.

I took a deep breath and responded. I looked Ed in the eye, and with a half-smile, I patted Ed on the back. "Have I told you how thankful I am that I have you for a friend? I . . . I mean, you really helped me through some tough days, and it's so good to have someone to talk to out here." I paused for a second and started again. "I really am sorry for how this turned out with Brock, but we have to just keep going. We need to trust God and press on. How much good will you be if you dwell on this?"

Ed stopped and looked at me. He took a deep breath and sighed. "We really are in a battle, aren't we?"

I added, "For sure, Ed . . . that's for sure. But we know who wins. We can read the last chapter, and we know who wins!"

Ed turned and began to disappear as he walked through the cold, white misty fog to his car. Without looking back at me, he bid me goodbye. "Take care, Levi. Talk to you Sunday."

"See ya, Ed. Have a good one, my friend." I got into my freezing car and started it up. As I waited for it to warm up, I prayed for Ed and thanked God for saving him and for the heart Ed has for others now. And I also thanked God for the great friend he was to me. And as I thought about things, I also asked God about Ed's friend Brock and that, somehow, he might have accepted Christ before he passed.

When I got home, Emma had dinner ready, and Katie greeted me at the door.

"Hi, Daddy," she called out. "Are you finished with school now?" She knew I was out for Christmas, but it sounded like she was asking if I was done with school forever, and that may have been what she meant.

"Well, sweety, I'm done with teaching until after the Christmas break. But then I have to go back."

She looked a bit puzzled. "But do you get to stay home with us for a few weeks?"

"Oh yes, dear, I do. And we'll have lots of fun together over the break. OK?" Katie nodded her head and smiled, and gave me a hug as I lifted her into my arms and walked into the kitchen.

Convenience

"Hey, Emma," I yelled across the room. "Did ya have a good day?"

She turned around and smiled at me, and jokingly asked, "Are you done with school now?" I smiled back.

But Katie jumped right in and explained, "He is still not done, but he gets a few weeks at home for Christmas."

Emma and I cracked up laughing at Katie's clarification. We regained our composure, and I thanked Katie for the clarification. "Katie, let's go wash our hands so we can eat some of that yummy chicken!"

I had a great dinner with the family, and afterward, Katie and I went out to the garage to find the Christmas boxes. When we moved in, I had piled all the boxes we didn't open over to one side of the garage with great plans to organize and store them properly some weekends. That weekend never came. So, Katie and I began rummaging through the boxes, making a huge mess, looking for the two Christmas boxes. Of course, they would be the last two we found. As we were making space and pulling the two boxes out from the corner, I heard a car pull up in the driveway.

When I looked out the window, I saw that it was Ed. That was strange, I thought. As Ed made his way into the garage, I was just lifting the Christmas boxes. I couldn't see my way since the boxes piled in my arms blocked my view, so Katie helped steer me to the entrance door. Ed got a little chuckle out of watching me nearly trip and throw the boxes into the air. But we made it into the house, and I thanked Katie for her great help and told her I'd be right in to unpack the boxes.

As I stepped into the cold garage, I yelled to Ed, who was still standing near the garage entrance. "Is there a ball game tonight that I forgot about?" Shaking his head, Ed began to walk toward me. He had a serious look on his face and was clutching a letter in his hand. Oh boy, I thought. Here we go again. Now, what's happened?

As Ed got closer to me, the serious look gave way to a smile as he began to speak. "You are not going to believe this, Levi; you are not going to believe this! I got a letter from God!"

"What?" I blurted out with a half-smile on my face.

Ed was panting as he stopped. He caught his breath enough to say again: "I got a letter from God." He began to laugh out loud, and I began to wonder if the kids at school had a point in thinking that Ed had finally gone off the deep end.

I looked at Ed and said, "Do you want to explain or just stand there laughing?"

Ed finally stopped laughing and looked at me and said, "Oh . . . oh, yeah . . ." he laughed out loud again, "Directly from God. It's actually from Brock. Of course, Brock is dead." Ed began to laugh again.

Yep, I thought, *off the deep end.*

Ed continued, "I got this letter today in the mail. Brock must have mailed it from the hospital a few days ago—just before he died."

I looked at Ed, waiting for more detail. He looked at me in my desperation, trying to figure him out. He drew a deep breath, trying to think of a clear way to explain. "OK," he said, "how about I just read it to you?" He took the paper from the envelope and started reading it to me.

Ed,

Thanks for stopping by. We've been friends for a long time, and I figured that if anyone might show up, it'd be you, and sure enough, you did. We've always been straight up with each other. So, when you told me about your experience with the Lord, I knew you meant it. I know it may have seemed like I wasn't even listening, but I was. When you told me that you had felt something was missing despite all you had been through and accomplished and survived in your life, I knew exactly what you were talking about. I felt the same way. And I guess since I was so close to death, it seemed like I was never going to find out how to fill that emptiness. I was kind of embarrassed to just jump right in as you were talking, and besides, I approach things carefully and need to think about stuff first.

Well, after you left, I read the little pamphlet over and over a bunch of times. You know, it all finally made sense to me. I couldn't get out of bed to get on my knees, but I think God will understand. Anyway, I prayed to him for the first time in probably fifty years, and it was the first time ever that I really knew what I was saying and meant what I was saying. I asked Jesus to forgive me of all my sins and to be my Savior. It felt so good; I wanted to jump right out of that bed and shout for a while (the nurses probably wouldn't have noticed anyway).

Ed, I have to tell you that I really feel great. The void is filled! And now I have Jesus in my heart! Thank you so much for being such a good friend all these years and for telling me about Jesus. Now that I've got this down on paper, I feel better. Come by, and we can talk about it.

Your good friend,
Brock
Semper Fi

Ed couldn't finish the last sentence without his voice breaking up a bit and tearing up. My eyes got a little "sweaty," too. We just stared at each other.

I finally broke the silence. "You did get a letter from God," I said with a smile breaking across my face.

Ed began to smile and then chuckle a little. And I followed suit. We were both standing in the garage, freezing and laughing our heads off as Emma poked her head through the door. She looked at us as if we were crazy. I looked back and stopped laughing for a moment, and told her, "He got a letter from God!" That got us both laughing again. Emma just continued to stare at us with a half-smile, nodding her head as she closed the door again. God is good! God is good!

Chapter Seventeen

The next day was Christmas Eve, and it was going to be a full day for sure. I got up a little early so I could prepare—but first, newspaper and coffee. I looked through a frost-covered front door window to the outside. I could tell it was going to be a clear, crisp, and freezing day. The smoke rising from the housetops down the street went straight up. I certainly wasn't a physics major, but I remembered the smoke rose that way when it was really, really cold. I almost hugged my cup of coffee, holding it close to help me warm up as I peered out the window. I figured it would be a great and exciting day. Then I remembered what happened on Thanksgiving Day, with Lynn's outburst, Brit going to the emergency room, and Mom passing out . . . what a night. Maybe I didn't want it to be quite that exciting, I thought to myself. I cautiously opened the door and reached down to get my paper. After ripping the frozen paper from the front porch floor, I quickly shut the door and walked back into the living room, and settled into my chair, coffee in hand and ready to dig into the paper. Then I heard Katie and Emma walking around upstairs. Katie was probably too excited to sleep any longer, so she awakened Emma. I tried to choke down my coffee and read the paper a little quicker because once they came down, I knew I wouldn't get another chance to casually read my paper. Emma had to pull out a roast and get it cooking soon, and Katie and I were going to get the gifts together.

The morning passed quickly, as busy as we were, and we soon found ourselves getting ready to go to Mom and Dad's. I went to start the car to get it warmed up before getting dressed and packing up the food and gifts. It was so cold when I took my first breath outside it seemed like my entire sinus system froze up inside my head. The handle of the car door was hard to pull open, and the door itself opened grudgingly. Everything seemed harder in this cold weather. I quickly got in and started the car. It slowly cooperated, and once I got it going, I quickly scooted back into the house.

When I got back in, Emma and Katie had all the food and gifts ready to load up. I looked at Emma, who could see my anguish with the cold weather. Smiling, she looked at me and said, "We have a few minutes yet, so let's wait till the car warms up before we go out."

I responded, "Let's wait till spring to go out!" Emma laughed, but Katie looked a little puzzled by that comment. So, I explained that I was just kidding; she smiled and came and sat on my lap as I sat down on my chair.

As I sat, I began to ponder the whole George and Brit thing. "Emma, what do ya think about George and Brit?" She looked at me, raising her eyebrows with a puzzled look, trying to figure out my very general question. "I . . . I mean . . . well . . . I guess I haven't seen them much lately. Wonder how they are getting along, and I wonder whether Brit is still feeling sick all the time and whether she still intends to . . . you know." I looked at Katie in my lap and was reminded not to get too detailed.

Emma smiled at me and asked, "Which question do you want me to answer?"

I smiled back. "Sorry, just hope this all works out, and I can be positive today."

Emma could tell I was concerned. "Levi, it seems to me they are getting along OK. But as this pregnancy gets further along, I'm sure the pressure is mounting for both of them. I can't imagine what it would be like to be that young and have such huge issues to deal with."

"Yep," I added. "That's why those Social Support shops are so successful in talking these desperate young girls into . . . you know."

Convenience

"Makes me sick," Emma added. Then her face perked up. "But hey, you're the one who said we just have to rely on the Lord. It's Christmas Eve, and we don't want to think too hard about stuff like that today. How 'bout we get into the car now?"

"OK," I agreed lightheartedly. "But I still think we should wait till spring." Katie giggled as she excitedly jumped off my lap and grabbed my hand. We all got into the car and drove off to Mom and Dad's.

When we arrived, Dad was peeking through the window. When he saw us, he started for the door, being careful not to open it too soon and let all the cold air in.

"Hello, guys," he yelled as we walked up the steps. "I had to shovel today; it froze my nose and toes," Dad said jokingly. Katie got a worried look on her face. "Well, not completely; I counted, and they are all still here," Dad continued, joking so Katie would get a laugh.

"Where's Mom," I inquired as soon as I got everyone into the house.

"She's in the kitchen, of course," Dad answered.

So, I called out, "Mom," a little extra loud. No one answered. "Mom!" I yelled louder as I started worriedly toward the kitchen door. As I opened the kitchen door, I yelled still louder, "Mom!"

Just then, she entered the kitchen from the back porch. "Why are you yelling so loud?" She had a big smile on her face and gave me a big hug.

"You didn't answer," I responded.

"I was out on the porch getting my cutting board. You worry too much. And there's my little sweetheart!" Mom said. She gave Katie a big hug exclaiming, "I missed you, dear. You need to come over more often." Katie beamed. Mom made her feel so special.

Emma entered the kitchen to deliver the roast. "Here you go, Mom."

"Oh, that looks really nice. Thank you, dear Emma." Mom hugged Emma and kissed her on the face. I knew what was coming next. Mom began to shoo us out of the kitchen, except for Katie, who would stay and help. "OK now, everyone out, so I can get the last bit of work done. Emma, you can stay if you like, and of course, I'll need Katie to help!" So, I strolled out into the living room to hang out with Dad.

"Well, how are you, Daddy?"

"Oh, I'm doing OK," he said with a sort of sigh.

Trying to lighten things up a little, I joked, "Of course, George is planning on being fashionably late." Dad didn't really get it, but he offered a courteous grin. I said hopefully, "Maybe he'll get here on time. He still has fifteen minutes."

We both sat down and tossed out some small talk. But I was curious about Mom and had to ask, "How has Mom been doing? Has she felt OK lately?"

Dad looked at me expressionlessly. "She passed out again yesterday. She had just finished washing dishes and came out here to talk to me. When she leaned over to me, her eyes sort of looked out into the distance, her eyelids fluttered, and she got really dizzy. I grabbed hold of her, and she passed out right in my arms."

"Did you call the doctor?"

"No, she woke up right away, and the first thing out of her mouth was, don't call the doctor. She said that they don't care about her, and she didn't want to waste anyone's time."

"Dad, what are we going to do?"

"I don't know, son. The sad thing is that she is right about the doctors." We both just stared off into space for a moment.

Just then, George's car pulled up to the front of the house. I could hear the music blaring over the loud noise his car made from the hole in the muffler. Wanting to change the subject away from Mom, at least for now, I quickly exclaimed, "Well, Dad, it looks like you were right. George did make it on time."

Chapter Eighteen

George and Brit scurried up the sidewalk; they both were wearing jeans with holes in the knees, and they were all too happy to get into the house and out of the frigid weather.

"Hey, bro," George yelled as he looked at me. His face lost expression as he turned to Dad and said hello. Dad looked at him, somewhat surprised that George even addressed him and responded with a hello. Brit was barely showing yet, but she was having a rough time with morning sickness. It was beginning to wear on George too. I know he wanted her to quit stalling about the abortion. He wanted to see the "little problem" go away, so Brit would feel better and they could get on with their lives. Brit, on the other hand, kept stalling, insisting that the Social Support people assured her she could get the abortion late into the last trimester if she wanted. And, of course, they offered to pay for the whole procedure. Trying to shake off the cold, Brit was rubbing her arms as she said through a shiver, "Hello, Mr. B," referring to Dad, "and hello, Mr. B," looking at me. We both answered at the same time, "Hello, Brit," which brought a little chuckle from Dad and me. "I guess there are three Mr. Bs," I quickly responded. Brit smiled. George didn't.

"Well, let's see what's cookin' if Mom will let us into the kitchen," George said as he motioned toward the kitchen door. Brit grabbed George's hand as they started toward the kitchen. Dad and I sat back down on the couch and continued our small talk. I purposefully avoided talking about Mom, so we could have a pleasant time. But I couldn't get the thought that Mom might have some serious health problem out of my mind. The most vivid, recurring image I had was of Mom lying on the kitchen floor the night we arrived and my fearing the worst as she lay there.

It didn't take too long before George got kicked out of the kitchen. I knew it was coming. He probably put his finger into things to make sure they were "done right." Sure enough, he came running out of the kitchen with a big grin on his face. Mom poked her head out the kitchen door, waving her shoe in her hand. She was half joking and half downright hot under the collar as she yelled, "Will you ever learn, son?!" Brit must have run for cover somewhere in the kitchen. Dad and I just looked at each other with a smile, both agreeing that George was no match for our little Italian Mom—armed with a shoe in her hand.

George's retreat sent him to the couch with Dad and me. I looked at George and asked, "What happened to Brit? Did Mom take her prisoner?" George smiled.

I loved it when he smiled. He did it so infrequently. He seemed so angry most of the time. Dad looked happy too. I wanted to talk to George so bad—really talk and enjoy a conversation with my brother. It seemed like we were so busy that I hadn't really talked to him for a month. On the other hand, I didn't want to set him off on some rage that would be painful for me and painful for Dad too. So, I tried to start out light and harmless. "So, what have you been up to, George? Seems like I haven't seen you in a while."

"Oh, you know, bro. Just working, going to school," he paused for a moment. "Oh, and watching Brit puke every morning. I can't tell you how glad I'll be to see her get rid of that . . . problem."

I was beginning to percolate inside but was determined not to boil over—not on Christmas. But I had to press a little. "So, when is Brit going to do . . . that?"

George looked at me with a stern, angry look. "I don't know. She says she's OK for now. Whatever that means. I'd personally drive her to the doctor today if she would just say the word."

I held my tongue and desperately tried to survive the conversation.

Convenience

"Is . . . is she still working at that taco place after school?" I asked, trying to change the direction of the conversation. "Maybe that is making her sick."

George took the bait. "She's still working there. Says she needs to help her mom out with the bills. Plus, we get free tacos any night she is working there. The only drawback is that she smells like a big taco," George added with a grin.

"Make sure she is getting enough rest, or she could get a virus," I told George, trying to be serious again.

And George followed my lead with a serious look, exclaiming, "I told you, bro, I have the solution. Get rid of the growth. That would solve all our problems."

Just then, Mom poked her head out of the kitchen and told everyone to gather around the table. I had been just about to go on the offensive with George. *Thank you, Mom, and thank you, Lord!*

We gathered around the table and grabbed our seats as Mom and Emma, and Brit brought out the food. George immediately began to grab food, but Mom stopped him, directing that no one got food until we all sat down and prayed. George rolled his eyes but listened to Mom, except for the handful of chips he had already grabbed. He munched on those while the ladies sat down.

Finally, everyone was in place. They all looked at me, waiting to pray. I grabbed Katie's little hand and Emma's and bowed my head. I couldn't help but wonder if George and Brit wouldn't partake in the prayer like the last time we did this. Before I started, I took a last glance at them. George was staring off into space, purposefully avoiding even listening to the prayer. But Brit . . . I was shocked. She had bowed her head, and her eyes were tightly shut. Could she have accepted Christ back in November when Emma talked to her in the hospital? She certainly had my curiosity up. I finished the prayer by thanking God for the year he had provided for us, thanking him for family, and most importantly, for sending his son Jesus Christ to die for our sins.

As usual, we all dug in and enjoyed dinner. We managed to keep our conversation light and fun throughout the dinner. The food was excellent, as usual. I couldn't help but wonder what was going on inside

Brit's head and heart. Certainly, way more than any teenager should have to deal with. We wrapped up dinner with some of Mon's scratch-made coffeecake. It was an old Ukrainian recipe—something Mom had learned when she lived in Ukraine for several long, hard years. Dad served the dessert as had been the tradition in our house for years. He would serve a piece of cake, kiss us on the head, and wish us "Merry Christmas." Katie was a bit in awe over the whole event, thinking it was a bit out of the ordinary. I'm sure that Brit was a little embarrassed as well. Growing up, she never had a father figure and that type of leadership symbol in her home, so this was something unusual for her. But she seemed to do OK with it all.

After dessert, we opened some gifts. We never went too crazy with gifts like a lot of other families. Plus, none of us were exactly flush with cash. But the gifts we exchanged always seemed thoughtful and complementary to the receiver. Katie was the most thrilled, of course, opening her presents with glee. Emma and Katie, and I saved our personal gifts for when we got home, so we could have a little family Christmastime later. Katie was thrilled when she opened the gift that Mom and Dad got her. What else but a little cookware set of her own?

After that, Katie and Emma, and I sat together in Dad's big recliner and watched Brit open a gift from George. As she opened it, George was acting a bit embarrassed, apologizing that he couldn't have gotten her something more. He was always a little nervous at such moments. And, of course, he was still a little too proud to show too much emotion. But as Brit opened the small box, she glanced over at George and smiled, which basically swept George off the planet and into oblivion. She opened the box to reveal a gold bracelet. It had pearls connected by gold links.

"I love it, George," she exclaimed as she immediately began to put it on. It wasn't super spectacular, but to Brit, it was like the crown jewels.

Everyone in the room could tell from Brit's expression that she deeply loved my little brother. Then Brit pulled out a box from a paper bag she had left by the door when she came in. No one, including George, really expected Brit to be giving gifts. She was our guest, and we knew she had no money to buy gifts. She smiled at George and handed him the box. He had a puzzled look on his face and almost seemed hesitant to open it. He was also at a loss for words—a thing none of us could recall happening too often. Katie came and sat by George, rescuing him from the spotlight a bit. Again, George was hesitant to open the package, almost afraid he might experience some emotion contrary to the hard callous exterior he usually portrayed. As he finally began to open the package and realized what was in it, he just stared at Brit—almost as though he was looking through her. The gift was a Bluetooth speaker he could use in his car. George loved his music. He seemed to escape from the pains of this world when he got in his car and cranked up his music. Brit understood his need to escape and his feelings about all that. Between the perfection of the gift, the fact that George knew Brit had no money to buy such a nice and expensive gift, and her loving smile, Brit scored a direct hit on George's heart. He had no idea how to react. He stared at Brit for a moment and then quickly began to show Katie how the speaker worked, trying desperately to hide any emotions that might leak out. Mom knew what to do; she seemed so wise sometimes.

"Who wants coffee?" Mom yelled as she marched off to the kitchen. Emma bailed out as well, following Mom, and Dad was not far behind. I looked at the procession with a smile.

"Wait for me! Oh, George and Brit, want any coffee?"

"I'm good, George answered, still looking down at the player, pretending he was showing it to Katie.

Brit piped in, "None for me, thanks." So, the four of us proceeded to make one pot of coffee!

Just as the coffee was ready to pour, George and Brit poked their heads into the kitchen, with Katie following behind. George mustered up a few words . . . the first he could manage to say after the shock of the present.

"Brit and I are going to her house," George said, trying to look at his stern self again. But he wasn't quite his normal self. His emotionless armor had been penetrated.

"Thank you for everything," Brit said enthusiastically as they both offered a final goodbye and quickly left the house. Mom yelled at George as he opened the front door. "Be careful. It's slippery outside and icy on the roads." George gave no response and shut the door as he and Brit left.

"Well, Mom," I began as we sipped our coffee, "We'll help with the dishes and clean up."

Mom quickly responded, "No. Alex and I can get this. You guys get to your own family Christmas."

Mom was so smart and so aware of the dynamics of the people around her. She knew we needed a separate family time of our own for Christmas. I wondered if I would ever become as perceptive and wise as she seemed to be.

"Well, we can at least help bring the dishes in," Emma volunteered. But before she could finish, Mom responded, "No, no; that's OK. Your dad can help me with that. You need to get home before it gets too late. Why don't you go start the car, Levi, and get it warmed up so my sweet little girl," Mom then looked at Emma, "and my sweet big girl don't get cold."

Emma smiled. "OK, OK; you win," She finally admitted defeat.

Chapter Nineteen

When we got home, Emma jumped into action with Katie in tow. They brought out some candles and matches and spread out some cookies on the coffee table in the living room in front of the tree. Then Emma turned on a Christmas CD and lit the candles. On cue, Katie was standing by to shut the lights off. Apparently, they had planned the event down to the littlest details. So, we listened to great music and, with just the light of the Christmas tree and a few candles, we sat on the floor and exchanged gifts. It was great, and I was so thankful for my little family. I knew Emma had been through a lot in the last year or so. With my accident and the move to a small hick town in the middle of nowhere, and it being the middle of the coldest, darkest part of winter, I really wanted to get something special for her. Of course, I didn't have much money, so I couldn't get her as much as I would have liked. But, after searching long and hard, I finally found a set of ruby earrings—small ruby earrings, but they exactly matched the ruby necklace I gave her on our wedding day.

I was excited to give Emma the gift but wanted to wait until it was the last thing. We enjoyed every minute of watching our girl's smiling face glisten in the candlelight. We finally made it to the last gift. I handed Emma the little box. She smiled and looked at me, and took the box. It didn't take long for her to open the little package. As she looked in, she immediately recognized the style of the earrings.

She looked up at me, saying, "Levi, these match the necklace you gave me on our" . . . ; overcome with emotion, she leaned to me and hugged me tightly. I could tell she was crying a little as she quivered in my arms. I think it was not only the gift but a release of the emotions from the stress of the season and the past year. She finally looked up at me and simply said, "I love you." I responded in kind, and we hugged for another moment. We both suddenly remembered Katie and looked over at her. She was sitting quietly, just observing us. We both laughed a little and grabbed her, and included her in our hug.

"Merry Christmas," I exclaimed.

Well, after that, of course, it was time for coffee again! After all, I figured we'd be up late playing with Katie and her new toys. She, in particular, had a grand plan to set up her old and new ponies and conduct several "activities" with Mom and Dad.

It was fairly late, and we had played for hours when the phone rang. It had to be near midnight by now. Thoughts raced through my mind. Maybe George had an accident. Mom told him it was slippery out tonight. Or maybe Brit had another emergency. Or . . .

Oh Lord, not Mom again! I had to stay calm as I moved to answer the phone. I looked back at Emma as I grabbed up the receiver. "Hello," I said in an inquisitive tone.

"Levi, how are you?" It was a woman's voice on the line—a voice the person assumed I would recognize as soon as I heard it.

"Hi," I responded. "Um, who is this?"

"Oh, Levi. It's Lynn. Have you forgotten me again already?"

"Hi, Lynn. How are you? We were hoping to have you over for the holidays. I left a message on our phone a while back."

"Yep," she cut me off. "I got your message." She paused for a moment. "Guess I got a little busy," she giggled. "I've had a lot . . . a lot going on lately," she snickered.

Then she hiccupped. She was definitely drunk. "Well . . . hey, Levi, I just wanted to wish you a Merry Christmas!" She snickered again. "Hope your family had a great day! I'm here all by myself!"

Her comment threw me off. I didn't know how to respond. "We would have liked to have you over to join us, Lynn."

Convenience

"No, Levi," she paused longer than she realized. "I mean, I'm really by myself!" Like no baby inside. She paused again as she began to get a little annoyed that I hadn't been following her. She paused a long time again. It seemed like endless silence. I was so off guard and confused; I felt like I was on an amusement park ride, not knowing which way was up. Then she continued, "I had an abortion last week. So, as I said, I'm really by myself now." She chuckled this time, then the long, long pause again. I could tell that she was holding back tears. She took a deep breath and then went on the offensive. "Guess you're happy now—your pious little self! Now you can tell everyone, "I knew Lynn would do it, right? You know, Levi . . . having a baby right now would just not have been fair. Now, I can concentrate on my career. This job is the most exciting thing that has ever happened to me! Do you get that? No, I supposed you don't." Lynn's voice began to break up a bit as she began to cry. "Maybe I'll have a kid in a few years when things are more convenient," she sobbed a little. I still hadn't said a word. She paused again as her tears turned to anger. She sniffled a little and then began again. "Well, just thought I'd call and say hello. Now, you can go back and enjoy your perfect little life even more! Merry Christmas!" She hung up. As I bowed my head, I strained, staring at my phone with no real expression on my face.

"Honey," Emma called from across the room with a worried tone. "What is it?" I looked up from the phone and looked at Emma.

"That was Lynn," I responded, still with no expression. "She wanted to wish us a Merry Christmas."

Emma knew there was something wrong and asked again, "Levi, what is it?" I tried to gather myself and my thoughts.

"Uh, she really wasn't too sincere with her holiday greeting. Emma, she was drunk." I paused for a moment, trying to explain the best I could. "She had the abortion last week. She seemed really disturbed and tried to joke about being alone on Christmas—really alone . . . as in no child anymore. Then she went on to sort of imply that it was my fault for how bad she felt. She said I could now feel even better about my pious little self. I don't get it, Emma; I just don't get it."

"Oh, Levi," Emma put her hand on my shoulder. I was speechless. So much had happened all day long, and to end it with this, well, left me speechless and staring into a dark kitchen. Emma gave me a hug from behind and laid her head on the back of my shoulder. Neither of us said anything for a while.

"Well," I finally blurted out with a deep breath, "we can't let this get the best of us." I turned and smiled at Emma. "I had a great day at Mom's with George and Brit and then together here with you and Katie. I couldn't be more blessed."

Emma smiled back and hugged me again. "Let's go to bed, honey," and she added, "Merry Christmas, dear."

Chapter Twenty

Well, thank the Lord for how he makes every day new and fresh. We managed not to think too much about Lynn for the rest of the holiday. I didn't think it would be good to try to talk to her again in the next few days. Emma, Katie, and I enjoyed our time together and got a lot done around the house. We even went on an evening sleigh ride at a ranch outside of town. Katie loved horses and was in awe the whole evening, which ended with a wonderful dinner in an old cabin while an old thick-mustached cowboy told a few tales about the Wild West. We all loved it. At times the cowboy would stop mid-sentence and look you right in the eye. The only sound was the firewood crackling. The shadows bounced off the fireplace and across the old cowboy's very serious face. It was certainly a night we will all remember. Well, as is always the case, the time off seemed to go by so fast, and I found myself with only a couple of days left to prepare to get back into school mode. But we had a great vacation. We hardly saw anyone else after Christmas Eve. In fact, I only talked to Mom on the phone, and we had lunch once together at a little shop in town. I began to wonder what George and Brit were up to. I also got to thinking about Ed and how he might be doing.

Then, on Saturday night, Mom called. I could tell she was trying to stay calm as usual, but something was up. "Hello, Levi," Mom began, "how are all of you?"

"We're good, Mom. What's up?"

"Oh well, George came over tonight and . . . well, he was in one of those grumpy moods." There was a silence that seemed to last forever.

"Mom, tell me what's going on."

"Oh," she said, "it's not a big deal, really. Well, I guess it's sort of a big deal. I'll be honest. I've never seen George so upset."

"Mom, I know how crazy George can get. This must have been bad for you to bring it up."

"It was, Levi . . . seems he got into a fight with Brit over the baby. They must have really had a big fight. He said she had no idea what she was doing with this growth, as he called it. Then he stopped and corrected himself. He said it was not a growth but more like a tumor. Can you believe that, Levi? He was really mad."

I continued to listen as Mom went on. "He called her all kinds of names and said he didn't want to see her again."

"What did you do?" I asked.

"Nothing," Mom replied. "I didn't do anything, but your dad had heard enough and told George to calm down and be quiet and to quit saying things he would regret." Mom paused then for a moment, took a deep breath, and continued. "Then George began to yell back at your dad. He said that Dad would never understand him or anything about kids these days and called Alex a few choice words. Then I tried to step in to get him to calm down. In his rage, he turned to me and said . . . well," she paused. "Maybe I shouldn't trouble you with all this."

"Mom," I broke in, "I'm part of this, aren't I? Tell me what he said."

"Well, he was just out of his head, and I know he didn't mean it."

"Mom," I interrupted again, "tell me what he said."

"Levi, he just blurted out and said, 'shut up, or I'll shut you both up for good!'" Mom continued, half sobbing, "Oh, Levi, I know he didn't mean it. You should have seen his face. He was angry and terrified at the same time. He stood there in silence, breathing heavily and looking at us." Mom paused again and then continued. "Levi, tears began to roll down George's angry, frightened face. Then he lowered his head, looking confused. He turned without a word and walked out the door. He slammed the door so hard that I thought it would break into pieces.

Convenience

"Oh, Mom, I'm sorry," I replied. "Are you guys OK? Any idea where George went?"

"We're fine. We've been around long enough to know he didn't mean any of what he said. I have no idea where George went, though. I just hope he and Brit are OK."

"What should I do, Mom? Maybe I'll go look for him and talk to him."

"Levi, I don't know; I'm just gonna pray about this tonight. I'm sorry to bother you with all this. Please be careful and take care of your own family."

"I'll talk to you in church tomorrow, Mom. Please call me if you hear any more. Oh, and please tell Dad I love him and that he is the best Dad anyone could have . . . and by the way, you're the best Mom."

"Good night, son. Thank you. I love you, and I'll tell your dad. See you tomorrow."

As I stepped outside, a cold gust of wind chilled me to the bone. I thought to myself, *"Oh Lord, what should I do?"* He answered. It occurred to me. A great thing about small towns way up north is that there are very few places you can go when it's close to thirty degrees below zero. We had one restaurant that would still be open this late. It was called Aunt Sally's, a little place that stayed open all night, mainly for the truckers. But the food was good and all freshly made. So, I explained everything to Emma and headed over to Aunt Sally's.

As I pulled up, it was still hard to see out the windshield of the car. It was so cold that the engine was not yet warm enough to clear the frost off the windshield. But as I peered through a small clear portion of the glass I had scraped off earlier, I could see George's car in the parking lot. He was there! "Thank you, Lord," I said to myself and asked God to please forgive us and bless this situation. As I got out of the car, I quickly made my way to the front door of Aunt Sally's. As I pulled the door open, the little bells at the top of the door announced my arrival to all that was in there. George saw me and got a little excited as his expression perked up a little. Then he came to his senses and literally shook his head as if to shake off the appearance of happiness to see me. He recovered and put his angry face back on.

I sat next to him at the table. "Hey, George. How are you?"

"Hey, bro. It's funny seeing you out this late," he added sarcastically. "Mom called you, didn't she?"

I smiled and ignored the question. "Just coffee tonight?" I asked.

"Well, it's warm anyway, and I'm a little low on cash."

As the waitress approached with a smile, I greeted her with a hearty hello.

"What would you like, sir?"

"Hmm," I said with a smile. "I'll have a coffee and two double cheeseburger combos." The waitress looked at me, kind of funny. "Oh," I said, "they aren't both for me, of course. One's for my friend, George. Oh, and we want just the cheese and meat and bun. No mayo or any of that lettuce and other stuff."

"OK," the waitress responded. "I'll get you some fresh hot coffee and get your order in."

I could tell that George was impressed and even a little touched that I remembered just how we both liked our burgers. I think it comforted him a little, but of course, he tried hard not to show it. I was just glad to start off our time together with something we had in common. And, of course, I could also tell George was just plain hungry.

"Wow, bro. Did ya miss supper? Eatin' late, and burgers at that. Are the health police gonna come and arrest you?" George asked with a half-smile.

"No," I responded, smiling back. "But I'll pay for it tomorrow," I added jokingly. Just then, the waitress arrived with my steaming hot coffee. I doused it with cream and took a sip. "Oh, that does warm a guy up, huh, George." Then we sat in silence for what seemed a long time. I was determined to do a lot of listening this time instead of talking. I looked at George. As much as he tried to put on an angry-but-in-control face, what really showed through was fear and confusion. His eyes and nose were still red, I'm sure, from crying. I really felt for him this time. Maybe in the past, even though I didn't set out to be, I was judgmental, wanting to "fix" George. I still thought the way he approached things was wrong. But this time, instead of trying to fix him, more than anything, I just felt for him. I thought to myself, *"Lord,*

Convenience

please help me through this and to do and say what you would have me do and say.

We still sat in silence, both playing around with our coffee cups, sipping and saying things like, "Ah, that's good." Then I noticed George with a stressed look on his face. He was, I'm sure, running through his dilemma with Brit, replaying them in his mind. I could see him getting angry all over again. It began to build up again. His face turned red, his jaw tightened, and he began to bite down on his lip. Then he turned and looked straight at me. Guess he had no other choice. He was going to boil over if he didn't talk to someone. As he began to speak, I could see a vein in his neck, and one on his forehead began to show. He even shook a little as he drew a breath.

"How could she be so stupid?" George said, trying to keep his voice from rising too high. I just looked at him, waiting for more. He continued, "We can't take care of a kid right now. We can't even take care of ourselves! Look at us!" His last few words were loud enough that a few people in the restaurant looked at us or stopped drinking their coffee for a moment with raised eyebrows. George noticed the others and stopped his speech for a moment lowering his head as if to drink a sip of coffee.

I tried to help his discomfort, commenting that he was too hard on himself and Brit. I added, "You guys are doing fine with this life thing. It's not easy growing up these days."

George was a bit surprised at the half-compliment I gave him. Guess he was expecting to do battle with me as usual. Then he took a long deep breath and responded. "Bro, listen to me. We are both kids. How are we supposed to take care of a kid? And—" he paused deep in thought for a moment. "This is the time in our lives when we are supposed to be having fun—no responsibilities, no cares or worries, just enjoying ourselves for a while!" He could tell he was getting too loud again. He took a sip and, gaining his composure a little, quietly added, "This is the worst, most inconvenient thing that could happen at this time in our lives." He sipped again as he thought some more and added, "I just don't get why she is waiting or what she is waiting for. We can quickly end this problem and get on with things. Everybody does it. When I talk about it with Brit, she nods her head like she agrees with me; then, she changes the subject really quickly. And we never get to the point where we put our coats on and go do this thing and be done."

Well, George was doing most of the talking, and I was certainly glad for that. But my heart was wriggling jelly inside as I tried to listen and even empathize with George as he saw Brit's baby as just a "problem" that could be "terminated" or exterminated, like a bug problem in your house. *Oh, Lord, help me,* I thought to myself as I continued to listen to George. Then, as George finished his statement, the silence returned. He looked at me for a response. I took a sip of coffee to stall a bit. As I looked up at George, the waitress approached our table with our food. "Oh yeah, here we go," I said with a bit of excitement, taking the opportunity to change the subject for a moment. George broke his lock on the conversation for a moment to dig in.

I bowed my head discreetly and thanked the Lord for the food, and took a hearty bite of my burger. As I chewed, I still wasn't sure how to respond to George, but I knew that I had to try. "Well," I began slowly, still munching on my food, "I guess you do still have time, right?" I was gulping back my emotions as I struggled inside at what I was saying. "I mean, you once told me that abortions can be done any time during pregnancy. You even mentioned they could be done up to a certain time after the . . . and the . . ." I couldn't go on with that thought. I faked a cough and then just ended with, "well, whatever it was." George kept eating. I wasn't sure if I made any sense to him with my last statement, and I wasn't sure if that was what he wanted or needed to hear.

Then, for whatever reason, George switched the topic. "Bro, I really let Brit have it tonight. I screamed at her." He paused in thought, tracing the episode in his mind. "She just looked at me. She didn't say anything. It was like she was waiting for me to calm down, so she could enjoy me again, love me again. But I didn't cool off, bro . . . I didn't cool off. I just turned and left. I left her standing there waiting."

"Then I went to Mom and Dad's house and blew up at them." George paused a bit. His eyes began to get moist and red again. He took another bite of his burger to stall a bit longer and clear his emotions. As he chewed, he looked around the restaurant a bit so as to recover further from his emotions.

I felt so bad for him but didn't know how to help. He had grown up in a world that had devalued life to the point that you could just switch it on or off. If a new life seemed too annoying or inconvenient, you could just switch it off, like a light that was too bright. In fact, it became your right to do so, and if someone questioned that, they were violating your privacy. It was such a twist of the truth.

Lord, please forgive us, I thought to myself.

George began to ponder again. "Who's gonna take care of the kid if we both have to work or go to school? Mom isn't healthy enough, and Brit's Mom works her whole life away."

"George," I responded, "I'm sure Emma would help sometimes, and I know that Mom would help no matter how she felt."

Silence again. George finished his food and began to get ready to leave. I knew I couldn't let him go just like that. "George," I began again and looked him straight in the eye. "You know I'm here for you and will help you any way I can." I took a long pause and finished my sentence, "no matter what."

George responded in a solemn voice. "Thanks, bro . . . really. I'm glad you came out." Being careful not to get too emotional and to keep it light, he added, "especially glad for that juicy cheeseburger and those greasy fries." He smiled and patted me on the back as we stood up.

"Listen," I said. "Go and make up with Brit. I can almost see her still standing there, waiting for you to get back to the person she seems to love so much."

"Not sure she wants me back, bro. Maybe I'll wait till tomorrow and try then. Good night, Levi."

"Where are you going?" I asked.

"Maybe I'll go back to our house and sneak in quietly."

"See you soon, George." I watched George leave in silence. I knew his heart was still heavy with all the issues he had tugging at him. I thought, though, maybe he was a little more hopeful and felt a little better. At least his stomach was full, and he could get some sleep. As he opened the door of the restaurant, a burst of cold, smoky air rushed in. Sitting near the door, the waitress, another customer, and I waited somewhat impatiently for the door to completely close again so we could warm up.

I took my last gulp of coffee to warm my insides a bit, paid the waitress, and struck out to my car. It was a freezing drive home, and I didn't even bother trying to warm the car. I just wanted to get to the house as soon as I could. As I pulled up, I noticed the living room light on and figured Emma couldn't sleep. I parked and dashed up the front steps and onto the porch with the sound of crackling ice crystals under my feet. Emma opened the door for me, wasting as little open-door time as possible.

"Hi, my dear," I exclaimed in a low voice.

"Hi, honey," Emma responded. "I couldn't sleep and thought I'd wait for you. Did you find your 'bro,' as he calls you?"

"Sure did," I responded. "We had a nice little talk . . . and a nice not-so-little cheeseburger and fries," I added with a smile.

Emma hugged me and gave me a kiss. "Hmm, yep. French fry breath."

We had a chuckle together, and I explained all that transpired, emphasizing that I was thrilled that at least I didn't leave with us both at each other's throats.

"Let's get to bed, Levi. We've got church tomorrow," Emma exclaimed as she started up the stairs to bed.

"Right behind you, dear," I responded as I double-checked that the door was locked and shut tightly so as not to let any cold air through.

Well, Sunday came and went. We had a great couple of services that did us all some good and got us charged up to get us back into the routine of school again. My Monday morning class dragged on a little slowly, with the kids a little less ready for the "routine" than I was. After dismissing class, I made my way down to the break room to get my lunch and brought it back to my classroom, and sat down to eat. Just as I was taking my first bit, someone slapped me on the back.

"Hey, Levi!" It was one of those slaps that were delivered in friendship, yet a little harder than the sender realized and pretty annoying to the receiver! I turned to see Ed Stone with a big grin on his face.

"Hi, Ed. How are you? Hey, if you had waited two more seconds, you could have slapped the peanut butter and jelly right out of my mouth!" I said jokingly but really half truthfully.

Ed laughed loudly as usual. As annoying as he was sometimes, I had to admit to myself how entertaining it was to see Ed so overjoyed with life.

"Church was great yesterday, wasn't it, buddy?" Ed asked. I nodded, now having a mouth full of food. "Well," he continued, "I'm gonna grab some pizza from the cafeteria, and I'll meet ya in the gym in a while."

"Pizza," I said, catching Ed before he left. "Is that your special diet? Are you sure that's a good idea since you're still recovering from a heart attack?"

"Now, Levi," Ed answered, "if I remember right, you were the one who smuggled in a large pizza for me the day after my surgery, right?" Ed laughed out loud again as he departed.

"Bye, Ed," I said with a mouth full of food again.

Well, Ed and I had a great time with the boys in PE class. The kids seemed to think it was almost unfair how much fun we had—with it being school and all. And, of course, as happy as Ed seemed, the kids still thought he had finally lost his marbles. After class, I quickly showered and headed for my last math class. As I walked the hallways, I remembered George and the weekend and that Brit was in my next class. I wondered how she might act and whether George had even talked to her. He hadn't, of course, called any of us since the blowup.

As class started, everyone was in their place . . . except for one empty chair—Brit's chair. I waited for a little extra long to start, which no one complained about. Still, no sign of Brit, so I began. I used the first few days after a long break for review. I thought that was best for math, so everyone could ease back into it and get a good review of the foundational stuff on which we would build for the rest of the year.

As I plowed through the material, I kept looking at that empty chair, wondering if Brit and George were OK. I hated the look of that empty chair. It stood almost as a symbol of Brit maybe giving up, checking out. She had finally put her trust in someone and put her feelings on the line with George. And now I wondered if she would think that maybe George was just like everyone else and that she might just give up hope and become a recluse. Even worse, I know she had drawn closer to the Lord throughout this year. I believed, like Emma, that Brit was putting her trust in the Lord to some extent, and I really hoped that she hadn't backed away from that. As I said, I hated seeing that empty chair.

I finished class and spent about an hour getting caught up on paperwork. As I worked, I kept drifting back to thinking about George and Brit. As I was deep in thought, my stupor was abruptly interrupted by Ed. He popped his head into my room and yelled excessively loudly, "Hey, Levi, ball game tonight?"

"Oh, hey, Ed," I stammered, gathering my thoughts. "Yeah, yeah, of course. I'll pick up some snacks on the way home."

"Is seven thirty good for you?" Ed asked.

"Sure, any time is good for you, pal!"

Ed smiled and disappeared as quickly and abruptly as he had appeared.

Things seemed to be getting back to normal. I had a great evening with Emma and Katie, and then Ed and the ball game. Emma watched the game with us until halftime and then slipped off to bed. Ed and I chatted, commented on the game, and had a few snacks. Still, I kept wondering about George and Brit. I kept wishing George would call or something. Anyway, as I watched Ed drive off into the cold night, I got an idea. I decided I'd stop by Mom's in the morning for coffee and to check up on George and get the update.

The next morning, I got up early, got ready, and made my way to Mom's. As I knocked on the door, she, of course, was already up and about the house, doing this and that. She answered the door with a big smile. "Levi," she exclaimed and gave me a hug. "How are you? Haven't seen you for a few days."

"Oh, I'm fine, Mom. How are you?"

She didn't answer my question but quickly invited me in. "Come in and have some coffee before you go to school." She knew just where to hit me—a warm cup of coffee on a cold morning.

"Just what I had in mind, Mom,"

I came in, kicking the snow off my shoes and removing my jacket. The house smelled of fresh coffee already, as if Mom had been expecting me. She was always prepared. As I sat down and sipped my drink, Mom and I had a nice talk about general things, but I finally got a chance to ask about George. "So, what's going on with George? Did he get things straight with you and Dad?"

"Well," Mom responded, "you know George. He didn't say much about that night. But I could tell he felt bad about what he said to us. He didn't come right out and apologize, but he joked around with both of us and spent a little time with us at supper on Sunday night. We both knew that was his way of saying he was sorry."

"Sounds like George, all right. Well, glad to hear that. Did he say anything about Brit? I didn't see her in school yesterday."

Mom pondered for a moment, sipped on her coffee, and responded. "No, come to think of it, he didn't really mention Brit at all." That wasn't the answer I was hoping for.

"Hmm," I responded. "What do you think, Mom?"

"I'm not sure what to think, Levi. They make a great couple." Mom stared off into the next room as she sipped her coffee again.

We both sat in silence for a moment. "Well," I finally broke into the silence, "I guess I need to be getting to school. Don't want to be late and have to get a tardy slip and hall pass," I said jokingly.

Mom laughed as she responded, "Ha, that would not be good!"

I headed for the door and got my coat, scarf, and shoes on, and bid Mom goodbye. As I walked back to the car, I thought of George again. Maybe they didn't makeup. Who knows?

The morning was pretty uneventful, pretty normal, and pretty slow. I guess I was thinking about the afternoon math class and wondering if Brit would show up. *Please, Lord*, I thought, *please don't let Brit fade away, give up, and let go of the vision she seemed to have caught for a good, happy future.*

Well, as my afternoon math class started, there was that empty chair again. I was continuing my review from the day before. As I got deeper into our review, I decided that Brit was not going to show up, so I began to forget about that and concentrate on my review. But as I turned back toward the class from writing on the whiteboard, there she was, in her seat, smiling at me. I was happy to see her but tried not to look too moved by it all and kept on with my review; after class, Brit stopped by my desk on her way out.

"Hey, Levi, . . . I . . . I mean, Mr. Bell. How's it goin'?"

"Hi, Brit. Good to see you. How are you?"

"Well, I was a little sick yesterday," she responded as she looked down at her stomach. "But I'm feeling fine today. Sorry, I missed yesterday, and I need to know what to do to make up the work."

"Oh," I said, not even thinking about schoolwork. "We've just been reviewing so far and haven't done anything new. I like to start slow after the holidays, so don't worry about it. Have you seen George lately?" I blurted out my question before thinking through that they may still be fighting and scared myself. Quickly backtracking, I continued. "I mean, I haven't seen him in a few days, so I was just wondering if you had seen him."

Brit rescued me from my awkwardness. "Yeah, sure. He's been at my house most of the week," she said as a big smile glazed over her face. I could tell Brit really loved my brother. And she had reaffirmed her trust in him and them. Relieved, I responded. "Oh, OK—well, glad he's OK."

Brit explained. "We had a little disagreement on Saturday, but we have definitely made up now." She couldn't keep the smile off her face. She seemed as happy as I'd seen her in a long time; it was as though she had some things finally straight and settled in her mind.

"Well, I'm glad to hear everything is OK," I said cautiously.

"Me too," Brit replied as she looked up at the clock. "Oh, gotta go. Meeting George downstairs. See you later, Levi—I . . . I mean, Mr. Bell."

"See you. And be careful down the stairs," I yelled as she flew out the door. "OK," Brit yelled back without looking. I couldn't tell what to make of Brit's happiness. She had not seemed like her normal happy self for months. And now she seemed almost jubilant. I was certainly glad to see her that way. It certainly had been a while since she had been really happy.

After the slow start back from the holidays, things seemed to pick up a little and get back to normal by midweek. The rest of the week zipped

Convenience

by as I found myself driving home from school Friday evening. Even though it was only four o'clock in the evening, we were so far north that this time of year that it was already dark ... not to mention freezing cold.

As I drove near Mom and Dad's house, the four tall cottonwood trees looked as though they had had enough of the cold dark winter. They seemed to stoop over a bit and looked weak and worn. I was certainly getting a little tired of the winter myself, but I knew it would be quite a while yet before spring would hit. As I focused back on the road, I noticed Lynn walking up the street ahead of me. A chill ran down my back as I remembered our last encounter on the phone. I didn't know what to do. Should I drive by and wave, or should I ignore her? Well, she helped me with my decision as she got to the corner of the block. She turned the corner and began to walk down a side street for whatever reason. Maybe she didn't even see me coming up behind her, or maybe she was avoiding me. *Oh Lord*, I thought to myself. *Please be with her. Bless her and let her know you love her. Please help her in what seems to be such a difficult time.* I drove home. It was completely dark now ... and colder.

Well, a couple of weeks went by fairly uneventfully. Brit seemed happier than I had seen her all year. She smiled and joked and acted as though she had no problems at all. George was just George through it all. I kept wondering what was on either of their minds.

We were now into February, and I was giving my class its first big math test since the Christmas break. It was going to be a tough test for sure. I gave it on Friday so that my students could recover after the blow over the weekend. As the top of the hour came and went, there was that empty chair again. I wondered if Brit was going to show up. Certainly, she wouldn't miss this day of all days. Her grades were solid Bs, and she couldn't afford to miss the test and maintain her grade. But at five minutes past the hour, I had to start the test—Brit or no Brit. And that's just what I did. Brit never did show up. Maybe she was sick again, I thought. Later, after the test and about halfway through grading the papers, I thought I'd take a break and call George.

"George, how are you doing?" I asked as I caught him between classes.

"Well, bro. I'm OK," he responded.

"What's up?" I continued. "How's Brit? Was she sick today? She missed my test. I know I'm a tough teacher, but . . ." I said jokingly.

George responded with a little laugh, "Well, I'm not sure where Brit is. I haven't seen her today either. When I called her this morning, she told me she wanted to sleep in a while, so I didn't need to pick her up. Didn't think she was gonna sleep all day, though. Whatever. I'll stop over there after I get a snack at the house. Oh, and about the test, just give her an A," George joked. "Sounds like a plan?"

"Tell ya what, George, I'll give her a nice big . . . second chance to take the test. No need to thank me, bro. It's the least I can do."

"You're right, Bro," George agreed. "It really is the *least* you can do." We both laughed and bid each other a good day.

As I hung up, I got ready to go home. I finished grading the last few papers and cleaned up my room a little. It was another cold and already dark night. As I drove home and passed by Mom and Dad's house, there was Lynn again, walking along the sidewalk. This time I couldn't avoid driving by her, and I couldn't pretend I didn't see her. She was waiting to cross the street in front of me. As I drove past, I made eye contact. She recognized that it was me, and as I drove past, she looked right at me expressionlessly and watched me drive by. I tried to smile a little, but she had absolutely no expression on her face. She looked pale, eyes sunken, and older than the last time I saw her. I forcefully held my smile through the encounter. *That was weird*, I thought to myself. I still couldn't figure out how to handle Lynn. *Lord*, I thought, *please help me to respond the way you would want . . . for her sake.*

As I turned into our driveway and parked, I noted the new snow that had fallen. And as I got out and walked to the house, I trampled the new three or so inches of snow on the grass and was formulating my grand plan for Saturday morning: drink a nice hot, huge cup of coffee and get caught up on shoveling the sidewalks! Katie was watching me through the living room window. Her eyes lit up as I drew closer. She had her hat and coat on and began to smile and jump up and down as I reached the door. Then, as I came in, there was

Convenience

Emma, also with a coat on, who jokingly joined Katie in jumping up and down.

"Hi, dear," Emma yelled from across the room. "Been cooped up all day in the house, and we want to go on a date! What do you say?" Katie's big beautiful steely blue eyes sparkled in the light as she smiled at me.

"How can I turn down an offer like that from the two most beautiful girls in the world?" So, I headed right back out to the car, and we piled in. Thankfully, the car was already warm from my drive home. We drove over to our favorite high-class Italian restaurant, Pizza Barn. It was the best pizza place in town—and the only pizza place in town. But it did have a warm, cozy atmosphere, and we had a blast as we discussed the week's events, laughing and just enjoying being with each other.

Through the course of the conversation, I was reminded about seeing Lynn again and explained the encounter to Emma. "What do you think, dear?" I asked. "I'm sure I'll run into her again. Not sure how I should handle it. I'd like to help her somehow."

Emma munched on a piece of pizza and stared off across the room. Then she responded, "Levi," she said as she was swallowing her bite of pizza, "maybe you don't need to do anything right now. Maybe you should just be there, ready to listen when . . . if she decides to talk to you. I feel terrible for her, but you can't fix everyone's problems, and I think she really needs a friend to talk to and will turn to you and me when she is ready. Then, we might be better positioned to be her friends and help her get through what seems to be a really hard time."

I pondered a bit and responded, "I suppose so." That was the best I could come up with. I quickly changed the subject so as not to dampen our happy mood.

Well, Katie fell asleep on the way home. As we parked, I got out of the car and picked up Katie, and tried to keep her as warm as I could as I carried her in. Then we had the task of getting her coat, hat, gloves, and shoes off without her waking up. She must have been pretty tired because she didn't wake up at all through the whole process. So, Emma put her right to bed. We stayed up a bit and talked some more before going to bed ourselves. I wanted to get up early, excited to do my shoveling duty outside. Just as I was getting ready to get into bed, though, the phone rang. The first thing I thought of was that maybe there was something wrong with Mom again, or maybe it was Lynn again. And what in the world would I say?

Chapter Twenty-One

As I answered and said hello, I was relieved to hear a "Hi, bro" on the other end.

"Hi, George. What's up?"

George began, but in a more serious tone than usual. In fact, his tone was more mature and straightforward than I had probably ever heard from him. "I'm at Brit's house, and no one is here. Her mom is probably at work, but I don't remember Brit having to work today. She has not been over at your house, by chance, groveling to you about missing that test, has she?"

We had gotten to know Brit better over the last few months, and she did occasionally stop by to talk with Emma and Katie. But we hadn't seen her lately. "No, George, she's not been over here. She must be working. You should probably talk to her about cutting back a little on hours and not working so late. It's not good for anyone's health to work that hard and be . . ."

"Be what, be pregnant? Don't start with me, bro!"

"No, George, I wasn't going to say that. I was going to say that she shouldn't work so hard and be in school. Remember, she missed my test today."

"Oh," George responded. "Yeah, whatever." He calmed down a little but still was worried about Brit. "Uh, guess I'll go pick her up at work then. Later, bro." He hung up. Emma was still in the living room reading a magazine when I turned out the bedroom light and went to sleep.

The next morning, I slept in just a little but slowly made my way to the coffeepot. It was sunny outside but still cold, and I could see the sunshine glistening off the snow in the front yard. I poured myself a nice hot cup of coffee and headed for the chair in the living room where I could read yesterday's paper and enjoy the sun. As soon as I got settled in, the phone rang. A little annoyed, I set down my cup, climbed out of the chair, and grabbed the phone off the table.

It was George. As he spoke, I remembered that he hadn't been able to find Brit the previous night, and this time he was frantic. His voice cracked a little as he explained. "Bro, I didn't find Brit at work, so I thought maybe I didn't catch her before she closed the taco shop and then missed her on the way home. So, I just went to Mom's and went to sleep.

Brit's mom just called me and told me Brit didn't come home last night, so she thought Brit was with me! Levi, we don't know where she is!"

"OK, George, calm down a little. Let's think about this." I had told George to be calm, but now I was getting very worried myself. I didn't want to show that to George, though. "Think about anywhere else she said she might be. Does she have a friend that she may have stayed with?"

"No. Not that I can think of—that she would stay with . . . unless Jenny may have asked her over."

"Who is Jenny?" my voice began to rise a little.

"Hold on, bro. I'm getting a call from Brit's mom. Let me call you back." George hung up the phone. Shaking my head, I was still trying to wake up and comprehend what had just transpired. I finally got my senses together and realized what I needed to do was pray. *"Lord, please bless us and let nothing be wrong with Brit. We've come to love her as our own, Lord, and she has such a great personality and such potential. Please, Father, let her be OK."* I decided to run upstairs and get ready for the day in case I might have to help George, God forbid, go look for Brit.

As I was climbing up the stairs, George called back. He was even

Convenience

more frantic. He told me that Brit's mother said she had found a note on the floor that was addressed to George. George asked her to open the note and read it over the phone. George explained the note to me. Brit talked about how much she loved George and wanted to do what was best for him. She said he was right about the abortion and that they couldn't have a baby right now and how it would make matters so inconvenient for everyone. She went on to say that she was at fault and wanted to make matters right. So, she decided to go to an abortion clinic in Sterling, which was not far away. She figured she could sneak away over the weekend and get the abortion done and be back to explain. Brit finished the note by assuring George that the abortion clinic said they would take care of everything and would cover the costs.

My stomach began to twist in knots, but I knew I needed to keep my composure and help George. "OK. What should we do?"

George didn't answer for a minute.

"George, you there?"

"Yeah, I'm thinking. Brit mentioned a family clinic up in Sterling a long time ago. Maybe that's where she is. Wonder why she won't answer her phone, though, unless the clinic doesn't let people bring in a cell phone."

I could tell George was out of ideas and getting really worried.

"Tell you what, George," I responded. "I'll try to call the place while I'm getting dressed, and I'll swing by and pick you up, and we can start making our way there."

George seemed a little taken aback by my interest and care for Brit and him. "Uh, OK . . . Uh, bro. I'll wait for you at Mom's and run out to the car when you come by." Trying to lighten things up and make himself more comfortable, he added, "I'm not standing outside to wait, though. It's too cold out there."

I bid the bewildered George goodbye, hung up the phone, and began searching the internet for the clinic in Sterling. There it was—it was an abortion clinic, all right, with a bright and shiny advertisement for free consultations and, in some cases, free procedures from Social Support. I got the number and gave them a call. As the phone rang, I thought about how sad it would be to learn that Brit had an abortion, but we'd deal with whatever happens. Still, I asked the Lord to please allow that not to be the case . . . somehow. As I heard the sixth or so ring, I began to wonder if there was anyone there. Then I was connected, but I only got an answering machine, stating office hours and saying that the clinic was closed for appointments on the weekends. Since it was Saturday, the place would not open for another two hours. I hung up, wondering what it all meant. Did she check-in and was recovering? Did she not go in at all? Where in the world was she?

I called George back and told him the story. He still wanted to drive up to Sterling, about an hour and a half north of us, and look for Brit. So, I got my clothes on and sucked down my coffee. Then I quickly told Emma the whole story and asked her to please pray, and I headed out the door.

Winter was really getting old and tiresome; by this time of year, I always thought that it should be getting a little warmer outside. But that, as usual, was not the case. As I stepped out and took my first deep breath, I was quickly reminded that winter was not even close to being gone yet. It was still freezing.

When I arrived at Mom's house, George was looking out the front window. He waved at me as I pulled up in front of the house. Before I could park, George was shutting the door tightly behind him and running toward the car. "Hi, bro," he exclaimed as he quickly got into the car, rubbing his hands together to generate a little heat.

"Hello, George. Are you OK?" I asked as I looked him right in the eye.

He paused for a moment, stared out the window, and answered, "I'm really worried about Brit. She has never done anything like this before. What if she's . . . what if she's, you know, hurt bad or like, unconscious or something?"

"George, don't think that way, man. Let's just hope she's fine—maybe her phone battery died or something."

"Oh, Lord, help us and keep Brit safe, please," I prayed without even thinking that George might not want to hear that right now. I looked over at George for a response, but he was still staring off into the white, slightly wooded field behind Mom and Dad's house. He finally looked at me.

Convenience

"Let's get moving, bro!" As I pulled out, I thought about what I should say, what would be a good topic to talk about along the hour-and-a-half drive. But when I looked over at George, he was already dozing off. He must not have slept much. So, I just told him to get some rest, and turned up the radio a slight bit, and kept my mouth shut for a while. The morning sun seemed so bright as it glistened off the snow-covered ground, especially as we got out of town and drove past the waves of white fields and a few trees here and there, surely planted by farmers long ago. The sunshine also seemed deceitfully warm, yet I knew better: it was still bitterly cold out and would be for a while longer.

As I thanked God for the beauty of this place, I also began to ask Him to please let Brit be OK. Even though I did my best to reassure George, I really couldn't think of a good explanation as to why Brit had not called yet. What if something went wrong with the procedure and Brit was in some sort of serious or life-threatening condition?

Oh Lord, I thought to myself, *please bless Brit, and please don't let anything bad happen to her.*

Thankfully, George slept nearly all the way. He began to wake up as we approached the main exit for Sterling. I remembered the town from when I was in high school. We used to play football and basketball against their high school team. Sterling was a smaller town than ours, and their teams were often made up of farm kids of various ages patched together to make up enough for a team. We usually beat their teams pretty handily. The place brought back memories of my high school days, especially since it looked nearly the same as it did back then. Nothing much had changed. But one thing was new, the abortion clinic. We figured it wouldn't be hard to find since there were only a few commercial property streets. But as we looked around town, we didn't see anything.

So, I pulled out the address I got from the internet and realized that the place was actually on the outskirts of town. As we drove about a mile past the last little residential area, we saw the building nestled between a couple of other office buildings but not much else around the area. The parking lot was empty. We pulled up to the front door, which was frosted over, so we couldn't see much inside. But George walked up to the door and tried to wipe away the frost to get a peek while I waited in the car. It didn't look like he was able to see much as he pressed his face to the glass. Then just as I expected him to start heading back to the car, I saw him pull on the door, and it opened. He slowly peeked inside, then quickly entered, the door shutting behind him.

"Now what?" I thought. I decided to wait for him in the car since I didn't think he'd find out much in the building. Little did I know how much was going on in there. As George peeked inside, he saw a figure sitting on a chair, asleep in the corner of the outside lobby. As he entered, he realized it was Brit! He ran over to her, yelling, "Brit, Brit!"

George threw off his jacket and wrapped it and his arms around her. As he did so, she woke from her stupor and raised her head to look at George. With a look of sheer terror on her face, she began to cry, "George, George, I'm so sorry, I'm sorry. I failed you; I failed you! I couldn't do it. I couldn't get rid of this baby. I'm so sorry, George. I tried to call you, but my phone died, and everyone was gone." She paused as she looked around the lobby. "I didn't know what to do. I'm sorry, George . . . I'm sorry." She looked up into George's face, tears rolling down her frozen cheeks. Her lips were blue, and she was pale as a ghost. Then she got that look of terror on her face again, and slowly her head tilted back as she passed out.

"God, help me," he shouted as he wiped away tears from his face so he could see clearly again. Then he bent down to pick Brit up. Just then, I walked through the door.

"Oh, Lord," I shouted. "What's going on?"

George explained that "she had slept in this freezing lobby all night."

"Why?" I asked stupidly.

George didn't answer. He just picked Brit up as he yelled for me to open the door and get the car warmed up. We got her into the car, and I turned up the heat. She was lying limp in George's arms in the back seat. Regaining my wits, I put the car into drive, and we sped off toward the hospital. As we pulled away, Brit began to come to again.

"George!" she yelled out before her eyes opened.

"I'm here, Brit," he responded as he tightened his hug. She opened her eyes and looked at George. Confused, she asked, "Where . . . where are we?"

"We're in Levi's car, heading to the hospital," he told her.

When he mentioned the hospital, it must have struck a chord with her. She got a fearful, distant look on her face, remembering the events of yesterday.

"George, I tried to do what was best. I went in to have the abortion." She paused again; her eyes were tearing up. "But I couldn't do it!" Her body sank even more as George propped her up.

"It's all right, Brit," George told her. "Don't worry about it. I love you, dear, and I want you to be all right."

She looked into his eyes, still with a confused look on her face as she continued her story. "At the last minute, I told them that I had changed my mind. I didn't want to do the procedure. The nurses seemed nice to me until I said that. They told me I should continue and that there was no way I could afford to have a baby right now. They got madder as they spoke. They said I would have no life if I had a baby right now. I couldn't go to school, go out, or do anything. I'd be a failure in life, and I would fail you. They said this was the most inconvenient time in my life to have a baby! Finally, the doctor came and leaned over to me," Brit paused for a moment, "and looked me in the eye. He kind of quietly said, with a smile, 'Don't be a fool, Brit, you can't have a baby now; this is ridiculous.'" Brit began to cry harder. "I screamed at him . . . I told him I did not want to have an abortion and to leave me alone!"

As George held her, she began to cough uncontrollably. "It's OK, Brit," George said, trying to calm her down. "You're safe now." She continued to cough and began to hyperventilate. Then suddenly, she began to breath more deeply. Her eyes rolled back, her head tilted back, and she passed out.

"Lord, help us," George cried out as he urged me to hurry.

As we pulled up to the hospital emergency entrance, I stopped and got out to help get Brit out. George carried her up to the big double doors that opened automatically. Brit was still unconscious. As George walked in, he began to yell for help. Two nurses ran up beside him, followed by a gurney pushed up by another nurse. They gently put Brit on the gurney and continued into the main lobby, where we were met by a doctor.

"What happened?" he asked.

George began to explain that Brit was from Franklin and was in Sterling yesterday by herself. He said that "she was stranded in the unheated lobby of an office building last night. Since the building was out of town a ways and her cell phone died, she had no option but to try to stay warm in the lobby all night. Being pregnant, she tried to protect her stomach and curled up in a ball in the corner of the lobby away from the door."

"But it was so cold last night," the doctor responded, now deep in thought. "Let's get an IV started and get her slowly warmed up. George, I'm sure she's in shock right now. It's a good thing you came along when you did. Any longer this way . . ." he paused and then changed the subject. "Was she awake at all when you found her?"

"Yes," George responded. "Although she was kind of delirious, she talked to me for a minute. Then she got like scared and started breathing heavily and passed out."

"OK," the doctor said, trying to calm George down as well, "Let's get her into a room." They wheeled Brit into a room across the hall from the main emergency room with George by her side. I stayed out in the hall.

"Oh, Lord, please help us through this, and please let Brit and the baby . . . and George be all right." While they were all in the room, I had a chance to call Brit's mom and Emma and give them an update. Brit's mom was, of course, beside herself, thanking us for finding Brit while at the same time asking over and over if she was going to be OK. I tried to calm her down, but she seemed to get more excited the more she talked. I finally butted in and told her that Emma could come and pick her up, and they could come to the hospital right away. That got her back to her senses, and she said she would be ready. Through a sobbing voice, she thanked me again and hung up. Then I called Emma and explained everything that had happened. Expecting that she might be needed to help, Emma already had herself and Katie ready to go. She said she'd be over at Brit's in a few minutes, and they would be on their way after that. I told her I loved her and hung up.

Convenience

I walked over to the room where Brit was taken and peeked in. They were still working on her, and she had still not regained consciousness. That worried me. George looked at me with a confused and worried look on his face as he sought some comfort or sense of all this, but I couldn't offer much except a smile and thumbs-up. That was very lame, I thought, but I couldn't think of anything else at the moment. I did get his attention again to tell him that Brit's mom and Emma were on their way. That little update seemed to encourage him. I could tell he was thinking about how much he loved his Brit, who was just lying there. I'm sure he felt helpless as he tucked the blanket under Brit's side as he struggled to do something that might help.

After about a half hour, as I was standing outside the room to get some air, I noticed Emma and Brit's mom, June, come around the corner. As June walked toward us, I really didn't know what to expect. I had only seen June once before, and that was only briefly, when she was at school once to pick up Brit. June looked older than she probably was. She didn't have fancy clothes or a great job or any of that. I knew she had poured every ounce of herself into providing for Brit through the years. I guessed that she probably had given up a lot of her personal life and aspirations so she could take care of Brit. And now her precious girl lay in a hospital bed unconscious.

As I hugged Emma, she asked, "How's Brit?"

June was right behind Emma now, listening attentively but at the same time looking around as though she was a bit confused. She seemed a little disoriented and had a scared look on her face. It was almost as though she was in shock. Before I could finish, she walked away and into Brit's room. We followed. Seeing Brit, June immediately grabbed Brit's hand and leaned her forehead into Brit's, touching her gently. Her body began to quiver as she began to sob quietly. George was still holding Brit's other hand, and I could tell he was feeling a little awkward. His head dipped a bit, and he looked away from Brit and downward. The doctor, whom we spoke to only briefly, now came over to June as if to comfort her. He explained that he was pretty sure Brit would be OK but was hoping she would regain consciousness soon, which would make him feel better about her recovery. June stared into the doctor's face for what seemed a long time. Her confused expression faded into a stern gaze to the point that the doctor looked like he was becoming a bit uncomfortable.

She finally spoke. "What about the baby?" The doctor was taken aback. He stuttered a bit as he began to answer.

"Well, I think it should be OK."

June fired back. "You think IT should be OK? Why aren't you even a little concerned about IT?" June began to turn red, and through tears, she queried the doctor. "Do you know that I was pressured by a doctor to abort Brit when I was pregnant? Had I decided to kill her in my womb, this beautiful young lady would not be here." The doctor was speechless, just staring at her. June didn't say another word. She just turned from the doctor and began again to look at Brit. The doctor, seeing an opportunity to escape, quietly slid out the door.

June still had not acknowledged our presence. Again, seeming like she was a little in shock, she simply stared at Brit for about a half hour. We stayed silent. Emma finally gently touched June on the shoulder and reminded her that she had to go to work in a few minutes. Emma offered to give her a ride if she needed it. June sort of snapped out of her trance and looked at Emma and me and George. She had calmed down a bit through the half hour.

"Ah," she sighed, "yes, please, that would be very nice. Are you sure it's no trouble?" As June came out of her stupor, she began to look at George, which made him feel even more uncomfortable. After a moment, June came around the other side of the bed, stopping right in front of George. He turned to her, barely lifting his head from its low position. She looked at him, still teary-eyed, put her arms on his shoulders, and gave him a hug. Then she looked him right in the eyes, pausing. Then she said, "George, thank you so much for saving my little girl." She leaned in a little closer. "You are a good man," she said, gently patting him on the shoulder. Then she reached for her coat on the chair, put it on, and walked out. Emma looked at me quizzically and followed June out the door.

I turned back to look at George. He had the most confused look on his face. "George . . . George, bro, are you OK?" He finally looked at me. I knew what he was feeling. Sadly, I don't think he had ever considered himself a "man" or "good," for that matter. I came around the bed and smiled at him.

He looked up at me and said, "Did . . . did you hear what she said?" His tired, sleepless face turned a little redder, and tears began to well up in his eyes.

"Yeah, and I couldn't agree more."

He hugged me as the tears began to roll down his cheeks. He sniffled a little, holding back more tears, as he looked at me. "I love you, bro," he said quietly as a slight but genuine smile came over his face.

"I love you too, bro," I responded, through a smile of my own. George then quickly regained his composure and turned back to Brit.

Chapter Twenty-Two

George and I spent the next half hour trying to regroup our emotions and concentrate on Brit again. After that, we both decided to go out in the hallway to the vending machine to grab a coffee and a snack. As we walked out of the room, the doctor was standing at the nurses' station and saw us. He dropped his clipboard and walked over to George; he pulled George and me aside into the hallway. He wanted to confirm that George was the father of the baby that Brit was carrying. George, a little insulted by the inquiry, answered that he was definitely the father.

The doctor smiled, responding, "It's OK, son. I just need to ask these questions as a formality." He patted George on the shoulder. "I also need to ask you another question." He took on a more serious look and sort of moved between George and me and looked directly at George. As he sighed, he spoke, for some reason a little lower and quieter, "George, this is a hard issue for you and all of us. But I need to ask you this. If we take the fetus out now, Brit could recover better. Her body would have more strength to recharge herself. While she is here, it would be a simple procedure."

George looked at the doctor. Then he looked away, down the hall where Emma and June had left earlier. He stared for a moment into the now empty hallway. Then he turned back to the doctor. "You mean abort the fetus?"

"Well," the doctor paused; with a half chuckle but a little uneasily, he said, "Yes. That's what I mean. The clinic that Brit was in last night called a few minutes ago. They said they were very sorry about what happened last night and explained that the janitor had overlooked Brit and they would ensure nothing like that ever happens again. George, because of their mistake last night, they are still willing to fund the abortion and the medical procedures here today." The doctor ended his talk with an upbeat smile. "What do you think?" George's face began to turn still redder, and he carried a half smile that I thought was just emotions welling up inside him and his body, not knowing what expression to portray. Maybe the doctor thought he was legitimately smiling regarding the option because he smiled a little nervously in return. Then George's jaw seemed to tighten, and tears welled up in his eyes. He spoke kind of through his clinched jaw.

"So, the fine clinic that left Brit for dead last night still wants to take . . . to kill this fetus, and that's how they will show their concern for Brit. How nice!" He forced himself to smile through his anger. George walked over to the window in the hallway and stared out, and paused for what seemed an eternity. He finally answered the doctor, "No . . . no, I don't think so, doctor," George responded, still looking out the window. That was all George said. I thought that maybe George was afraid to show his anger and that he might really lash out at everyone there had he turned to look at the doctor.

Next, the somewhat dejected doctor turned to me, pulling me aside. "You're his brother, right? Can you talk some sense into him? It would be an easy opportunity to simplify this situation and make Brit's recovery much simpler and more convenient. We should do this for Brit's sake and convenience."

Now feeling the anger well up myself, I took a deep breath and looked the doctor in the eye. Now my jaw began to tighten. "So, it would be more convenient, you say." I began to really get hot. "Convenient, like having a remote for your TV is convenient, or a drive-through latte at the coffee stand." The doctor's serious look began to fade somewhat into a puzzled one. "Convenient like that, right? Except this involves killing an innocent life!" I moved in closer to his face. "What's next, doc?

Convenience

Maybe it's more convenient to be able to kill babies up to the first year of life. Of course, only by their mother because it's her *right*." The doctor moved back from me and rolled his eyes.

"No, really, doc. What's the difference? It's a mother's right, as you say. It's her body, right? That's the argument. Maybe the mother could make the final call on a person's life—their whole life!" I was yelling now. "Hey . . . hey, how about me?" Still with a clenched jaw and looking the doc right in the eye, I angrily and roughly rolled up my pant leg to expose my prosthetic leg.

"Maybe you should call my mother to ask if she wants to end me! I . . . I mean, look. I don't even have two legs! It'd be more convenient for the rest of you if you didn't have to mess with guys like me, right?" Now I had a slight but angry grin on my face. I moved in closer to the doc again and lowered my voice. "Oh, doc, you need to be a little more careful. You're looking a little bloodthirsty. I see the excitement in your eyes. Tell me this, please. How can someone try so hard to save life sometimes and, minutes later, try so hard to destroy it?"

I walked away from him and over to George. George had heard everything I told the doctor. He looked at me through his tear-stained and tired eyes and managed a slight smile. He struggled a bit to speak but managed to get the words out. "I . . . I thought I was the one who was supposed to lose his temper and shout." That's all he could say. His eyebrows began to crinkle up, and his smile faded as he held back tears again. We looked at each other for a second, and he reached out to hug me.

"It's OK, George; everything will be OK. I'm proud of you, brother—really proud of you.

As I looked over to the door, I noticed that the doctor had slipped away. So, George and I made our way back to Brit's room. Things seemed calmer. A different doctor showed up and explained that Brit was stable and the baby was all right. He was getting ready to move Brit to a regular room. He cautioned, though, that Brit was still not conscious, and he hoped she would come too soon, but it could take some time. We could tell that point worried the doctor a little bit. George grabbed Brit's hand again and walked with the group as they moved Brit down the hallway.

Alec Marchi

Things had settled down a bit, and George and I got a little rest for the remainder of the afternoon. It was nearly seven o'clock when I woke up from a short nap in the hospital room chair. George was also asleep in a chair next to Brit. She still had not regained consciousness. As George stirred, he suddenly remembered where he was and what had happened and looked up to see if Brit was awake. Disappointed, he looked down at the floor for a moment. Trying to help, I offered to go get us a little food from the cafeteria. George looked at me and nodded as he responded. "Sure, bro, I'll stay here." So, I went downstairs to the first floor, somewhat relieved to be out of the room for a minute and to be able to stretch my legs.

Chapter Twenty-Three

Since it was evening now, all I could find to eat were those unhealthy, highly preserved microwave sandwiches in the ever-faithful, ever-ready vending machine. But as hungry as I was, they seemed like fine dining to me. I got a couple out and popped them into the microwave, got a couple of soft drinks out of another machine, and headed back upstairs. As I walked into Brit's room, I found George exactly the way I had left him, staring at Brit. The TV in the background had a basketball game on, and I tried to divert George's attention for a moment by asking who was playing. He didn't even look up as he attempted to answer. "Huh, oh, . . . ah, thanks for the food . . . I'm not sure who's playing, bro." Then George grabbed the sandwich and began to eat it quickly, barely taking his eyes off Brit for even a moment. We sat and enjoyed our "healthy gourmet" dinner; not saying much, both were still well-worn from the day. As we finished, George went back to his position of holding Brit's hand and looking at her. Then he laid his head down next to her arm to rest. I began to watch the ball game on TV.

Around eight o'clock, George called out to me. "Bro, look." He looked at his hand that was holding Brit's. Her fingers began to move a little and squeeze George's hand. He looked at me and then back to Brit. Her eyes began to twitch a little. Then, suddenly she got this fearful look as her eyes slowly opened. I thought she probably was still reliving the scare she had at the abortion clinic. She tensed up and acted as if she wanted to sit up but couldn't. When she fully opened her eyes, she was staring right into George's.

She began to speak, but George, with a calm, slight smile, put his finger to her lips as he said, "Shhh." He smiled at her for a moment, still staring her in the eye. Then he finally began to speak. "Don't worry," he said as tears again welled up in his eyes. "You are gonna . . ." He paused to fight back more tears. "You both are gonna be OK. I love you—I love you both. And we'll be kids with a kid!" Tears now streamed down both their faces as George dropped his finger from Brit's lips so he could kiss her. After their embrace, they looked at each other and began to chuckle a little but still just stared at each other, smiling. I loudly cleared my throat to get their attention but got no response from either.

So, then I said, "Ah, I need to step out for a minute, be right back." Not sure they heard a thing I said, but I slipped out to give them a moment. As I got into the hallway, my emotions finally caught up with me. I stopped, sat on a bench, and put my hands in my face. Overcome by fatigue, fear, anger, and now immense joy, I sat there and wept. I thanked God first for saving Brit, and for my brother George, and for getting us through this terrible night. Then, as I continued to cry, I thanked God for saving the life of this baby— for allowing it a chance for life. And I asked that it be blessed and grow into the great person God intended and that this person would do great things. I sat for a bit and regained myself, wiping my eyes and taking some nice deep breaths.

As I stood up and walked a little further down the hallway, I heard Emma coming around the corner. I looked at her and smiled, trying to hide my emotional state. "Hey, dear." She knew me well and could see that I was yet a little emotionally off, and she got this scared look on her face, preparing for the possible bad news. I just looked at her again and said, "It's all good, my dear. Brit woke up and is going to be OK." Tears again welled up as I hugged Emma and added, "and . . . and the baby is . . . is OK too! They are both gonna be OK." Emma finally broke down too, and I could feel her body quiver as I held her tightly.

After a few moments, I looked up through my teary eyes and saw Brit's mom coming down the hallway. She noticed us and quietly walked over to where we were standing. I, again, didn't know exactly what to expect, having not had a chance to talk to her earlier in the day. Maybe she blamed her troubles on our family, I thought. I wasn't sure what to say as she approached. She walked straight to my side and said, "Levi, I need to tell you something."

"Oh boy," I thought, here it comes.

"Levi," she began to tear up as she paused for a moment. "I . . . I just want to thank you . . . and your family . . . and George for how good you have been to my Brit. We've always been, well, sort of looked down upon in this little town. Believe me, if I could have left here, I would have moved somewhere else. But you and your family are different. You made my girl feel . . . well . . . special." She again paused to regain herself and asked, "Is she OK?"

I smiled, "Yes, yes, she is awake now and going to be OK." She hugged Emma and me together, and we walked to Brit's room.

As we walked into Brit's room, Brit's mom seemed a little more together now and a little more tuned in. She had a big smile on her face as she made eye contact with Brit. George immediately pulled back slightly from Brit as he saw her mother come toward them. He seemed to understand that they needed a moment. Brit's mom grabbed her hands, leaned down, and gently pressed her forehead on to Brit's. "I love you, my little girl," June said quietly.

"I love you too, Momma," Brit responded.

June asked, "How are you feeling?"

Brit responded with a surprising, "How are *you* feeling?"

June giggled a little and said, "I'm perfect now that you are OK." We all slipped back out of the room and gave them a little time together.

Chapter Twenty-Four

Although he was extremely tired and worn out, George seemed more at ease than I had seen him in a long time. He didn't talk much, which was also strange for George, but he smiled at Emma and me as he walked down the hallway toward the bathroom.

I sat down with Emma for a minute on a bench in the hallway. "How was Katie today? I missed her, but I guess she had a good time with Mom."

Emma responded, "Well, your mom wasn't feeling too well most of the day, and so Katie spent most of her time with Alex while I was out." I sighed and took a deep breath.

"You mean Mom was sick all day? Did she have any more fainting spells?"

Emma paused for a moment, and then she explained: "Your mom had a spell this afternoon but was sitting down when she passed out, so she didn't get hurt. Levi, I don't know what we should do with her. She doesn't seem to be getting over this, and the clinics and hospitals won't even give her an appointment unless we bring her in while she has a spell. How are we supposed to do that? And what will that show? They don't seem to care much about her at all."

I started to get mad all over again, "Well, next week, I'm getting her an appointment if I have to jump on the nurse's desk. This is ridiculous. Wonder if Mom's just too old for them to even care or expend resources. What have we come to in this place?"

Just then, George walked over to us. We sat and talked for a few more minutes and then wandered back into Brit's room. Her mom had left the room for a minute, but I figured she was going to stay as long as she could through the evening. And I knew George was planning on a nice night, sleeping in the chair next to Brit.

As we bid our goodbyes, Brit looked at Emma and me for a moment. She smiled and teared up a bit but didn't say anything. She didn't have to. We smiled back as Emma put her hand on Brit's shoulder and bent down to give her a gentle hug.

As I was leaving, I looked at George, still sitting at Brit's side. "Do you need anything else, bro?"

He looked over at me and smiled, and paused. His face now calm and happy, he said, "No, bro, I have everything I need." He paused again, still looking at me, and finally said, "Love you, bro." His words pierced straight into the depths of my heart.

I smiled back, answering, "You too." Then I turned and left, catching up to Emma, who was already in the hallway. We talked the whole way home, praising God for how he took a very difficult and long day and turned it into one of the most victorious we could imagine.

As I thought through it, I told Emma, "You know, Brit could have been completely done with all this. She could have taken the doctor's 'professional' advice and awakened without care. I . . . I guess it would have been more convenient for her. But what courage Brit showed, at eighteen years old, to stand up to the 'pros' and decide on life." I couldn't continue without choking up.

Emma responded, "I guess her mom faced the same thing and made the same choice. She followed in her mom's courageous footsteps."

All I could say was, "Thank you, Lord!"

As we drove on, I looked at Emma, "I almost forgot, where's Katie?"

Emma answered with a smile, "She's at your mom's house, of course. She might be asleep, but we can go pick her up and get her back home."

"Hope Katie's OK. It's been a long day for her too." Then, I added. "And what about Mom? Did you talk to her?"

"Yes, about an hour ago. Mom is OK now, and she and Dad are still up."

Convenience

We quickly parked at Mom and Dad's house. It was still really cold out, so we wasted no time making our way to the door. Mom was waiting for us and knew just how to make us feel good: hot chocolate. Katie was asleep in the bedroom, so we sat in the living room and huddled around each other for a minute, warming our hands with our cups of hot chocolate and talking about the day. I again explained how the Lord had taken a really scary and difficult beginning and turned it into a wonderful victorious ending. Mom and Dad sat on the edge of their seats, listening attentively and excitedly.

As I came down from my high to tell the story, I got a better look at Mom. She looked pale and off-color, and I could see she wasn't quite feeling her best. She played down her fainting spell from earlier in the day, but I was worried. "Mom, I'm gonna take you to the hospital this week for a checkup again."

She quickly answered, "Levi, you know they are just going to tell me that there is nothing they can do unless I'm in the middle of a fainting episode. I don't think I rate any further or advanced tests, as they say. I always feel like they don't have time to mess with an old person like me and don't think they want to waste their 'advanced testing' on me. So, all that ends up happening is they are wasting my time."

"But Mom, I know there is more they could do. This is ridiculous. I'm going to call and get that appointment and get something done here first thing tomorrow."

"OK," she relented, "but I don't think we are going to get anywhere. I'm too old." She gathered up the empty cups and walked into the kitchen. I looked at Emma, nodding my head in disgust about the situation, and finished up my hot chocolate. Dad's face went from the joyful thrill of hearing George and Brit's great news to a worried look again.

After I finished my drink, I got up and went into the kitchen. When I opened the door, I saw Mom, teary-eyed and crying a little, as she washed the cups. "What's wrong?" I asked as I reached for her shoulder. She looked at me and slowly responded.

"Wrong? Nothing's wrong, son. I am just so happy—happy that you came here to live, I mean." She paused for a moment to hold back more tears. "I know it isn't easy sometimes for you and Emma, living in this small, cold little town. But you have been such a blessing. You have literally saved lives: You saved Brit and her baby, and you saved George." She stopped again, overcome by emotion. "You saved George from his anger and bad outlook, and you reconnected George and your father." She broke down again, and I gave her a big hug. She looked at me again and said, "Thank you, son . . . thank you."

"Mom, it's not me. It's God. *He* brought us back together. *He* got things right." We hugged again and then gathered ourselves and returned to the living room.

We got Katie's coat on without waking her and quietly departed. We were too tired to say much more as we quietly rode home. I thought to myself, *God is good . . . God is good.*

Chapter Twenty-Five

The next few days flew by. The doctors wanted to keep Brit in the hospital through the week. George couldn't stay with Brit during the days since he had missed so many school days through the year and couldn't afford to lose anymore and still graduate. So, Emma and I spent time through the day with Brit, and George and Brit's mom covered the evenings. I took most of the afternoons off and helped keep Brit up to speed with her studies, especially math. She needed to pass math this year if she was going to graduate in the spring. Ed covered my afternoon PE classes by himself for the week. I knew that was a lot of work, but I really appreciated the time to help Brit. So, we all pitched in and worked our way through the week.

One of the first and most frustrating things I did on Monday morning was to call the clinic to get an appointment for Mom. But, as Mom said, they wouldn't budge on getting her in to be seen unless we could somehow catch her in the middle of a fainting spell. I was disgusted and knew there were other tests they could do. I was convinced that if she were younger, they would offer those tests.

"What do I have to do to get you to see my mother?" I was nearly shouting into the phone by then.

The nurse responded, "Sir, please lower your voice. These calls are recorded, by the way, and I don't appreciate your tone."

"Well, it's good to know that this call is recorded. So, you're telling me that there are no other tests that can be done for my mom. I guess I shouldn't say other tests since you haven't given her any yet." The nurse responded somewhat nervously.

"No, there are a number of tests that could be done, but there are a lot of other patients that have shown more symptoms of serious problems and simply have priority over your mother's case. I can fit her into our schedule in June."

"June! As in three months away? Or do you mean next year, June?" I asked sarcastically.

Not wanting to engage in my level of sarcasm, the nurse kept her cool and said, "This year, sir. That is the best we can do. There is simply no room to see her sooner unless it's an emergency."

"If she was your mom, I bet it would seem more of an emergency to you." She didn't respond. "All right," I said.

"Please make an appointment for her then." She gave me a date in mid-June and told me they would call to confirm a week prior to the appointment. I knew deep down inside that mom was just too old for them to show concern. Ever since medicine became socialized and virtually taken over by the government, it seemed as if the medical professionals didn't care like they used to. It also seemed very convenient for those in control to push older people aside to conserve resources and time for younger people. It thoroughly disgusted me. It seemed more convenient not to help older people like they were sort of in the way and had no value anymore and were just taking up space and resources.

As the week progressed, Brit regained her strength and stayed right on track with her schoolwork. She seemed to have more drive and motivation than I had seen since last fall. I was so thankful to see George and her so happy and purposeful. I was, on the other hand, a bit worried about Ed having to handle PE classes all by himself. Those boys could be a handful, even for both of us. But when I'd talk to Ed on the phone, he seemed fine and was happy to be a part of our family's efforts to help Brit and George. I invited Ed over on Thursday, though, just to make sure he was OK. There was a great ball game on TV, and he brought over a few snacks. It was a great time for both of us to relax. Emma knew I needed

Convenience

a few hours to chill out a bit, so she was happy to have Ed over as well. We both rushed to the door when he rang the doorbell.

"Howdy," Ed yelled loudly, as usual. We both smiled and greeted our good friend. It was truly great to see his bubbly, loud, obnoxious self again. Ed had two large pizzas and a couple of bags of chips in his hand. And he could barely pull the door shut behind him.

Emma gave Ed a hug and grabbed the food to take to the kitchen. "You gonna eat it all yourself?" Ed laughed out loud at his own joke as Emma walked to the kitchen.

"Are pizza and chips on your healthy diet plan?" I asked, adding to the lively discussion. Ed just looked at me and smiled.

"Levi, it's just once in a while, brother. I can't eat the nasty healthy stuff all the time." Ed settled in, and we sat down in the living room.

"How did PE go this week? I know those boys can wear a guy out pretty quick."

"Oh, they were fine," Ed answered.

"Well, we appreciate the help this week, and I was able to keep Brit up to speed in school. Just don't want you to overdo it."

"Overdo it?" Ed answered back. "Ha-ha. First, I'm still a Marine at heart, you know, and there's no such term in our language! Second, with God at the center of my life now, there's no way I can overdo it any day. I'm so glad for every day and enjoying life so much now, brother!"

I kind of laughed and patted Ed on the back. "Well, tomorrow I'll give Brit her math test at eleven, and then I can come back out to school and do PE. Hey, why don't you take the day off and get some rest? I can cover it. I'm guessing after forty years of teaching, you have a few days of leave saved up?"

Ed beamed as he made himself comfortable on the couch. Emma joined us for pizza and then went off to bed. Ed and I enjoyed a great ball game, talking all the way through it, mostly criticizing the coaches for making decisions that we thought we could do better! As the night wound down and Ed put his coat on to leave, I patted him on the back as I helped him to the door.

"Great to see you, my friend," I said, smiling.

He smiled in return and said, "You too, brother. See you tomorrow."

"Yes, I'll be there to help you once I give Brit her test at eleven. Ed, why don't you take the day off and let me handle the boys in PE?" Ed just laughed.

"We'll see, brother. Goodnight."

The next day, I got up early. The weather was getting a little warmer, and it was going to be a sunny day, but still pretty cold out. After I warmed up with some oatmeal and coffee and talked to Emma for a while, I set out for the hospital, excited to give Brit her math test and hopefully see her get released later in the day. After scraping the frost off my car windows, I jumped in the freezing thing and prayed it would warm up quickly. As I drove off, I thanked God for this day and for all he had done in the past week.

When I got into the hospital, I moved quickly away from the door to warm up. I was excited to get up to Brit's room and give her the math test. Brit had been studying with me all week during the day and studying with George in the evenings. As I entered her room, she was already up and finishing her breakfast.

She smiled at me and said, "You're late for class!"

I returned the smile and said cheerfully, "Good morning to you too!" Brit looked healthier than I had seen in a long time. The color was back in her cheeks, and her smile was full and energetic like I hadn't seen since Christmas. "Are you ready for your test?"

Brit pushed away her breakfast cart and adjusted her pillow, so she could sit up straight. She pulled up the sheet to her waist and flipped the rest over toward me as she said with a smile, "Look, no cheat sheets . . . get it?!" I rolled my eyes, responding to the corny joke, and we both laughed out loud. The nurse, already used to our antics, walked in just then and asked us if everything was all right.

"Great," I responded, "but if there is a cup of coffee somewhere that I could get, it would be even greater."

The nurse smiled, "I can get you one, Levi."

As the nurse left the room, Brit looked at me again and said, "You know, Mr. B, I've been through a lot of trauma this last week. I think you should have some pity on me and cut me a little slack on this test. I may still not be totally healthy."

Convenience

I quickly responded, "I haven't seen you look healthier, stronger, and happier in the last four months!" I paused for a minute, though. Then with a more serious tone, I said, "I'm sorry. You have been through a lot. Didn't mean to make light of all you have been through."

As I looked at Brit, she stared at me—emotionless for a moment. Then, a smile crept over her face that she couldn't hold back, and then a laugh as she said. "I was just joking about the trauma and all that. Where's your sense of humor?"

I smiled back, shaking my head, and said, "OK, OK, you got me on that one. Let's get this test going, shall we?" I pulled the test paper out of my bag, along with some scratch paper, pencils, and a calculator.

Brit became more serious and focused on the test. She really did want to do well on this test. This would probably be the most important one left this year, and if she did well, she and I knew she would likely pass the rest of the year's material and finally pass the required class, which of course, would mean she could graduate on time. As I passed her the material, she immediately situated herself and the test items and, with an intense and focused look on her face, began the test.

I didn't want to disturb her, so I kept my mouth shut, except to tell her that she had one hour. I turned my chair to look out the window and catch a little sun, propped up my good leg on the other chair, pulled out a book from my bag, and began to read. Deep into the pages of my book, the hour seemed to go by pretty fast. Realizing Brit had only ten minutes left, I turned to her to remind her of that fact.

She looked back at me before I could speak. "I know, only ten minutes left. I'm just checking my answers and going back over two questions that I skipped before." She shifted her focus right back to the test. As test time drew to a close, I closed my book, put it back into my bag, stood up, and stretched.

I held out my hand, and Brit passed me her test, scratch paper, and other things. I took a quick scan through the pages. As I looked at Brit, she smiled. "I think I aced it, Mr. B." I smiled back at her.

"Well, I was going to grade your test at school, but maybe I'll just grade it here, so you can know what you got right now." She looked at me and nodded in agreement. So, I sat down and pulled the test key from my bag, and began to go through the pages of the test. I turned my back to Brit so she couldn't see my markings.

When I finished, I turned back to her and said, "You did very well. You got an eighty-five percent." Excitedly sitting up to hear the news, she then slumped back on her pillow as she heard the score.

"What? Are you sure about that?" I looked up from the paper and back to her again.

"Well, let me see." I paged back through the test. When I got to the last page, I stopped. "Oh, maybe I should grade the last page." I looked up at Brit with a smile and a laugh that I couldn't hold back.

She sneered at me and responded, "Not funny."

I quickly said, "Just joking. Where's your sense of humor?"

Still a bit annoyed, Brit smiled and said, "OK, OK, you got me. Now can you finish grading the test, please?"

I smiled again and said, "All right, I guess I can do that." I quickly finished grading the last page and calmly looked back at Brit. "OK, looks like you got a ninety-five."

She looked at me, emotionless for a second, then screamed out, "Woo-hoo, woo-hoo!" And she began bouncing on the bed. I laughed as I watched her joyous outburst . . . until the doctor came rushing into the room— this was the same doctor who thought we were a little crazy the last time he came into the room. I dampened my big smile a little, and Brit stopped bouncing as we looked at the doctor.

He paused for a moment before speaking. His eyebrows were raised up a little, and then a smile came over his face as he looked down at his chart and said to Brit. "Well, looks like you are ready to go home." He looked back up from his chart with a more serious look again. "I have some vitamins for you to begin taking. You should probably have begun taking them a month ago, but you and that baby should be fine if you start taking them from now on. And I have a schedule of regular checkups I'll give you. Do either of you have any questions?" Brit paused for a moment and then looked at the doctor.

With a rather serious expression, she told the doctor, "Thank you, sir, for taking care of my baby and me." Her sincerity was clear, and the

Convenience

doctor was taken aback for a moment. I thought he might actually show a little emotion through his professional outer shell.

He looked Brit in the eye as he said, "You're welcome, dear, and thank you for brightening up this place a little. We get so about our business around here that we forget the joy of life, sometimes." He paused again, collecting himself, "Well, anyway, you are good to go, young lady. Levi can arrange for your transportation, and we'll see you in two weeks for a checkup." The doctor then quickly slipped out.

I looked at my watch and realized that I needed to get to school since I promised that I'd take the PE class for Ed, so he could take the afternoon off. I told Brit that George would come by in a couple of hours to pick her up and that the hospital bill was already taken care of.

As I gathered my things to leave, Brit stopped me. "Mr. B," she paused for a second, "I just want to thank you one more time." Holding back a tear, she continued. "You and your family have been better to us than anyone I can remember." She turned and looked out the window, pausing again; then, turning back to me, she continued. "I want to thank you for saving my life in more ways than you know."

Now I was choked up as I responded. "No, thank *you*, Brit." She looked at me with a puzzled look. I continued, "Thank you for brightening our whole family's days and for your sense of humor, and for saving the innocent little baby inside you." She smiled. We didn't say another word as I turned to leave her room.

Chapter Twenty-Six

I got to school as fast as I could since I was a little late coming from the hospital. I even skipped lunch. As I pulled into the teachers' parking lot, I noticed that Ed's truck wasn't there and thought that maybe he had decided to take my advice and take a whole day off. I went straight to the gym and started changing, so I'd have a few minutes to prepare for the boys' PE class. Just as I finished changing and began to walk out to the gym floor, I got a call on my cell phone.

"Hello, Mr. Bell. This is Nancy Stroudson. I'm the head nurse on the fourth floor of the hospital. Mr. Stone has had another heart attack."

My own heart sank. "How bad is he?"

She said, "We are working to find out now. He is conscious, though, and asked to talk to you."

A little relieved that he could talk, I responded. "Oh, yes, could you put him on the line?" Ed's voice was weak, and although he would never admit it, I could tell he was in a lot of pain. He struggled to tell me a joke as soon as he spoke.

"Don't let those smart-aleck boys push you around, brother." A smile came across my face. It was good to hear my friend's voice.

I responded in kind. "Told you not to eat that pizza last night, and don't expect me to sneak one into the hospital this time!" My smile quickly faded as I could tell this was serious. "I'm gonna come out there. I'll get someone to watch the boys."

Ed insisted, "You don't need to do that. Just come out after class."

"No," I'm heading back now." I paused for a second. "Don't want you to be alone, brother."

Ed quickly responded, "I haven't been alone since I met the Lord Jesus." He caught me off guard. Tears quickly formed in my eyes and rolled down my cheek.

"You hang in there, my friend. I'll be there soon."

The nurse got back on the phone. "Mr. Bell, Ed is stable for the moment, and the doctors are deciding what procedures to take if any. He's in room 402."

I thought the "if any" comment was a bit odd, but I didn't want to waste time talking. "OK," I said, "I'll be there in thirty minutes." I quickly threw on pants over my PE shorts and contacted the principal. He said he would cover for me. As I began driving to the hospital, it occurred to me that I had just been there and wondered if Ed was there while I was on a different floor.

Parking at the hospital once again, I quickly made my way to the fourth floor. As I turned the corner, I got room 402 in sight and prepped a smile for Ed. I wanted to be upbeat and encouraging for my good friend. I walked into the room, beaming... only to find the room empty... and quiet. My lower jaw dropped as I looked around the room, trying to figure out what was going on.

Just then, a nurse walked into the room, carrying fresh linens for the bed. I double-checked the room number and was about to ask the nurse what was going on when a doctor walked into the room. He somewhat sharply told the nurse to hurry up and make the bed as the room was needed right away. Barely noticing me, the doctor walked around me to leave the room. As he passed by me, I tapped him on the shoulder and said, "Excuse me, doctor. Do you know where Ed's room is?"

He looked puzzled for a moment and seemed distracted as he looked toward the door, intending to dash out as he responded, "Oh, you mean the old man that was in here? He died. His body's in room 110 downstairs." The doctor then quickly stepped toward the door. My heart dropped, and I felt faint. Overcome by emotion, I followed the

Convenience

doctor into the hallway and grabbed his arm. I yelled, "The old man had a name. Ed, that's his name—Ed Stone!"

A tear rolled down my cheek. I'm sure it was a scary sight. "I know to you he's just some meaningless thing taking up precious space in your hospital! What happened to compassion for human life?" Then I got right into the doctor's face. "He was my friend, my best friend." I could feel my face getting red-hot as tears streamed down both cheeks. The doctor was now definitely scared; without taking his eyes off me, he told the nurse to call security as he backed away from me. Not taking his eyes off me, he reached for the elevator button and pressed the button several times nervously but got no response.

The nurse pointed to the out-of-order sign, reminding him that the elevator he was trying to use was not working. Annoyed, he yelled back to her, "I know, I know," and he pressed the other button for the elevator next to the broken one. Still keeping his eyes on me, he backed into the elevator and disappeared. I blinked and shook my head, trying to clear my vision from my tears and come to my senses. I leaned on the hallway wall and shook my head again. Looking through my tears, I saw a nurse coming toward me. I wasn't sure what she was going to do, detain me, help me, or maybe ask me to leave. I looked up at her as she reached out to touch my shoulder.

"Sir, are you OK?" she asked.

I took a deep breath and answered, "Yes . . . yes, I'm OK." Then she followed up by telling me that Ed's body was in room 121 and that she could take me there if I wanted.

"No . . . no, it's OK. I can find my way down there. But thank you." I answered with a confused look and made my way to the elevator.

As I got out of the elevator, I made my way down the hall, following the numbers on the doors, around the corner, and there at the far end of the hallway was 121. There were no lights on in the room, only the sunlight squeezing through the closed blinds. I looked to the corner of the room, and there was Ed's body. Tears immediately began to flow again. I stood over him, looking down at his body. He looked like he was asleep. I reached down and touched his forehead with the back of my hand. It was shockingly as cold as the cold dark room he lay in. That set me off again. Tears streamed down my face as I began to get angry inside.

I thought to myself, *Why, why now? Why God? Why . . . why now? He was such a joy to me and to everyone around him. He was so happy.* My emotions churned inside me as my mind began to lose control. I thought: *Why had I dragged my wife and daughter to this awful, cold, dark, lonely place?* I began to sink into myself. *I'm all alone now . . . all alone.* As my emotions continued to ball up inside me, I felt like I couldn't take it any longer. With a clenched fist and clenched jaw, I began to slowly shake my head and softly pound my fist on the side of the bed. Just then, a hand touched my shoulder and jolted me back to reality. Gasping for a breath, I turned and saw a nurse standing there. I cleared my tears away and looked at her.

"Hello, ma'am. I'm . . . ah . . . sorry for being so emotional."

She said, "It's all right . . . it's all right." Then she just stood there, looking at me.

Finally, she walked across the room and grabbed a chair. "Here, please sit down." I followed her request as she went to grab another chair and sat beside me. "My name is Jen. I've been a nurse here at the hospital for about four years now." She stopped for a second, her smile giving way to a more serious look, and glanced at Ed. "He was a good friend of yours—I could tell. I don't know if you remember me, but I was Mr. Stone's nurse the first time he was in here after his first heart attack."

She paused for a few seconds, peering into the darkness, "I watched Ed today and could tell right away that he was, well, unique. I . . . I don't mean strange in a bad way." Smiling, she continued. "Actually, it was the opposite. He seemed so happy." The nurse looked out toward the window as she continued, "He seemed happy and unafraid." She looked down for a moment, then back to me, "He was happy, cheerful . . . and unafraid." She looked me in the eye now, very seriously. "Do you know how many people come in here terrified, looking to me for some reprieve, some comfort?" She took a deep breath. "Anyway, I'm sorry if I scared you, but I wanted to ask you something." She paused again, and looking at me intently, she asked, "Why was he so happy and so unafraid of what might come?"

Convenience

I looked at her, still trying to regain my composure and understand why she was saying all this.

Then a smile came over her face for a second. "I remember Mr. Stone from when I was in high school. We called him 'stone face.' He was so different then—always angry and sarcastic. I didn't want to be around him for one second. Yet, when he was in here, he was so different. He had such joy. What made the change?"

Now totally tuned in, I thought to myself for a moment. *God, how wonderful you are. Here I am, nearly cursing you in my self-pity, and you gently put your hand on my shoulder, remind me that you are in charge, comfort me, and put the next one who needs you right in front of me.* I pulled together a smile, wiped the tears from my face, and began to answer the nurse.

"Well, you see, Ed became a Christian. Ed spent his first sixty years searching for a way to fill the void in his heart. He thought that achievement, finishing college, being in the Marines, or victory on the battlefield might fill the emptiness. Then, like a lot of people, he hoped to find fulfillment in his marriage and in having a child. But somehow, that didn't work out as he had planned, either. He was never close to his son, who, for some reason, didn't exactly follow in his father's footsteps. I don't know the whole story, but his son moved away after high school, and they didn't talk much after that. His wife moved out a few years later."

I stopped for a moment and swallowed heavily, and took a deep breath. "Then, his wife found out she had cancer and died only a year later. After that, Ed sort of shrank into the angry, sarcastic guy you talked about. When I got here last year, there he was, just the way you remembered him."

I smiled and let out a little chuckle under my breath. Then I continued. "He didn't think much of me for sure at first. He could tell I was a Christian and told me a few times how he thought religion was a crutch. But somehow, after a while, I became more of a curiosity to him. Somehow, he couldn't quite get under my skin the way he thought he could, and I continued to be happy and not too bothered by him. We both shared the responsibility for the physical fitness program for the high school boys, and somehow, after a while, we got to be friends. Anyway, I'm talking too much. I'll hurry. One day, after a frustrating time with the boys in PE, he really let his guard down and shared his feelings and concerns with me. So, I explained my belief in God. He didn't seem very moved by my explanation. But during the Christmas holiday, I asked him to join my family and me in church. He finally agreed, and I remember that day so well."

I continued, "At church, he was like a kid, glued to a movie, on the edge of his seat, and hanging on every word. Afterward, he went and talked to the pastor and asked a ton more questions. I think it all came together for him. He finally realized that Jesus was real— that Jesus really died for his sins and made way for him to be forgiven, redeemed, and on his way to heaven. After Ed accepted Christ as his Savior, it was as if God restored their relationship from despair and loneliness to what it was meant to be all along. Sixty years of guilt and emptiness and loneliness just melted away. Suddenly, Ed had a purpose in life, and it all made sense. He was thrilled and wanted to live every moment of the rest of his life serving the one who saved him, fulfilling the purpose God had for him."

I stopped and snickered as a smile crept over my face, "The PE kids who thought Ed was a little off before were sure he was crazy after he became a Christian." I paused again and, with more seriousness, continued, "But he really did get to work on his new mission. In Marine fashion, he was pretty, straightforward with people, sharing his faith. Actually, he was kind of like a bull in a china shop, but he was doing things the way he knew how, and I believe God used him just that way. He shared his faith with one of his best old friends, Brock, who accepted Christ just before he died. He really became a joy to everyone he was around."

Tears welled up again and spilled down my face. "He was especially a joy to me; we were really good friends. He was one of the few friends I have here." With that, I stopped.

Jen leaned toward me in her chair and looked at me. "I'm sorry about your great loss. He definitely seemed like a great guy to have as a friend." She smiled and looked at me. I took a deep breath and smiled back.

Convenience

"Thank you for helping me. Would you like to join my family and me for church sometime?"

She smiled again, "How about this Sunday?"

"Absolutely," I responded. Then I looked back at Ed's body. "I can be the point of contact for the funeral. I'll try to get the word out to Ed's son, and I can arrange a service in the next few days with the funeral home here in town. I'll call them on my way home."

Jen responded, "I'll let the folks here know that you are the point of contact." She stood up and reached out to shake my hand. "Thank you," she said. I thought to myself, *She saved me from my downward spiral, and she is thanking me?*

"Well, thank you, Jen. Thank you very, very much." We shook hands, and she left. I walked over to Ed's body one more time and, in silence, thanked God for Ed and for all he had done in Ed's life and was still doing, even after Ed's death. Then I was going to say goodbye to Ed but really couldn't bring myself to do that for a couple of reasons. That wasn't really Ed lying there anymore. It was his body, but the real Ed was with the God who saved him now. So, I just looked upward and told Ed, "I'll see you later, good friend."

Chapter Twenty-Seven

On the drive home, I tried to figure out how I was going to tell Emma. It was cold and dark, and I didn't see anyone out. As I pulled into the driveway, I could see Emma in the living room, waiting for me. She turned the outside light on as soon as I pulled in. I still hadn't figured out how to tell her. As I got to the door and opened it, Emma was there, with a cup of coffee for me in her hand. I just said hi and began to take off my coat. After I took off my coat and took a sip of the coffee, I set it down and looked at Emma. Tears welled up, and my lip began to quiver a little. I didn't say anything. Emma began to tear up and looked inquisitively at me as if she was asking for confirmation that Ed had died. I looked at her through my tears and nodded my head in confirmation as I reached out to hug her. The emotions peaked again, and I held Emma tight as the tears began to flow down my cheeks.

After a moment, I regained myself and looked at Emma. "Ed's gone," is all I could say for the moment. Then, I struggled to add, "but God is so good." Emma looked at me through her tears with a bit of confusion about what I had just said. I half smiled and added, "Really, it's quite an amazing story."

She half smiled back. So, we sat down, and I explained how I got into a squabble with the doctor and thought I'd be thrown out by hospital security and then how I found Ed in the cold, dark room. Then how I did a nosedive emotionally, ready to lash out at God for losing Ed, this place, and anything else I could pile onto myself. And just when it seemed that I would totally lose it, a hand reached out and touched my shoulder. "It was almost as if the hand of God reached down to rescue me from myself."

I explained the whole thing quickly to Emma and how the Lord was so good in his rescue of me. He even put another person in front of me with whom I could share his Word. He was always looking to bless and share his truth.

Emma just sat and listened carefully. A slight smile came over her as I spoke. "I want to hear more detail, but you should go up and see Katie before she goes to bed. Hey, how 'bout you put her to bed, and after that, we'll spend some time together?"

"You're right; I need to see my girl and spend a little time with her." I wiped my eyes with a napkin from the table. "Do I look OK and not like I've been crying?" I asked.

"You look fine, dear," Emma assured me as I got up and headed up the stairs.

As I peeked my head into Katie's room, she saw me, and she smiled. "Hello, my dear girl. How are you?" I walked in and gave her a big hug, and she reciprocated.

As we hugged, she looked a little closer at me and stared for a moment, and then asked, "Daddy, are you sad?" I stopped for a moment to think and then answered.

"Well, I'm sad, and I'm happy. I'm sad because my friend, Mr. Ed, went to be with the Lord today, and I won't be able to see him here on earth again." Katie looked at me inquisitively. "But Ed knew Jesus and is in heaven now, and I'm happy that he is there and that someday, I'll be able to see him again in heaven." That was more than enough for Katie to compute. She looked at me and didn't know what to say.

So, she simply smiled and said, "Do you want to play horsees?"

I smiled back and told her, "Of course, I'd love to play horsees."

We played for nearly an hour. What a joy it was to spend time with my daughter after the day I had. I stopped for a moment to look at her and tell her how much I loved her. We really had a good time. Then she picked out a book for me to read, and I tucked her in bed, sat beside her, and began to read. She must have been pretty worn out because I barely made it through the first few pages before her eyes began to droop. She was soon asleep with a slight smile on her face. I kissed her on the forehead, shut off the light, and proceeded back downstairs.

Emma was reading on the couch. This time, she had hot chocolate for me. I sat beside her and explained the whole day again in more detail. Emma and I were again amazed at how it all transpired. Then she helped me think through how to take care of the funeral and all the arrangements. The only next of kin that I knew of was Ed's son, to whom I would send a note. We made a plan, and I agreed to call one of the funeral homes in town first thing in the morning. We ended the long day by again thanking God for all his blessings and for how amazing He was—and for each other.

The next morning, I got up early and called Blackson Funeral Home. I didn't particularly like either of the options for funeral homes in town and thought both were somewhat less worried about their jobs and more worried about making money. But that was sort of unfair since I really didn't know either and had never dealt with them directly. As it turned out, Mr. Blackson told me that Ed had set up an account with a small amount of money in it to cover his funeral. So, I met with Jim Blackson later in the day. He covered all the concerns almost as though he was reading from a checklist. We decided on a funeral to be held on Tuesday at the church where Ed and my family worshiped; we would have a short ceremony after the service at the burial site.

Then I had the less-than-exciting chore of picking out a casket. I couldn't believe there were so many styles and price ranges from which to choose. Then we went over the agenda for the service. I picked out three of Ed's favorite songs, and the service would include me speaking for a short time after the pastor. I made sure that the service included a message by the pastor, as I knew Ed would have wanted. We also put together a short obituary for the newspaper, which included the announcement of the funeral time and place. The whole ordeal was difficult since I kept thinking about Ed and how I'd miss him, but Jim made it very efficient and comprehensive, and I felt good that we had done our best for my friend. Once I got home, I spent the rest of the day hanging out with Emma and Katie, trying to forget about the whole event for at least a little while. The rest of the weekend went well, except for church, which was tough without my loud-mouthed, smiley, happy friend.

Chapter Twenty-Eight

I knew there would be a lot of people at work who would want to talk about Ed, and I was not looking forward to that. It would be painful and difficult. So, while I was at church, I asked Mom if I could come by in the morning for coffee just to help me prep a little for the day. She, of course, was glad to have me over in the morning, and as usual, she had coffee hot and ready for me when I got there. It was still pretty cold outside in the mornings, and I was glad to get out of my freezing car as quickly as I could and get into Mom and Dad's house. I left my car running outside to get it nice and toasty for when I returned.

"Hey, Mom," I shouted as I entered the half-opened door.

"Hi, son," she responded as she quickly showed me in so as not to let too much cold air into the house. I threw off my hat, coat, and gloves and made my way to the kitchen. Grabbing a hot cup of coffee, I warmed my hands and took a wonderful first gulp to warm my insides.

"Oh, that's nice and warm," I exclaimed. My joyful face turned serious as I stared past the edge of my cup while I took my next sip. "Mom, it's gonna be tough today. Everyone is going to want me to tell them what happened. It's hard enough to think about it. I'm gonna have to explain it all day long." Mom, being the wise one as usual, then looked away from me and out the window.

"You know, Levi, you told me about how great the Lord was through the whole ordeal; how great the Lord was to give you Ed as a friend; how Ed came to the Lord and became such a special, fun person after that; and how Ed was certainly on a mission after that. It's a wonderful story. Maybe God wants you to use the opportunity to tell it to others and enjoy the good memories today." Now I looked away from the top of my cup and right into it as I took my next sip, pondering what Mom said. She was right. I was already forgetting God's goodness and thinking about myself. *"Didn't take long,"* I thought to myself. I took a deep breath and smiled.

"Yeah, good point, Mom, very good point." We chatted about a bunch of less important things for the next few minutes until it was time for me to go. As I got my coat and other items on, Mom prepared to quickly open the door. I kissed her on the cheek as I said, "Love you, Mom, and thanks for the coffee . . . and for getting me back in focus again." I quickly made my way to the well-warmed car and on to school in a much better frame of mind.

I managed to get to school early, even with the coffee stop at Mom's, so I popped into the principal's office to tell him what had happened. He was glad to see me and listened attentively as I explained what had transpired over the last few days. I ended by letting him know that the funeral was set for noon on Tuesday, and he said he would be there. He also made an intercom, all-area announcement once everyone was in place during the first period. Over the loudspeaker, he talked about how Ed had been a faithful teacher for over forty years and how many, many of the town's citizens remember him to this day, and how he helped shape their lives. He ended by letting everyone know the funeral time for the next day and that those who wanted to attend could do so over an extended lunch period. The rest of the day was, as I expected, a bunch of people, curious and slightly excited to ask about Ed and what happened. But I was ready for them, ready to tell the wonderful story of God's goodness.

Of course, once they saw where I was going with my answer, some of them soon realized that they were "late for class." Brit patted me on the back as she came into a math class that afternoon. I hadn't seen much of her outside of class since she got out of the hospital. She and

Convenience

George seemed busy catching up on their lives and preparing as best they could for graduation and having the baby. Even in her larger state and knowing she didn't always feel good, she usually smiles from ear to ear. Today, she was a little more somber but still gave me a smile. The rest of the day was pretty normal, and I made my way home as hastily as I could. Emma and Katie were ready with dinner, and we had a nice, quiet evening. I stayed up to write down a few words to say at the funeral the next day and to remember Ed again sitting on my couch, being annoyingly loud as we talked about the ball game we were watching and laughing the evenings away.

I had arranged with a couple of teachers to fill in for me the next day, so I could concentrate on taking care of the funeral and making sure all went smoothly. As I got up and began to get ready for the day, I wondered if anyone would show up for Ed's funeral. He didn't have many real friends.

"Well," I decided, "we'll just have to make the best of it." Over morning coffee, Emma helped me review everything to make sure we wouldn't let things fall through the crack. She then proceeded to get herself and Katie ready and promised they'd be waiting for me by eleven o'clock. I left early to make my way over to the church and check everything there and then planned to come back and get them before the service. As I got into the cold car, I thought to myself, *Well, here goes, never done this before.* And I asked God to please help us all through this day.

Thankfully, as I got to the church, I saw Jim, the funeral home guy, already there and with everything in place. I shook his hand and thanked him for the great work on this.

"Sir, that's my job, and we know that loved ones are still grieving and not always thinking straight." He smiled at me and patted me on the back.

I guess I was the only "loved one" he was referring to, so I answered, "Thanks . . . thank you so much." By then, the pastor had made his way over and helped me out of the somewhat awkward moment by asking if we could go over the schedule. We all grabbed the already-in-place bulletins and reviewed the schedule together. Then Jim reviewed who would stand where and when and how we would all proceed to the cemetery after the service.

After everyone was clear, the pastor went back to his office, I think to study or to pray, and Jim went outside to ensure everything was in place there. Then he looked at me one more time to make sure I was OK, and then he made his way to the kitchen for a cup of coffee. I just stood there looking around the church, stopping my scan when I saw the casket. I made my way over to the casket that was open and looked at Ed's body. It was certainly Ed's body, but his skin color was not quite right, and his face was sunken in a bit. That sort of annoyed me, but I reminded myself that Ed wasn't there, just the old body that carried him around. How thankful I was that there was more to it than just this cold, lifeless body. Ed was in such a better place now, and how happy that made me. I decided to go into one of the classrooms in the building and review my notes.

Taking Jim's lead, I grabbed a cup of coffee from the kitchen and made my way to a quiet room to review my notes. I tried to envision being in front of the church as I practiced what I was going to say. As always, I asked God to please help me and speak through me. I had hopes that some of the people from the town or school might show up and that I could help share Ed's . . . and God's story.

The time passed quickly as I remembered that I still needed to pick up Emma and Katie, so I jumped back into the car and made my way home to pick them up. We didn't talk much on the way, and I'm sure Katie was wondering what was going on. Katie remained curious and cautious with the whole event and held my hand or Emma's as we walked through the parking lot and into the church. Once we were seated, I got up to make another round to check on things. A few people started arriving as I made my way to the door. As I walked around, I wondered if very many would show up. I also remembered that I had not heard from Ed's son, which made me a bit sad.

Chapter Twenty-Nine

As the hour approached to start the service, to my surprise, the church seemed to be filling up. As I took my seat, I chatted with Emma quietly for a few minutes. Then, as I turned to look around, I couldn't believe my eyes. The church was full. There were at least ten or so boys from the PE class and a few other students that I didn't know. It looked like a lot of teachers and the principal was there. As I scanned the crowd, I stopped short, made eye contact with George, and smiled. He and Brit were seated, as usual, near the back entrance. He had grown up so much this year, and so had Brit. I was so thankful for that. Mom and Dad were there, in their usual seats off to the side, about halfway up. I thought I knew everyone in this little town, but there were people there that I didn't think I had ever seen before. Finally, my scanning was interrupted by the organist, who began to play "How Great Thou Art." The pastor walked up to the front and sat down as he and the congregation sang. Afterward, he stood up to welcome everyone. His words seemed to help everyone relax and focus on God and on Ed. After some candles were lit and a solo was sung, the pastor called me to come up and speak.

As I walked up and took my place in front of the podium, I was again amazed at how many people had shown up. I began, maybe awkwardly, by looking over the crowd, stopping and smiling at those I recognized. And I finally broke the silence by greeting everyone.

"Well, good morning. Thank you for coming this morning. As you can see, Ed certainly was well-known and well-liked, and he had a lot of friends. I'd like to take just a few minutes to tell you a story, a story of a great man, who did great things, yet spent most of his life searching for the meaning of it all and for fulfillment. Some of you know that I grew up here, and then after college, moved away, and just returned here with my wife and daughter at the beginning of this school year."

I smiled slightly as I continued. "I have to tell you that Ed didn't really like me at first. We taught boys' PE together, so we were forced to spend time with each other. I guess he picked up on the fact that I was a Christian somehow, and he used to tell me that religion was a crutch. But somehow, and for some reason, one day, he decided we would be friends, and he began to talk to me on a more personal basis. He had a lot of questions about being a Christian. At first, I thought he was just getting more material with which he could make fun of me. But, after a while, I realized that he was genuinely curious. One day I invited him to church, and he met my family and me there. He sat on the edge of his seat as the pastor presented the truth of the gospel of how God sent his only son to humble himself and come to the earth he had made to take our place in our just punishment for sin. Ed sat right there, in that seat," I pointed, "on the edge of the seat, in fact, and hung on every word. After the service, Ed went to talk to the pastor for more details. He looked as though he had found the greatest treasure on earth, something he had looked for all his life. And maybe he had. Ed accepted Christ as his personal Savior later that day. And well, as many of you saw, he was never quite the same. As I mentioned, Ed was like a guy that had found a long-lost treasure. And I believe he did.

I added thoughtfully, "Ed finally found the meaning of life, the purpose of his existence, and man, was he happy. Those of you who were around him know what I mean." A low chuckle came from a few in the crowd, which made me a little more at ease. "Ed couldn't keep the smile off his face: he couldn't keep from talking about the Lord. He had such energy, and the light of Jesus shone so brightly through him everywhere he went."

I paused for a moment to catch my breath and change direction a little with my speech. "Ed was a marine's marine, tough as nails. He earned a Purple Heart for being wounded and a Silver Star for saving a large group of marines trapped on a hillside by charging a machine gun nest. He had a family and worked hard, in his own special way, to help build young folks in their understanding of physical fitness for many years. Still, he knew something was missing from his life, and after sixty-five years of being lost and searching for truth, meaning, and purpose, Ed finally accepted Christ as his Savior and found it all. He became so different and so 'saved' that at church, he would often tear up during a hymn. His emotions were so great during those moments that he had to release them somehow, and he would grab the hanky out of his pocket and wave it above his head," I smiled, "almost as if he were waving to God." I paused again to shift away from getting too emotional myself. After taking a deep breath, I started again.

"One of the men that Ed saved on that hillside during the war was Brock Johnson. Brock lived here in town for the last twenty years of his life. He died earlier this year from a long-term illness. Ed would visit Brock in the hospital from time to time. I'm sure they would reminisce about the war and all that has changed since then. But one day, Brock could tell Ed was different. He had a different outlook on things and a glow about his face. Ed explained to Brock about accepting Jesus as his Savior. Brock humored Ed and listened but didn't appear to respond to Ed's message. Shortly thereafter, we learned that Brock had died in the night—alone in his hospital room. But a few days later, Ed received a letter—from Brock! Brock had sent the letter to Ed because, for some reason, he couldn't say the things he wanted to say in person. Brock told Ed that he had accepted Jesus as his Savior and that he was happy as he could be." I smiled again and looked at the crowd. "So, Ed helped save Brock twice—once on the battlefield of war and then on the battlefield for our souls. Ed and I talked about how the Bible says that when a person accepts Jesus, there is rejoicing in heaven, and we thought that there was probably a rejoicing crowd to meet Brock as he entered heaven. Now I wonder if Brock was part of the reception crew for Ed."

"So, we'll miss Ed very much. I will miss my best friend greatly, and we'll all be a little lonely without him here with us. But we celebrate the fact that he is the happy Ed we remember, up in heaven, now and forever. And I look forward to Ed being on my reception committee one day and seeing him again."

With that, I took my seat again next to Emma and Katie. The pastor then rose from his chair and gave a short sermon, and spoke himself about Ed. He told the crowd about how accepting Christ changed Ed. The natural energy Ed always had was no longer released through anger, sarcasm, and arrogance. It was released through joy, love, and sincerity. He said, "When Ed came down that aisle after the service and wanted to talk to me more about Jesus, he was so excited. Everything suddenly made sense to him. As he sat on the edge of the chair in my office and I explained more, it was as if I was providing more pieces to a puzzle." The pastor went on to explain that salvation was a free gift from God for everyone and that he hoped everyone would accept this free gift. He offered to speak in more detail with anyone, just as he did with Ed anytime. As he closed his sermon, he invited anyone who wanted to follow the procession to the cemetery where they would lay Ed's body to rest. He bid everyone a good day and gave an uplifting benediction, and closed.

As we all began to leave, a younger man caught me in the aisle. He was tall, in his early thirties, and had a pleasant smile. I thought it might be one of Ed's former students from years ago. He shook my hand firmly and looked me in the eye as he spoke.

"Hello, sir," he said. And I responded in kind, and he continued. "I'm Ed." Shocked, I still hadn't picked up on who it was I was talking to. Then he cracked a slight grin and said, "I'm Ed . . . Ed Stone." My mouth dropped open a bit, and I stopped in the middle of the handshake. My brain was still trying to compute this. Seeing my surprise, he tried to clarify, "Junior, Ed Stone Junior." Then I regained myself and remembered Ed talking about his son, whom he had grown far from after his son moved away after high school.

Still in shock, I managed to put together a sentence, "Um, well. . . . Welcome, Ed." I smiled. At that point, Ed broke the staring contest and helped me out.

"I'm glad I could make it here today; I wish my wife and daughter could have come, but my wife is sick and couldn't make the flight."

Finally, coming back to my senses, I responded. "I'm glad you came too. It's a pleasure to meet you, sir. Sorry for my slow response, but I guess you caught me off guard."

"I'm sorry too," he responded. "I know it must be a little shocking to meet me here today, but I'm so glad to meet you, and your story and the message today were so wonderful."

I smiled and responded, "Is there anything you might want to say at the burial site?"

Ed quickly responded, "Yes, I'd like to offer up a prayer if I could."

Just then, Emma came up behind me. "Hello, dear," I smiled. "Let me introduce you to someone. This is Ed Stone." I smiled a little and waited for her reaction. She searched hard for something to say. The light finally came on.

"Oh, oh, my goodness, wow; this is pretty amazing; so nice to meet you, Ed." She shook his hand, still a bit shocked. After a brief exchange, we all proceeded to our cars and to the cemetery.

It was still pretty cold and breezy as usual, but the sun came out and made things a little more pleasant. We drove up near the site. There was a little awning over the area, and people had begun to gather there. The pastor caught me as we approached, and I told him that Ed wanted to say a few words and pray, so we rearranged the schedule a bit. No one wanted to stay too long out in the cold, so we tried to get things going as soon as we could.

As the pastor began, he again thanked everyone for coming out and then introduced Ed. Similar to my reaction, I could see in the crowd that they were a bit shocked. They certainly had Ed's attention as he began to speak. As Ed made his way to the front, he passed by the casket and stopped for a moment, running his hand across the top as though he wanted to touch his dad one last time. He got to the small podium, looked over the crowd, and smiled slightly to offer a greeting to everyone. Then he began to speak.

"Good morning, everyone. Most of you don't know me or may not remember me, but I'm Ed Stone Jr., Pastor and Levi, and all of you. I want to thank you for allowing me to say a few words here. I know it's pretty chilly out, so I'll try to be brief." Ed smiled again and paused for a moment to gather his thoughts.

He looked toward the casket as he began again. "My father was an amazing man, as Levi and the pastor have mentioned. I loved him very much, but I want to tell you the story of us, and our relationship . . and God. I was fifteen years old when I accepted Christ as my Lord and Savior during a summer camp. Mom had died the year before, and it was the first summer that Dad and I had together. And doing the best he could, Dad tried to keep me busy, so he sent me to a Christian summer camp for a few weeks. When I came back from camp and told Dad about the Lord, he kind of shrugged it off as no big deal. Maybe he thought I'd forget about it after a while. But I didn't. It was real to me and changed me, and gave me a whole new outlook on this life. Dad and I were never really close anyway, and after that, we grew even further apart. So, as soon as I graduated from high school, I moved out and ended up moving to Ohio, where I met my wife and settled."

Ed paused again for a moment, deep in thought. "We stayed in touch over the last five years, but not like a father and son normally would. Dad didn't make a lot of effort to talk to me, but I didn't make much effort either. You see, I thought it was my task in life to get my dad saved. I really loved my dad and thought it was up to me to lead him to Christ. Well, I didn't do a very good job of that. Every time I would bring it up, Dad would comment that my faith was just a crutch, and I believe he thought it made me weak."

Ed took a deep breath, and tears began to form in his eyes as he continued. "But I underestimated God's great power and the fact that he is in charge. You see, I just needed to pray for my dad and watch God do the rest. I didn't recognize it, but Dad was searching, seeking God, and God provided. He sent Levi from across the United States to settle back here and lead my dad to Christ. I needed to tell you this because I want you all to know how good God is and how much he loves us. What a blessing it was to hear my dad tell me he had accepted Jesus and to hear him so happy—probably happier than he had been certainly since Mom died. He called me a month or so ago and told me all about his new life in Christ. I was so thrilled." Ed stopped again. This time a lot longer, looking at the casket.

He was trying to hold back his tears, biting his lip a little and rocking slightly back and forth. "But God didn't stop there," he managed to get out while battling his tears. "When Dad called me, we probably talked for an hour. I could tell he was actually enjoying talking to me, and I him." Ed paused again and began to quiver a little. "Then he told me something I had longed to hear all my life." It took everything Ed had to continue. "He said he was proud of me and proud of the man I had become." Ed stopped there and, overcome, began to cry. He quickly composed himself again, apologized, and continued. "You see, God doesn't just stop when you give your life to him; he just gets started. He wants to heal you, heal your relationships, and bless your life. So, this story has a very happy ending."

He turned to the casket again. "Dad, I'm sorry I missed seeing you again here on earth. The family and I will greatly miss you. But I look forward to sitting, maybe under a big shade tree, with a nice hot cup of coffee, chatting with you, and having a few laughs in heaven. So long until then."

Ed closed by asking everyone to bow their heads as he prayed: "God, I'm sure I didn't do justice in explaining how wonderful you are and how great your love is for us. But I hope it made sense and that it sank in for some here. I pray you to bless everyone here, and again; we thank you for Ed Stone . . . Senior, and we look forward to the great reunion you have planned for us. Amen."

Ed didn't say another word after that. He lowered his head and made his way back to his seat. As he passed by me, I smiled and shook his hand. He smiled back and took his seat.

After the pastor came back to the podium, we all sang one of Ed's favorite hymns, "Victory in Jesus." I sang it "loud and proud," as Ed used to say, just like Ed would sing it. I grabbed Emma's cold small hand and squeezed slightly. She had tears in her eyes but was still smiling as she looked at me. I smiled at her, and we hugged for a moment. As a tear rolled down my cheek, and I watched the casket be lowered into the ground, I thanked God for everything and leaned toward Emma, speaking softly in her ear, "God is good . . . so good."

Chapter Thirty

After the service, I caught up with Ed and invited him to dinner before his flight back later that night. He gladly accepted. First, we all went to our house and changed into more comfortable clothes. Ed really appreciated a place to change into comfortable traveling clothes, and it gave us another chance to talk. As we waited for Emma and Katie, Ed and I sat in the living room.

"Ed, I didn't even think of this, but how did you find out about your dad? I guess I should have looked you up myself."

Ed responded, "You were probably too shocked to even think about it. And I think my dad probably didn't mention me much, so I understand you not thinking about that. It was a nurse from the hospital. I . . . I'm not even sure why she called, but she said she met you and my dad both times he was in the hospital. She said that Dad mentioned me a few times, and she knew someone had to notify me. I talked to her for a little while, and she was kind of disgusted with the hospital staff, who didn't even bother to try to find out if Dad had any relatives around. She said they just quickly moved dad out like they were happy to have the extra space."

I could see the discussion was making Ed upset and sad, but it reminded me of how cold and callous they were when I went to find Ed just after he died. I sat in silence for a moment and then responded. "Yeah, they seemed a little rushed when I got there." I didn't tell Ed that they didn't even call his dad by name, and the doctor just referred to him as the old man. Thankfully, our conversation was interrupted by Emma and Katie coming down the stairs.

"Sorry, we took a little longer." She looked at Katie with a smile. "We girls have to make sure our hair is combed and that our makeup is on the right." Katie smiled back. We then quickly made our way to the car and drove to a place called Granny's for dinner.

As we pulled up, I recalled eating at Granny's a few times with Ed Sr. We entered the restaurant quickly since it was still pretty cold out and especially as the sun was going down. As we opened the door, the familiar little bell rang, announcing our arrival. Most people were used to the bell but still looked around to see who was coming in. I smiled and made a general hello to a few people I made eye contact with as we made our way to a table far from the door. We took our coats off and sat down, and immediately the waitress was there to serve us coffee and take orders. They were really fast at Granny's; we usually got our food in just a few minutes. We kept the conversation light through dinner as we enjoyed our burgers. As Ed finished nearly his last bite, he stopped for a moment, grabbing his napkin and wiping his mouth; he stared out across the room with a distant stare. Then, he stopped and looked at me as he spoke.

"Levi, I . . . I just want to say thanks one more time to you and your family." He looked at Emma and Katie for a second and then back to me. Pausing long, he took a deep breath. "I know how it is to live here—small town, freezing weather, dark, and lonely sometimes. I'm sure it hasn't been so easy for you and your family to get through this winter." He smiled. "You could have stayed in Atlanta, surrounded by friends, a million things to do, and sunshine, . . . and probably better medical care for your leg." Stalling to finish his point, Ed took his last little bite and chewed it. His eyes glazed over as he chewed. Swallowing his bite, he continued. "It would have been much more convenient to stay in Atlanta. But I believe you followed God's leading and obeyed Him, and because of that," he paused again, "my dad got saved." A tear ran down Ed's face as he paused again.

To break the silence, I chimed in. "Ed, thanks, but it was God who did all this. And we were the ones blessed, blessed to have Ed for a friend." Emma nodded in agreement. And Katie, seeing her mom nodded, nodded too, which made us all smile and chuckled a little bit as Emma hugged Katie. All that brought a smile to Ed's face as he paused again and looked at us. "OK," Ed responded, "but I just needed to get that out. Like you said at the church, God is good!"

Wanting to change the subject to lighten things up, I asked Ed how he met his wife. "Well," he responded, "we met at a church in Ohio. I left home right after high school and moved to Ohio to attend college. I had just finished my degree in physical therapy, and she was a junior in college, studying accounting. We both started attending a Bible study for singles and, well . . . we just sort of hit it off pretty quickly." Ed smiled. "In six months, we were married. I know that sounds a bit crazy, but I kind of knew that Jan was the one from the first time I saw her. Most of Jan's family was from the local area, but I only had a few folks from my side attend the wedding. My dad came out for the wedding and then came out to visit when our son was born, but as I mentioned, I didn't see him much after high school.

Finished with my meal, I slid my plate to the center of the table and moved my coffee cup closer in. After a long sip, I looked at Ed. "Well, I know I lost a great, great friend a few days ago, at least for a little while. But I feel like we gained a friend too. Ed, if there's anything we can do for you here, please let us know. Or if you just want to fly over from Ohio and watch a ball game with the family and me, that would be great," I said with a smile.

Ed smiled back and responded. "I'll have to come back and take care of the house soon. Can I leave a key with you to check on things once in a while?"

Emma chimed in. "Ed, we'll go over tomorrow and check on the house and take care of the remaining food and other things that need attention."

"Ah, I hadn't even thought about that; I had been so tuned into the funeral."

"Thank you," Ed responded.

We finished up our meals, I picked up the check, and we left. We dropped Ed off at the airport a few minutes later. As we waved goodbye, I turned to Emma and said, "God is . . . " "good," she smiled as she interrupted me and finished my sentence. The three of us hugged for a minute. Exhausted, we drove home and dropped into bed. Since it was a school or work night, I prepared as quickly as I could and got right to sleep.

Chapter Thirty-One

When my alarm went off, I felt like I had gotten about three hours of sleep. After hitting the snooze twice, I remembered that I was supposed to go to Mom's for coffee. She had invited me the day before, and I told her I'd be there. I began to get madder and madder at myself for sleeping in, especially as I thought of Mom standing near the door with coffee in hand, ready to give to me as I entered the house. Annoyed with myself, I struggled to get up and call Mom to let her know that I accidentally slept in and now wouldn't have time to make it over. This was really not the way I wanted to start my day.

The only upbeat thing about the start of my day was that it was a little warmer out for the first time this year. In fact, it felt a little like spring was slowly sneaking toward us. Little bits of snow began to melt on the sidewalks and streets, and I could see the water running under some portions of ice near the curb—a telltale sign that spring was not far off. As I crackled through the slush and thin ice to the car, I remembered that my best friend, Ed, who always had some smart remark for me as I parked and marched my freezing self into the building, would not be there. It made me sad to think about that, but I immediately thought about the good day we had yesterday and getting to meet Ed's son.

As late as I was, I still had time to check in with the principal, Jim Garner. I needed to chat with him about how we would handle the boys' PE class for the rest of the year. Ed and I worked well together and had the class and the boys under control; we had made good progress with them throughout the year. I dreaded the thought of breaking in someone new but really didn't want to continue to do the job without help. Jim was busy with typical Monday morning needs of the school—phones ringing, people running around and asking questions. He was on the phone talking while I walked up to his open door. He made eye contact, acknowledged my presence, and motioned for me to come in while he finished his phone conversation.

As he finished and put his phone down, he looked at me. "Hey, Levi. How are you? Glad you stopped in." Just as he began his next sentence, a student poked his head into the office.

"Mr. Gardener, is the gym still open to having our pep rally for the track meet? We need the gym at one thirty instead of two o'clock, so we can prepare."

The boy looked at me and smiled. "Oh, hello, Mr. B. Good to see you, sir."

Jim's face went from smiling to complete annoyance as he reacted to the boy's comment. "It's Mr. GarNER, not GarDENER."

The boy was not greatly moved. "Oh yeah, right. What about the gym, sir?"

Still annoyed, Jim looked at the daily schedule on his desk. "Ah, yes . . . yes, you can have the gym at one thirty."

"Great, thanks," the boy responded. "I have to get to class." He turned to me and smiled, and said, "See you later, Mr. B!"

Jim looked further annoyed as the student left. "Why can't he remember my name? We are almost at the end of the school year, and he still can't remember my name." He paused for a moment, looking at me. "But he had no trouble with yours," he said, as his frown turned upward into a smile. "These kids really like you, and you've done a great job with PE this year."

"Well, thank you, sir, but really, it was a team effort with Ed. Ed Stone and I worked together well, and Ed was really the one who led the class and built great relationships with the boys."

Jim's smile changed back to a look of slight agitation. He turned

Convenience

toward the window for a quick moment, scanning the parking lot for stragglers as he continued. "Oh, yeah, right, Ed Stone. Ed was a good man and had worked here for a lot of years. Levi, that brings me to my point this morning." Jim turned back to me.

"Levi, with only seven weeks left in the year and with the last week being pretty slow, well, I'd like you to finish out the PE class by yourself. It would help us out a lot. From a financial standpoint, with Ed being gone now, we could save some funds and get caught up a bit on our end-of-year budget." Jim ended his sentence with a half-smile and almost seemed relieved that Ed was "gone now."

Now, I was the one with the annoyed look and a bit disgusted that Jim seemed to have no regard, no respect for Ed's death. Jim could see it on my face. "Ah, oh, I mean . . . we'll miss Ed, of course, but well, let's be honest. Ed probably should have retired a few years ago, anyway, when he was around sixty-two. That would have left room for some of the younger teachers like you to move up. Anyway, this is a financial break that can help us, but you'd have to do the class alone for the rest of the year. What do you think?"

He returned to his smiling face again. I was beginning to boil inside while at the same time trying to contain my emotions and not get outwardly upset. I took a couple of deep breaths and looked at Jim.

"Well, to be honest, Jim, I can finish the year out myself, but it won't be of the quality that Ed and I had with these boys. We really made some progress with these boys physically and in helping build young men. Ed was really liked and respected by these boys, especially this second semester."

I moved in closer and looked Jim in the eye, "But money is money, right?" I paused with a smile and patted Jim on the arm. He looked back at me, raising one eyebrow. I continued. "So, I'll finish the class myself as you requested." I smiled again and began to turn for the door. "I should get to class now."

Before I got to the door, I stopped and turned back to Jim. Rubbing my chin as though deep in thought, I looked at Jim. "So, if you thought Ed should have retired to open positions for some of the younger teachers, well, I guess you're considering retiring soon, yourself?" Jim was now the one boiling inside but maintaining his composure. He looked at me, working with all his might to produce a forced smile, but didn't respond. "Just a thought, but really none of my business."

Jim nodded, still maintaining that forced smile. I smiled back and turned again for the door. "Have a good day, Mr. Gardner. Sorry, I mean Garner." I shut the door a bit harshly on my way out.

As I walked down the hallway, I thought to myself that maybe I was a little rough with Jim . . . he sure made me mad . . . maybe I should have been more polite . . . maybe I'll lose my job. I left it at that. I prayed to myself, *"Lord, please forgive me. I'm sorry. It's so hard to see people who seem to have no regard for life and for those around them. I'll try to do better with Jim. And please, Lord, help me through PE class this morning."*

As I approached the locker room and thought I was ready to do this, the feelings about Ed came rushing back so vividly. I got a sinking feeling in my heart. We had such a great time together, here in this stinky old locker room, joking and carrying on. I changed my clothes in silence and made my way to the gym floor. The boys were sitting in the bleachers, as always, waiting for us to guide them. I forced a smile and made my way to the front of the bleachers where they were sitting.

"Good morning, men," I looked them straight in the eyes. They responded with a lackluster good morning and remained a bit melancholy. I took a deep breath, looked at them again, and began to speak. "Look, guys, I miss Ed really bad myself, but you know we have to press on." I paused. "You've done such a great job this year, and both Ed and I were . . . are extremely proud of you." I took another long, deep breath and continued. "Ed was great and certainly is in a great place now, and I look forward to the day I can see him again. But in the meantime," I smiled, "you're stuck with me."

"It'll be a little tougher with just me, but it's probably time for you seniors to learn a little more about leadership." I had six seniors in the class. "Each of you seniors will take a turn working with me to lead the class. It'll be great practice for you. That's what the world is gonna expect from you soon enough." I smiled again. "As I said, I'm proud of you and proud to be a part of this class with you. Jon, come on up here." One of my most mature senior boys bound down the bleachers. "Get them lined up for calisthenics and then a half-mile run inside. I'll be on the court waiting for you all to finish, and we'll play some four-on-four hoops today." Jon took the class down to the floor and lined them up, and began the routine. *"Lord, I prayed again; please help me—help us through this."*

We ended up having a good class, and using the senior leads (something I came up with on the way to class) seemed like it would work well. The boys regained their normal moods after a while, and we ended on a positive note, joking and laughing. The weather seemed to help make everyone a little happier too. It was sunny and warming up nicely; the snow was melting at a steady pace, and a few spots of dry pavement were visible here and there. *Thank you, Lor*d, I thought to myself as I finished my shower and headed for the lunchroom.

As I worked through my afternoon classes, a lot of people asked me about Ed, and I tried to stay upbeat and answer their questions. My last class was math, and I was looking forward to a little relief and checking up on Brit. I hadn't talked to her for a few days since I had been out a lot over the last few school days. As usual, she was one of the last ones to get to class. But these days probably had a good excuse: she was far along in her pregnancy now with only seven weeks to go: the same amount of time left in the school year. Brit moved a little slower and was probably getting pretty tired, but she was still happy and bright. I was so proud of her. After struggling to pass math for the last three years, she was finally doing well in math and school in general. She would have no problem passing math this year—and graduating. She and George were hoping to walk to receive their diplomas together. At two minutes to three, Brit walked in.

"Hey, Mr. B! How are you? Very sorry for your loss—you know, Mr. Ed and all." She had a serious expression as she finished her sentence and looked at me.

"Hi, Brit," I responded with a smile. "Thanks for thinking of Mr. Ed. He was a great man, and I'll miss him a lot. But I'm glad to see you here, and on time . . . barely," I jokingly said with a smile. She smiled back.

"Funny, Mr. B. But if you were hauling this extra little guy around, you'd probably slow down a bit." She looked down at her belly, rubbing it gently and smiling from ear to ear. I could see how much she loved her little baby already. What a joy it was to see her so happy. As she smiled, she looked back up at me and took on a more serious face. "Ya know, Mr. B., you taught me math so well that I've already calculated that I could miss the entire final test and get a zero . . . and still pass."

My expression went from gleeful to serious. I looked at her. "You wouldn't want to do that. You'd probably get a C instead of, well . . . possibly an overall A!" Brit smiled back at me again.

"Mr. B., even though I could, I wouldn't do that." As she looked at me, her smile faded a little, and her lips began to quiver. What on earth, I thought to myself, did I say now? She began to speak through her half smile and teary eyes.

"You see," she stopped to hold back tears. She dipped her head a little and began to speak in a low tone. "You see, you and your family taught me so much more than just math this year. You taught me the value of life . . . of my life, and my mom's," she paused longer, . . . "and my baby's. You could have taken the easier road, the more convenient option, and just blown my family and me off like the rest of the people in this town always did. But you made me feel special. You showed me hope and a future and that I was somebody."

Tearing up more now, she stopped, unable to continue to explain. A tear rolled down her cheek and over her smile and dripped onto my math papers. "Whoops," she said with a smile, discretely wiping her eyes and using the event to change gears. "Don't worry," she smiled again, "I'll do my best, of course. Guess I'll sit down now." She said awkwardly as she turned and proceeded to her seat.

I thanked God for how she had turned out and how she had grown this year. It certainly made my day, and so did the sunny weather. It was tough enough trying to keep my students' minds from wandering out the window and imagining what fun they could have outside, but I even caught myself a few times daydreaming as I soaked in the sunshine through the window. What a difference the spring had made after such a hard, dark, and cold winter. If I had the authority, I would have called off school for the day, so we all could enjoy the sunshine.

When the school day wrapped up, I immediately headed home.

Convenience

Almost running down the stairs and out into the parking lot, I hopped over and around the maze of one-inch-deep puddles and steady-flowing streams of melting snow making their way across the lot. What a difference, I thought, from the cold dark evenings when Ed and I would start our vehicles and stand outside of them and talk for a while until they were warmed up. The exhaust from the cars would rise, clouding up the night air and making it hard to see anything. I did miss Ed, I thought for a moment, but I didn't miss that weather. It felt so good to have light and warmth and see the snow melt and things begin to grow . . . and live again.

Chapter Thirty-Two

When I arrived home, Emma and Katie were having a snowball fight, trying to get one last bit of fun from the remaining snow and taking advantage of the warmer weather. As I pulled into the driveway, they diverted their attention to pummeling my car with snowballs. I stopped and got out, and chased them around the front yard. We had a great time.

As we were walking to the door, still out of breath, Emma turned to me. "How did your visit with your mom go this morning?" I turned to her and responded. "Well, I stayed up so late the night before with Ed's son that I just couldn't get up on time this morning and only had time to get to school. So, I skipped Mom's house. I meant to call her but forgot. Had a lot on my mind, but I did get to stop and talk to the principal and had a great day at school. I'll tell you all about it. So, I'm guessing Mom called you. I know she usually does that when I mess up the plans."

Emma pondered for a moment. "No . . . actually, she didn't call me all day. That's a little odd 'cause you're right; she usually calls if things aren't going the way we planned. Maybe you should call her."

"Right—as soon as I get these wet clothes off." We all gleefully ran into the house.

After we got dried off, I got on the phone and called Mom. Strangely, Dad answered the phone.

His voice was cracking, and he sounded very flustered. "Son, I was just going to call you. I'm at the hospital. Your mom had a heart attack. They are working on her now. I think she's stable, but they are still working on her. Son, I . . . I don't know what to do."

"Dad, what happened? Did Mom fall down?"

"No, no, son; she didn't fall down. She had a heart attack." My own heart sank as I listened. Dad's voice began to crack a little as he continued to explain. "She, she tried to walk to the store since it was such a nice day. I guess on her way back; she got chest pains. But . . . but she kept walking, thinking she could make it home. Oh, she's stubborn sometimes. She walked a little farther and then couldn't walk anymore, so she sat down on the curb. Someone saw her and called the ambulance, and they picked her up."

Dad's voice got higher and shakier. "Son, they lost her in the ambulance for a few seconds; I don't know exactly how long. But thank God she came back, and she was awake when I saw her a minute ago. She is critical but stable at the moment. The doctor said she had some damage to her heart, but he can't go in and repair it for a day or two until she gets a bit stronger and more stable." Dad began to cry a little. "Oh, son, can you come over, please?"

"Of course, Dad, I'll be over there right away." As I hung up, I turned to Emma, who could tell something was wrong. "It's Mom," I began. "She had a heart attack." I quickly explained what Dad had told me. Emma listened attentively as her eyes began to gloss. As I finished telling her what Dad said, I stopped for a second to gather myself. Rubbing my tired eyes, I took in a deep breath and looked back to Emma. "You know, I . . . didn't stop over this morning . . . and then I didn't even call Mom later in the day." Emma recognized me drifting out there in my thoughts and quickly tried to bring me back to reality.

"Levi, stop with those thoughts, please. Let's think about what we need to do. You need to get over there, don't you?"

"You're right, Emma. Sorry. Yeah, I need to get over there." I began to move toward the living room again to get my coat. Emma followed and continued to help me get my head together.

"I'll stay here with Katie for now," she said as she followed me. "And

Convenience

I'll call George, and maybe Katie and I will come over later." Finally coming to my senses, I stopped and turned around to her. Grabbing her hands, I looked at her closely and smiled.

"That's a great idea, my dear."

She smiled at me in reassurance. "I'll also call your sisters and fill them in," she added. "They will want to come over from Minneapolis."

"Man, I didn't think of that. Thanks, dear."

As I entered the living room and began to get my coat on again, Katie looked at me. With disappointment, she asked, "Daddy, why are you going out again?"

I stopped for a moment and sat down beside Katie. "Dear, I have to go see Grandma. She is sick, and I need to visit with her for a little bit."

"But you went to see her this morning, didn't you? Why do you have to go again?"

"No, Katie," I explained, "I was running late and . . ." I stopped for a moment and turned away as if I was looking for something. The emotion grabbed me again. I took a deep breath and composed myself as I turned back to Katie. "I was running late and didn't get to see Grandma this morning. I'll be back as soon as I can, though." I hugged Katie and kissed her head. "See you in a little bit, dear. Everything's gonna be all right."

I reached for the door and looked back at Emma and Katie one more time, and smiled. Then I shut the door securely behind me and headed for the hospital, praying all the way.

The hospital was only a few minutes away from the house, so I got there promptly and found the closest parking spot I could. I walked up to the door briskly and found a nurse who told me where my mom and dad were. As I rounded the corner of the hallway, I saw Dad and smiled, trying to calm things. He looked tired and worried and a bit confused. He hugged me as he spoke.

"Son, I'm so glad you are here. I called George and the girls. George said he would be here in a minute, and the girls are going to drive over in the morning." Trying to be strong, Dad finally slowed down enough to look at me. When he did, his emotions caught up with him. He teared up as he said, "Son . . . I'm scared . . . I'm sorry . . . I'm trying to keep calm and be strong here, but I'm scared."

I quickly responded. "It's OK, Dad. I understand, and I'm worried too. But God will take care of us."

He smiled and patted me on the shoulder. "Let me take you to the room," he said as he took a deep breath and smiled back.

"All right, Dad." As we walked, I tried to prepare myself to see Mom. The thought of her lying on the floor last fall flashed through my head again and brought a cold shiver over me. *"Lord, help me please"* was all I could think.

Dad pushed the door open gently and let me go first. I looked at Mom and immediately, almost uncontrollably, grabbed her hand as she looked at me. Acting on sheer emotion, I grabbed her hand and touched my forehead to hers. "Momma, I got here as fast as I could."

She smiled at me and responded. "Glad you're here, son. Sorry for all the trouble and for worrying everyone." I held her hand and smiled, brushing her hair back from her forehead with my other hand, and listened as she explained what had happened. I made a point to enjoy every word coming from her mouth and to enjoy looking into her faded green eyes. We sat and talked for a good while.

George finally made his way to the room. He had just gotten off work and got the call from Dad, and came right over. He chatted with Mom for a while, as I did. Mom finally insisted that we all go home and get some rest. We agreed it would be best for all and said our goodbyes, and left her alone to rest.

Then Dad and George, and I talked to the doctor for a few minutes on the way out. He explained that Mom had some heart damage but was stable, and they would do more tests in the morning to determine what to do next. Emma called and told me my sisters would be coming and would be there by the next afternoon. Wow, things happened so fast that night. I couldn't believe it was so late and that so much had transpired. Dad assured me he was OK and said he would go home and try to get some rest. So, George and I left, and I headed for home.

Chapter Thirty-Three

I got home just in time to kiss Katie goodnight and let her know that Grandma was OK. I apologize to Emma for not getting her over to see Mom. Exhausted, she and I went to bed and planned to get up early and get an update at the hospital.

The next day, I got up bright and early. I had called the school and gotten the day off so I could find out more about Mom. So, I went through my normal routine and was reading the paper and drinking my coffee when Emma came down. She was carrying my phone, which I had left upstairs.

"Better check for any missed calls," she said as she handed me the phone.

"Thanks, dear," I responded as I punched the buttons on my phone, but there were no messages. I wanted to call Dad but also wanted him to get some rest, so I sat in my chair longer than normal, talking to Emma and enjoying the sun shining right on me through the window. Emma and I spent the next hour talking as I took advantage of the time off.

We both were able to get ready for our day and for breakfast before Katie woke up. With breakfast ready, I went up to Katie's room and quietly tip-toed to her bed. I nudged her a little. "Katie, dear, it's time to wake up."

She seemed glad to see me still at home as she opened her eyes. After giving me a big hug, she popped up out of bed and bounded down the stairs to the kitchen. As we sat down together for a bite, my phone rang. It was George, who I guess couldn't wait any longer for Dad to wake up. He had called him and set up a rendezvous at the hospital in thirty minutes. With that, I shifted gears and quickly ate breakfast with the girls. Still too hot to drink too quickly, I tried my best to slurp down my last bit of coffee. Trying to get a last word in and maybe trying to stall my hasty departure a little, Katie spoke up.

"Daddy, are you going to see Grandma again?" We had explained that her grandma was sicker than we thought and had some heart trouble, and was in the hospital.

"Yes, dear," I answered. "I will be there for a while today. Maybe you can come over later to see her too."

In the middle of taking a drink from her sippy cup, her little eyes lit up as she looked over the top of the glass. A muffled "OK" came out from under her glass.

I smiled at her and Emma as I got up to get my coat on and leave. "I'll come back to see you and Katie later today . . . miss you," I said as I smiled and turned for the door.

"Miss you too, dear," Emma said.

I still wasn't sure what time my sisters would get into town, but George and Dad, and I would be there to meet them at the hospital. My sisters, Melissa and Rebecca, lived about a two-day drive from our place—not a drive you wanted to make too often, especially during the winter. We had been close growing up, but we were all so busy these days that I seldom got to see them. They had plans to visit this summer for a week around July 4th. Melissa texted me while I was on my way to the hospital and told me they would both be there at noon.

As I pulled into the hospital parking lot, I saw George standing at the door of the emergency entrance. It seemed like spring but still pretty cold in the mornings. Not wanting to move any more than he had to and not wanting to remove his hands from his pockets, George raised his chin a little and struggled to make eye contact with me as I drove by him, and he waited for me to join him after I parked.

"Hey, bro. How are you?" George asked nervously. He was trying not to show emotion but was clearly worried.

Convenience

"George, I'm OK. How are you?" George raised his eyebrows as he shrugged his shoulders and looked at me, sort of implying that he was as good as could be expected in this tough time. I just smiled at him. I myself was also pretty nervous about Mom but didn't want to show it. We moved into the lobby, where it was warmer. George and I chatted for a few minutes, getting caught up in each other's lives. We hadn't seen each other for a while, and both enjoyed our chat. A few minutes later, Dad showed up and seemed similarly worried about Mom. With him leading the way, we made our way to Mom's room. We quieted our chatter as we entered for fear she might be asleep. Mom, on the other hand, loudly announced our entry.

"Hello, my men," she said with a big smile. We immediately responded in kind. We spent the next hour talking to Mom, recounting the event, and trying to brighten each other's day. We explained that the girls would arrive in an hour or so, around noon. Breaking through our light conversation, the doctor entered the room and professionally and somewhat solemnly introduced himself and shook all of our hands. He gave Mom a cursory, again professional, smile and then turned to Dad. "Mr. Bell, can I meet with you and your children later this afternoon just to explain what we believe happened and where we can go from here?" Quieted by the doctor's demeanor, Dad cleared his throat.

"Ah, yes, doctor, once my daughters get here, we can come to your office. Thank you, sir." Dad immediately looked over to me after speaking, probably for a little comfort since the doctor sort of made us all a bit uncomfortable. The doctor gave us another professional smile and quietly left the room as quickly as he entered. We paused for a moment and then went back to talking to Mom. I was thrilled to see her awake and energetic. Time seemed to fly by, and around noon I got a text that my sisters were entering the parking lot. I looked up at Dad and George and announced, "They're here and looking for a parking spot." Mom smiled. George looked back at Mom and then at Dad and me again.

"I'll stay here, and you guys go meet Melissa and Rebecca," George suggested.

Dad and I went out of the hospital lobby and watched their car pull into a parking space nearby. They hurriedly got out, slamming the car doors and nearly running toward us.

Rebecca, who was always the more talkative one, yelled from across the row of cars, "How's Momma?"

"She's OK at the moment," I yelled back, trying to quell their concern in hopes they would pay attention to the parking lot and not get out in front of a car moving through.

"What does OK mean?" Rebecca asked, almost yelling.

"Calm down, sis. She's stable and awake, and we all can go see her."

"OK, OK. Well, let's get up there," Rebecca exclaimed as she walked right past us toward the lobby entrance. Melissa just looked at us, shrugged her shoulders, and followed behind Rebecca. Dad and I looked at each other and fell in behind them. We talked more on the way up to the room and explained all that had happened.

As we entered the room, the doctor put his pen into his white coat pocket and asked us all to sit down. He introduced himself to my sisters and then quickly focused his eyes on a white board. Clearing his throat, he began. "Well, our tests show there's a problem with Elisa's heart," the doctor explained as he moved to the whiteboard on the wall. He quickly drew a picture of the parts of a heart for us as he explained that Mom's heart had sprung a leak and how the fluid and blood had built up in one of the chambers. His drawing was not of any artistic quality, but it got the point across.

"What is it? What can we do about it?" Dad quickly responded.

Seeing George and I get a little nervous about the doctor's comment, the doctor motioned to us, stretching his arms out, hoping to calm us down.

Then, calmly, he again explained that Mom's heart had basically sprung a leak. Fluid had built up in one of the cavities. The situation was serious. Further leakage could cause her heart to become more and more ineffective to the point it wouldn't function at all. The doctor's plan was to perform open-heart surgery and repair the leaking area by closing the small hole that had been torn.

He didn't want to operate until Friday, so Mom would have two days to regain her strength from all the trauma. Since school was out for spring break, I had plenty of time to spend at the hospital. Dad joined me, and we spent the entire day Wednesday just enjoying each other's company. Mom was surprisingly cheerful and seemed to be feeling well. I could see fear in her eyes, though, the realization that possibly, these could be her last days.

We read her Bible together, and Mom reaffirmed her belief and trust that Jesus Christ had paid the penalty for her sins and that she had accepted God's free gift of salvation, and that she was sure she had an eternal home in heaven as a result.

We laughed and talked and enjoyed our day. I remember that at this particular hospital, they would play the baby lullaby song every time a baby was born. Since Katie was born in a hospital in Atlanta that did a similar thing, it meant all the more to me to hear that song on the loudspeaker. It made me think about Katie and Emma. I missed them both. They had been over in the morning to see Mom for a short time, but Katie had a play date with neighbor friends, and Emma had a few errands to run, so they went home for most of the day. They planned to spend more time with Mom on Thursday. The baby lullaby sounded out three times that day. Each time it did, Mom would look at us, forgetting about her predicament, and smile.

Later in the evening, we "kids" went to get something to eat. Dad decided to stay back with Mom. I could tell he wanted some time with his wife of fifty years. Right before I left the room, I watched the two of them for a moment. Dad looked at Mom with a look that went straight to her soul and to the memories that only they shared together. Mom returned in kind. As they looked into each other's eyes, fifty years of living flooded their thoughts: the hardships of escaping from communist tyranny with nearly nothing, the struggles of raising a family in a new country, and the wonderful life they had been given together and as a family.

"You have always put everyone in the family first, before yourself," Dad said as he reached for Mom's hand. Tears welled up in their eyes. "I wish I was more like you . . . I'm sorry I wasn't better to you."

"Stop," Mom looked right into Dad's eyes. "Stop. You were wonderful. We were and are a great team. We both sacrificed a lot, everything really, for this better life for our family and us. I couldn't have been happier with you and our lives. No more about regrets. You are a great man and a great husband and father. I'm proud of you."

Tears streamed down Dad's face as he replied, "And I couldn't have been happier with you, my love." As had been the case all their lives, in their lowest moments, they drew together as one. Realizing I probably had stayed too long, I quietly left the room.

After dinner, I came back to check on Dad and sat with them both for a few minutes. When Mom dozed off that night, she seemed healthier than ever. As I sat near her, I thanked God, for she seemed to be OK. Dad was still in the room, sitting near the window behind me. Just then, Emma and Katie came back to pick me up and quietly entered the room. We all looked at Mom for a moment. I smiled and picked up Katie, and gave her a kiss. Emma and I decided to take Katie home so we could all get a good night's sleep. As we walked into the hallway, Katie tugged on my hand and pulled me back into Mom's room. She asked me to lift her up so she could give Mom a kiss on the forehead. Mom opened her eyes slightly and put her hands on Katie's cheeks, and smiled back.

I looked over to Dad as we began to leave and asked him if he was OK; he took a deep breath and looked at me, and said he was fine. I could tell he needed someone to talk to, at least for a moment. I smiled at Emma and Katie and told them I'd meet them downstairs in the lobby. As I watched them walk into the elevator, I turned and put my arm around Dad, and we walked toward the vending machine in the hallway.

He began explaining what was on his mind. "Son, I just want to tell you that I think you are a great man, a great husband, and a great father. I'm so proud of you and thankful you are my son." He smiled as he looked at me. I thought to myself, *That's it?* Then I realized there are some things we wait so long to say or we never get the chance to say to our loved ones at all.

"Thanks, Dad. I love you." We walked toward the elevator. I still had my arm around Dad's back.

"I'm taking a sleeping pill tonight, so I can go to sleep. Will you come pick me up in the morning?"

Convenience

"Sure," I said. "Do you want me to let you sleep in a little?"

"No, I want to get back to the hospital early."

"OK, Dad, get some rest, please. Goodnight." I hugged him and headed for the lobby.

Emma and Katie, and I felt a little more confident and relieved that Mom would be OK that night. We went home and got some rest.

Chapter Thirty-Four

The next morning, I drove over to Dad's around eight. I figured he'd give me a hard time for getting him up at what he would consider pretty late, but he didn't. He was completely focused on Mom. By eight-forty-five, we were at the hospital. George was there, and Brit was with him, her belly clearly showing her pregnancy.

"Hi, Mister Bell. I wanted to stop by and say hello to your mom. She has always been so nice to me. I hope she'll be fine soon."

"Thanks, Brit. I know that means a lot to her."

Dad also chimed in. "Yes, thank you, Brittany," Dad said as she and George walked toward the elevator.

"Dad, do you want to grab a quick cup of coffee on the way to her room?" I asked.

George and Brit waited outside the elevator as Dad and I got our coffee. "Yeah, it was nice of you to come here," George said to Brit as he wrapped his arm around her.

"Are you kidding? I think your mom's great. She's one of the people who's always treated me nice," she said with a smile. "She always just treated me like everyone else, even . . . like I was a little bit special." That was the last thing I heard as we rounded the corner, and the elevator doors closed. We secured our coffee lids and waited for the next elevator.

Brit was right, I thought to myself. Dad would never have accepted Brit without Mom's approval and prodding.

Dad and I got on the next elevator. Brit and George met us when the doors opened on the floor where Mom was—or was supposed to be.

"She's not there. She's not there," George said, terrified.

"What do you mean?" Dad asked.

"Well, the receptionist, I . . . I asked Mom what had happened to her. She said she was moved to the pre-op area down the hall."

"No, no. She's not supposed to have surgery until tomorrow!" Dad yelled.

Just then, the head nurse for the floor came around the corner to explain.

"Elisa had some unusual signs of bleeding, and the doctor was concerned," she told us with a calmness that could be mistaken for her not really caring all that much.

"He canceled his schedule for today and instructed us to immediately prep her for the surgery."

"What's the matter with her? It's that bad?" I asked.

"Well, she had some unusual signs of bleeding; that's all I know." Again, the calmness made me even more apt to think the nurse didn't care much. My eyebrows furrowed as I took a deep breath and looked at the nurse.

"I heard you say that! What does that mean?"

The nurse sensed my annoyance . . . or maybe even anger. "Calm down, sir. I'll take you to Elisa's and to see the doctor before surgery."

She again, somewhat carelessly, pointed to a room down the hall. George ran. The rest of us followed the nurse.

As we got close, I heard Mom's weak voice say, "George, my baby." We entered the room as the nurses were installing another IV. Mom paid no attention to them. George was squeezing her free hand when we came in. Mom was staring at him. Her beautiful, faded green eyes began to moisten, and she managed a smile.

"Georgio, my son," she paused and smiled. "I don't know if I'll make it through this one."

Then she looked up at us, and Dad came charging in from behind us and grabbed her hand, and sobbed. "I love you," he told her, but she was already nearly unconscious from the medicine. I scooted near and tried to touch her, any part of her. I put my hand on her hot soft cheek.

"Love you, Mom."

The nurses asked George to move as they began to wheel her away. Dad stepped back, and George secured her hand again. His eyes were wide open, and he began to tear up. I couldn't remember the last time I'd heard her call him Georgio. That was her father's name. He turned around and made eye contact with Brit. He couldn't speak. She came closer as they walked down the hall and put her hand on George's shoulder as we all walked together with Mom.

The doctor followed soon after. He stopped to tell us only that "we have no time to lose." What did that mean? I thought to myself and could read the same sentiment on all of our faces. He would explain more after the surgery, he said.

Now, the four of us stood in the hallway as they took Mom into the operating room; we were quiet and in shock. We turned again to the elevator, stopping at the nurse's station to let her know where we would be. She smiled and pointed out a waiting area where there was a lounge and some vending machines on the first floor. I thanked her and worked on smiling back. She could tell we were agonizing over what had just happened. As we walked to the elevator, I wondered how the nurse handled seeing desperate people all the time, just waiting to hear news about the ones they loved the most. We got into the elevator without saying much. Dad seemed strangely composed, or maybe he was so shocked, he didn't realize the situation for what it was . . . Mom was in a very serious situation.

Trying to change the subject, I mentioned that I needed to call Emma, and I slipped out into the hallway. I strengthened myself as the phone rang on the other end. I knew that if I was going to lose it, it would be while talking to the one whom I confide in and love the most. Emma answered with an excited tone, wanting to hear the update.

"Hello, Levi, what's going on? Katie and I have been working and cleaning and doing anything we could think of to pass the time." When I didn't respond right away, Emma knew something wasn't right. "Levi," her tone changed. "What is it? Is Mom OK?" I braced myself but felt myself slipping into an emotional answer.

"Mom," I paused and took a deep breath trying to remain composed. I couldn't do it and began to tear up, and my voice cracked as I spoke. "The doctor had to take her into emergency surgery. Seems her heart or somewhere started bleeding internally. He barely had time to talk to us and got her into surgery right away. He said he'd give us an update in thirty minutes or so. Dear . . . dear," I paused again. "Pray for her and us. I wish you were here. I . . . I just don't know what to think or do." As I composed myself again, I realized I was just scaring Emma and not helping the situation. "But I'm trusting the Lord, and we all need to do just that, I guess. Sorry for losing it a bit, dear."

Emma immediately responded that it was all right, and she understood. "What can I do to help? Can I bring you guys something or just stop in?"

"I'd like you both to come right away—you all should be here." I paused again. "I love you, dear." That's all I could say. "Guess I better get back in with Dad and the others. I'll let them know you're on your way." I paused again. "Love you, dear. Talk to you soon."

As soon as I hung up, I headed to meet the others and let them know Emma and Katie were coming soon. In a few minutes, Emma and Katie pulled into the parking lot. I was waiting for them there and ran to the car to help with Katie. When I leaned into the car to get Katie, Emma leaned over and grabbed my hand, and looked at me, nearly expressionless for a moment. It helped both of us calm down a bit and focus. As we walked into the hospital, I began to explain more details about what was going on.

We got to the waiting room and greeted everyone, hugging and encouraging each other. Once we got settled again, we all realized it might actually be hours before we might hear from the doctor. Two long hours passed. I had snuck off to the chapel to pray and read my Bible for a while and came back, still waiting for news. When I returned, I saw my twin sisters running into the waiting room. They had just arrived from the hotel. Dad, who had held his emotions back thus far, stood up and hugged my sister Melissa. I guess it was finally too much for him, and he began to cry on her shoulder. My other sister, Rebecca, hugged both of them. He tried to explain what had happened that morning, but he couldn't get it out, and the girls began to cry too. George, sitting by Brit in the next row of chairs, watched. Finally, the girls turned to George and the rest of us. They gave us each a hug while they both continued to cry. Melissa and Rebecca had only briefly met Brit once before. After a minute or so, George reached for Brit's hand and pulled her over to him, and they hugged. He then turned to Melissa and Rebecca.

"You guys remember Brit?"

They both, regaining their composure a bit, smiled, and Melissa said, "Of course." She paused for a moment and continued. "I know you got to know Mom pretty well. She talked a lot about you and how much she liked you." Brit began to tear up and shake a little. "I know this must be really hard for you too."

Brit regained her composure and smiled back, and responded. "Yeah, I feel like your mom is a close friend if that makes sense. I visited her at times, even when George was working or busy. She is such a . . . " she paused as emotions began to stir. She then continued with tears welling up and her voice cracking, "She is wonderful." George wrapped his arm around her.

Rebecca then turned to me. "Where are Emma and Katie?" I explained, "They're in the children's waiting room. We weren't sure if Katie should be right here and see all this." Melissa chimed in. "I think you should tell them to come on over. We can help watch Katie. Why don't you run and get them."

The girls both gave me a quick hug and a kiss on the cheek and headed over to George. They were all hugging again as I headed out of the room to find Emma and Katie.

Chapter Thirty-Five

Three hours later. We had thought we might hear something in thirty minutes or so, but it was three hours later before the doctor came in to speak to us. He looked absolutely exhausted and a bit traumatized.

"Hello, folks," he said. "I'm sorry that I didn't get back to you sooner as I promised." He paused as though to hold back some personal emotions that he had invested in Mom's case. He cleared his throat and started again. "I have been working on your mother for this entire time. It seems that as soon as I repair one area of the heart, another part ruptures and springs a leak." He paused again and looked at us even more seriously. "The walls of your mother's heart are so thin and weak that they are rupturing when pressure builds, even normal pressures of the heart action. I . . . I'm not sure there is much else I can do." The room somehow seemed to get even quieter than it already was. As I looked at everyone's faces, I could see a mix of emotions: sheer terror, desperation, panic, and bewilderment. Seeing our expressions, the doctor broke into the silence. "But I'm going to take a short break and keep trying." He smiled and could no longer look into our eyes without revealing his emotions. He left without another word.

We stood there, looking at each other, not saying a word. I didn't know what else to do. So, I grabbed the hand next to me, and we all joined hands, and I began to pray and ask God to intervene. I thanked him for Mom and for the time we had together and asked that if it be His will, he would allow us a little more time together here on earth. "Mom seemed to have so much more yet to give here on earth, Lord," I said, pleading with God to heal her. "But . . ." I stopped for a moment, "Please give us the strength to handle whatever happens, Lord."

Three hours later. The doctor walked in again. I didn't think it was possible, but he looked even more exhausted than before. He pulled his mask and hat from his head in one fell swoop. He took a deep breath, paused again, and looked at us. "I continued to patch the holes for the last three hours. They just kept coming. So, I have put a sponge in her cavity in hopes that it may help stop the bleeding and begin the healing process."

"Healing," George interrupted.

"No," the doctor followed, "Please don't get the wrong idea here. The sponge is a last attempt to get your mom's heart to stop leaking in hopes that we may make some progress. I also used a synthetic patch to cover the opening I made in her chest. It . . . it's not worth closing now until . . . unless we see some progress. I am putting her back into the next room over. Please don't get the wrong idea here," he said again. He sighed. "We are only keeping her alive with our machines right now. There . . . there is very little chance that she will stop bleeding now, on her own. Give the nurses a few minutes, and they will come and get you, so you can see her."

He left without another word. I don't think he could take being around us anymore. He tried to remain impartial and professional, but he seemed to have let himself get emotionally wrapped up in this. Dad was in shock. He just stared out the window like he was trying to find some other place to be right now. I put my arm around him to try to bring him back from wherever he was.

"Dad, Dad, are you OK?" Dumb question, I knew, but I couldn't think of anything else to say. He finally looked at me and pulled together a smile.

He sighed as he responded. "Yes, son. I'm OK." He looked down at the floor after he spoke. I think his heart was hurting so bad he almost

Convenience

physically winced in pain. No one else spoke. We just tried to give encouraging looks to each other.

Emma and Katie had been down the hallway and had just arrived back in the room where we were. Emma could tell by the looks on our faces that things weren't good. She came over to me and just looked and tried to smile. I didn't say anything, either. We hugged, and I gave Katie a big hug as well.

Finally, I spoke up, "They are moving Mom to a different room now. She is only being kept alive by the machines. It doesn't look good, dear." I began to tear up again and turned my head so Emma wouldn't see my face. She reached out and touched my shoulder. I composed myself again. Emma had always been really close to my mom; she began to tear up, and I sensed she needed a hug again. Katie just looked at us in amazement. She'd never seen us this way. We finally came back to ourselves and looked at little Katie standing there like a good soldier, waiting for instructions. I reached down and picked her up. I told her that Grandma was really sick and may go back to Jesus. We would miss her, but we believed that Jesus had made a way that we could see her again in heaven.

Just then, the nurse poked her head in the door and told us we could come over to room 204. I mentioned that we should all go in separately first, so we could have a moment with Mom on our own. Then we could all go in together after that. Everyone agreed. George quickly moved to the door and made his way down the hall. He hadn't said much throughout this whole experience, but I could tell he was hurting. We all sat rather quietly as we waited for each one to come back from the room. I was the last.

As I entered the room, I dreaded seeing Mom like this. I took a deep breath and looked over at her. She didn't really look like herself. Her face was swollen from all the fluids they were pumping onto her body. But when I touched her forehead, it was the same soft skin that was her trademark. Even at seventy-five, she had always taken good care of her skin, and it was soft and moist. As I looked at her, I began to remember her voice and happy smile—how she enjoyed life and her family. A smile came over my face as I remembered. I just sat and held Mom's hand for a few minutes, remembering those moments. I didn't want to leave but knew I needed to. As I left the room, I felt like that would be the last time I would spend with her.

As I approached the waiting room, I began to think of how in the world we would get through the next few moments, and I asked God to please help us. I looked at everyone in the room and could tell they had the same thoughts that I had. The nurse said we all could go into the room together now. We walked down the hall, not saying a word. As we walked in, we all stood around Mom's bedside. Dad was near his dear wife's side. George was across from Dad, looking down mostly and not saying anything, with Brit at his side holding his hand. I was next to Dad, trying to be supportive of him. Emma was by me, and Katie was next to her. My sisters were at the foot of the bed, both sobbing quietly.

The doctor came in next. He went straight to Dad. He was still struggling to stay professional. He looked down at his feet and cleared his throat. "There is really nothing else that can be done." He looked away from Dad for a moment, I think, to avoid crying. Clearing his throat again, he continued. "She is being kept alive by the machines. There is really no hope for her heart now. It's bleeding from many places and won't stay together or heal now."

He struggled very hard to say what he would say next, "We can turn off the machines if you like."

Chapter Thirty-Six

Dad looked at the doctor—his expression totally confused again. He looked back at me to translate. "Dad, maybe we should turn the machines off." Dad was still speechless, as his red eyes looked to me again and then to the wall over Mom's head. We didn't say anything after that for a few minutes. I finally looked at everyone and suggested we sing. We automatically held hands, and we sang all the verses of "Amazing Grace." Tears were rolling down all of our faces. Mom loved that song, and so did I.

Then, God stepped in. All of a sudden, Mom's vital signs began to drop. Slowly they dipped down until they were all at zero. Mom was gone. At that moment, as I was holding her hand. I could almost imagine myself handing Mom over to Jesus. It was as if I turned her over to him, and he took her . . . her soul, that is, home to heaven with him. All that was left with us was that sweet little body that used to hold Mom. But it wasn't Mom anymore. She was not there. She was gone. The nurses then came in and asked us to step out and wait in the waiting room for a moment while they unhooked all the machines. We would all each get another chance to come in one last time.

The nurses called us back after a few minutes. Again, we each went down that cold dark hallway, one at a time to spend a last moment with Mom. This time it would be to say goodbye. None of us spoke. We just looked at each other. I grabbed Dad's hand. As I held it, Dad's hand began to shake, and he began to shake as I hugged him, and we all hugged him together. He had been through so much in the war and getting to America; he had family members die far away, and yet he had never shown so much emotion as he did tonight. He let out an agonizing groan from the depths of his heart that shook us to the core. After that, he got calm again and looked up at me and smiled, and dropped his head again. I hurt for him and hated to see him in such agony. We sat down on a couple of comfy lounge chairs as I motioned to the others to go ahead and start going, one at a time, to see Mom. Emotionless, George walked to the door, and Brit followed close behind. I watched as their outline faded into the dark hallway. As each left and came back, even Dad, they all seemed to show little emotion and didn't really speak much. We sat in the room in near-total silence.

Then, it was my turn to go. I struggled to draw a deep breath as I stood up and made my way down the hallway. It was quite a bit different now, with the darkness and quietness of the night shift. I looked to the room ahead of me now, agonizing over all that had happened and how I would handle seeing Mom in that room. A thought came to mind as I walked. I remembered how Mom looked that first night when she passed out at her house, and we didn't know what to do . . . how she looked almost lifeless lying there that night . . . and how it scared me. Now I would face that same image of Mom but for real this time. I took one last deep breath and walked into the room. Again, it was so different from hours ago when the room was lit up, and loud gadgets were making all kinds of noises . . . beeping and banging, the movement and suction of the respirator . . . and all the indicators and graphs measuring and monitoring. Now . . . all that was gone. It was dark . . . and so quiet. Mom lay there with her hands folded on her stomach. I reached out to touch her hand . . . shock . . . it was stone-cold, and I could feel no life left in it. I reached down and kissed Mom's forehead. Again . . . shock . . . it was so cold and so without life. Just then, I was reminded that this wasn't Mom anymore. This was God's way of reminding me that I had seen and felt the real Mom, her soul, and spirit, leave her and go to be with the Lord. How could I have forgotten so quickly?

I'm so sorry, God, I thought to myself and probably said it out loud to myself in the room. I paused for a minute and started to get angry—I breathed in harder and harder. "Why God, why?" And then, taking another calmer deep breath, I thought about it. I looked up at the ceiling. "Lord, I'm sorry. Actually, you gave your son's life on that cruel cross. You had to watch him suffer and die one of the cruelest deaths known. You did it all for me and us. You made a way for Mom to trust and be able to be with you now and forever, and you made a way that I can be reunited with her and all of our loved ones forever. Oh, thank you, Lord, for what you did for me and for us!"

I'm sure I was speaking out loud and wondered if some nurse might come to see what or who I was talking to. A peace came over me, and even a hint of joy that Mom was not here. Lying in front of me was just the sweet little body that once held Mom. I was reenergized. I didn't spend much more time in the room. And quickly, I walked out and down the hallway. As I returned to the waiting room, I was sure everyone in the room could see the somewhat regenerated emotions on my face. They all looked at me like I had finally lost it. I looked at all of them and explained, "Mom's not here. She is with the Lord forever, and we'll see her again." They all still stared at me, except for Emma. She understood, and she smiled at me.

We sat again in the waiting room for what seemed a long time, really not knowing what to do next. Finally, the doctor came in. He sat down for the first time since we had met him. He took a deep breath and began.

"Folks, I know this is a hard time. I just want you to know that I did everything I possibly could to try to . . ." he paused and looked at his watch. I think he was again getting emotional and trying to hide it. He was desperately trying to stay professional. "I did everything I could to try to save Ms. Bell. She seemed like a really great person, spunky, happy, a real strong personality wrapped up in a little package." He smiled as he spoke. Then he got serious again.

"Now, I know this will be hard, but there are things that need to be done, and you need to think clearly about all this." He reached into his shirt pocket and pulled out a pamphlet, and opened it. "You have two funeral homes to choose from to handle the body and funeral. Either one is good and will do a good job handling everything." I could see Dad's eyes glaze over again as the doc spoke of the details of all this. "So, Alexander, which of these do you want to handle this?" He put the pamphlet in front of Dad. Dad looked at it but really didn't see it. "Alex, we need to choose one, so they can pick up the body, take it to their facility and prepare it. In a day or two, they will need to go over what you want for funeral arrangements, which church you want, cemetery plot location, ceremony at the cemetery, all that."

I could tell Dad was about to lose it again. I jumped in and made the decisions for Dad. The doc understood. "OK then. Again, I'm sorry for how this turned out. I hope...." He had to stop and look at his watch again. "I hope that you all get through this as best as you can." That really didn't come out the way he wanted, but I guess it was the best he could come up with. He silently and quickly left the room after that.

Again, we were stuck staring at each other. "OK, there's nothing else that needs to be done now. Why don't we all go home and get some rest?" I suggested. We quietly all hugged each other and left.

Just like that . . . it was over, and, for me, life changed forever. As I walked with Emma and Katie to the car, it felt like some jewel in this crazy world was missing, and the world was a little less shiny now and a little emptier.

Chapter Thirty-Seven

The next morning, I woke up early, just like every other Saturday. As my eyes opened and I saw the sun shining through the window, I got that "great, it's Saturday" feeling and got excited to get my day going. Only for a short time, though, and then I remembered that Mom was gone and that today would be a tough, tough day for us all. The weight descended on my heart again as I ran back through the last day in my mind. But I remembered how God had comforted me too, and that helped me get back into focus.

I got up quietly so that Emma and Katie could continue to sleep. I made my way downstairs and got some coffee going. I peeked out the front window as I waited for the coffee to brew. What a contrast to several months ago when it was freezing cold, dark, and uninviting. Now the sun beamed proudly on the grass and trees, and there seemed to be life out there. And it was warming up nicely out there, even as early as it was. It further reminded me of God's goodness and his presence and lightened the weight on my heart a bit. After getting my coffee just right with a little cream, I grabbed the paper from the door and sat down, and began to read. As important as it was to get over to Dad's and get this day going, I decided to let him sleep in a little and waited an extra hour or so to get ready and make my way over to his house.

Once I finally got myself together, I drove over to a breakfast place and got a couple of burritos and a fresh coffee for Dad. As I drove up the familiar drive, I was unprepared for the memories of Mom that rushed at me. Tears immediately filled my eyes to the point that I could hardly see well enough to park, but I managed. I pulled myself together, trying to be strong for Dad. I got to the door and knocked hard. No answer for what seemed to me like a long time. I knocked again. Listening carefully, I finally heard some movement inside. It took Dad a long time to get to the door. As he answered, he tried to produce a smile. He looked like he hadn't slept a wink, and that was probably the case.

"Good morning, Dad. I brought you some breakfast and fresh coffee." Dad didn't say much.

He just looked at me and pulled together a smile and said, "You're a good son, such a good son to me."

Dad slowly opened the door, and we walked to the living room, where I pulled out the burritos and spread them out on the table. We sat down, and I thanked God for the food and the day, and Dad began to unwrap his food. I took the opportunity while we were getting settled to call George and my sisters to make sure they all understood we needed to be at the funeral home at two o'clock. I first got George on the phone.

"Hey, bro," he answered.

"Good morning, George. Did you get any sleep?"

"I got a little . . . very little, actually. I thought that over time, it would be easier, but I keep replaying all that happened yesterday." He paused long to hold back from becoming emotional again.

"You know it's gonna be tough today—at the funeral home, picking out a casket and discussing the funeral," I said. Long pause again.

"Yeah, I know. No good way to prepare for this but to just do our best, I guess." I smiled, thinking about how much George had changed since I saw him last year when we arrived. He seemed so soft-hearted now and matured, as compared to how hard he was to all of us before. God is good, I thought to myself.

"Ah, yes, George, brother; it's gonna be tough, but we have each other, and you are such a comfort to me." Long pause again on the line . . .

"I love you, bro." Now it was me who was pausing to hold back tears. He rarely said that to me.

Convenience

"I love you too, bro. See you at two, OK?"

We hung up, and I proceeded to call the girls. I had a similar quick conversation with them as well. As I ended my calls, I noticed Dad listening to my conversations. It certainly got him thinking about Mom again as well. As I hung up and looked at him, his eyes glazed over with tears. He looked at me and took a bite, and began to chew. I know he was trying to be strong, but with each bite, his eyes filled more and more with tears until they were rolling down his face. He finished his bite and looked at me, tears streaming now. And he let out another groan from the depths of his heart—it was pure agony, made audible. He put down his food, and I hugged him for a minute. Then, as suddenly as his pain flared, he dried up, sniffled, picked up his food, and began to eat again. He managed to smile at me. I tried to think of something to say that might help him.

"You know, Dad, I don't have much experience with all this, but I'm told that with time, the pain will subside, and this will all get easier to handle." *Lame,* I thought to myself. *That's all you can come up with?*

Dad responded, "Yes, son; I'm sure it will. And with God's help, I'll be fine, I promise." He smiled. I thought to myself that he was comforting me so much better than I was comforting him, which is what I had hoped to do. We finished our food and sat and chatted a little more while we finished our coffee. Then Dad decided to lie down and rest a little, and I cleaned up his house for him. Then I headed back home for a while before coming back to get Dad at one thirty.

As I pulled into our driveway, I tried to prepare myself for how I'd be around Emma and Katie. I always seemed more emotional around them, but now I needed to be strong and supportive of them. As I pulled up, Emma came out onto the porch, her cup of coffee in hand, standing in the morning sunshine. I could tell she was the one now trying to be strong . . . for me. She was so beautiful, standing there in her sweatpants in the sunshine.

"Thank you, Lord," I thought to myself. I walked up the steps without a word as I smiled at her and gave her a hug. She was such a comfort, and I'd hoped to be that for her. Still, without a word, we walked back into the house. She poured me a hot cup of coffee.

"Medicine for the ages," I joked, and Emma snickered.

"How's Dad?" Emma asked. I looked down and paused in thought.

"I think he's just trying to maintain right now. I've never seen someone so wounded in their soul. But I think he'll slowly heal. How are you?"

Emma took a deep breath, paused, and looked to the floor. Then she looked back at me. "I'm hanging in there—could have used a little more sleep, but I guess all of us are in the same boat today." She smiled. I could tell she didn't want to talk beyond what we had already said. "Hey, how about we get a couple more hours of sleep then? We're gonna need it later today."

Emma smiled as she stood up, and we headed for bed again. Katie had miraculously slept through the morning. We slept for a couple of hours, and it was probably the best sleep we had gotten in the last twenty-four hours. But I had to go through the same process again as I woke, feeling good that it was Saturday, then feeling my heart sink to my shoes as I remembered all that had happened . . . and that Mom wasn't with us anymore. Making the adjustment, I rolled out of bed, trying not to wake Emma, and got dressed. I looked at Emma, sound asleep, before I left the room. I covered her up a little more, looked at her for a moment, and headed down the stairs quietly. Out I went again, quietly shutting the door behind me, and drove over to Dad's.

As I walked up the sidewalk, I smiled when I saw him open the door for me. "Hey, Dad, how are you?"

He forced a smile. "I'm doing fine, son. Don't worry about me." I looked into his eyes as I entered the house.

"Are you sure?" He squinted a little, probably to hold back tears.

He sighed. "Son, I'm really, really sad." He stopped for a moment. "But I'm gonna make it. I'm so glad I have you and the others to help me through this . . . thank you." He smiled again. This time with less forced effort. I smiled back and hugged him. After a moment, we both dried up and got ourselves out the door, and headed to the funeral home.

As we drove up to the funeral home, the director was out front waiting for us. I couldn't help but think of a used car salesman with a

Convenience

fat tie and a fake smile, but I had to remind myself that he was probably sincere and just trying to do his best.

"Alex, Levi, hello." He smiled gently and carefully with just the right tone and loudness so as to show enthusiasm without coming off as callous.

He reached out his hand to shake Dad's. "I'm Jim." His expression changed slightly from a smile to serious just at the right time as he looked at Dad. "I'm so sorry for your loss. We'll do everything we can to make this as easy as possible for you and your family. Let's go in and sit down." He reproduced his smile again at the end of his sentence. With that, we entered the somewhat creepy place. George and my sisters were already in the meeting room. We hugged, and all sat down to discuss the plan. Very organized, Jim laid out a plan and schedule for the funeral for us.

He explained, "After we discuss the plan, we'll go into the casket room and let you pick out the casket. That will give you time to think about the schedule, and we can come back in here and finalize it all." He smiled again and handed out a generic schedule, and went over each portion quickly before suggesting we go and pick a casket.

We were all still shocked at everything that had happened. And I'm pretty sure none of us had ever reviewed a funeral schedule before, except for me. I was now remembering the process I went through with Ed's funeral. With all that, we sort of looked at each other and half-listened to Jim as he reviewed the plan. Again, shocked by it all, we had no comment when he asked. So, we filed out and went upstairs to the casket room. What a gloomy place, with caskets lining the walls on special shelves to allow for three rows stacked along each wall. I knew viewing caskets was going to be tough but also wanted to make sure we did a good job . . . a good job . . . picking out a casket? It all seemed so weird. As we entered the "display room," Jim began to explain things.

"Alex," he touched Dad's shoulder as he spoke. "I know this will be a rough day. Are you OK?"

Dad looked at him with all the strength he could muster, desperately trying to maintain his composure. "Thank you for asking, Jim. I'm OK right now. It kind of comes and goes."

Jim nodded in agreement, carefully studying Dad's response. After a polite pause, Jim looked at me and started in on his explanation. "There is a large variety of casket options and associated costs. Your mom and dad had put away a good sum of money for a plot and caskets, so you have money already available for this purchase."

I could hardly stand the thought of what seemed almost like car shopping for the "best deal," and it was killing me. I could tell everyone else was struggling too.

"Well, let's make this simple and choose this one. It's in the range of cost and seems very . . ." I cleared my throat . . . "nice and respectable." Relieved, everyone, including Dad, quickly agreed. I still fought myself inside, thinking: *Who cares what it looks like since it's going to be in the ground?* Then I'd feel bad for thinking so callously. We all agreed quickly on my suggestion and just as quickly moved out of the "display room" (showroom?) and back into the meeting room.

Dad didn't say much through that whole process and continued to float above it all to avoid the pain. I know he was glad to have us there to make sure we made a good decision. As we sat down, Jim handed us a sample service schedule again, and we all studied it quietly for a moment. As we looked over the sample, I noticed a man walk by our room. He did a double-take when he looked at me. His eyes got bigger, and he quickly looked the other way and walked by. I recognized him right away. He was the one who did Brock's funeral last winter and made me so mad. Ed and I were the only ones in attendance, and he seemed to want to get it over with as fast as he could. I remembered again how cold and callous the whole ceremony seemed. It made me mad all over again. But then I remembered finding Brock's letter and him writing that he had accepted Jesus. A smile washed over my face, and I forgot about Brock's funeral and that guy.

As we studied the sample ceremony, I had a comment. "Jim, this looks pretty good, but there's no space for the pastor's message."

Somewhat surprised, he responded. "We generally don't include that since we want to keep the service moving smoothly and quickly." He smiled as though he had solved the problem with some simple logic.

He didn't know I was not exactly a logical or rational person at times.

Convenience

"Well, I think that's the most important part of the service. I'd like to include time for the pastor to speak. Mom would have wanted it that way for sure."

Jim was a little surprised but smiled and responded. "Of course, if you want to include that, by all means, we will, and we'll give you a moment to speak for the family as well."

"That would be great," I responded. "I'd like to have some time to talk about a special time that each of us kids remembers with Mom." Jim quickly smiled and nodded.

Just then, George looked over at me and smiled. I thought for a moment about how he had changed over the past few months. His hard shell seemed to have melted away, and his tender heart had finally shone through. We moved on and talked about an opening and closing hymn and details of the service. We all agreed on those details kind of quickly, worn out as we were from experience. I could see Dad starting to drift a bit from the strong front that he had kept up all day. I reached over and hugged him.

"Dad, this sounds like a good plan, don't you think?" He smiled at me and paused for a moment.

Making an effort to look strong again, he said, "Yes, son. I think this will be fine." He was definitely hurting and almost forced the words out as he spoke through his pain.

Experienced in this process, Jim spoke up quickly after Dad's answer. "Thank you for leading us through this today. I think we have everything as your mom would have wanted it."

"Let's go over the whole ceremony quickly one more time, and we'll be through for today." He quickly reviewed the entire plan one more time and added how we would all drive to the cemetery and what we'd do there. No one had any comments when he was finished. We all thanked Jim and left, all relieved that it was over. I got Dad home, and I could tell he just wanted to rest and be alone, so I dropped him off and headed home, wondering how we would get through the funeral.

I headed home and spent the evening with Emma and Katie, and we all turned in pretty early. I talked to Emma about the day, and she seemed relieved not to have had to be a part of all that.

Chapter Thirty-Eight

The next day passed swiftly, and the funeral was upon us. Emma and Katie, and I readied ourselves almost without a word. Guess we were all thinking about the funeral and realizing this would be the last time we would be with Mom's sweet little body here on earth, although we knew we'd see her again. As we finished up in the house and got into the car, we were still not talking much. I occasionally smiled at Emma and Katie but couldn't really generate much talk. After I started the car, I reached over and held Emma's hand, and looked back one more time at Katie.

They both smiled back. "It'll be all right. We'll get through this. We have great memories that we can keep alive, and we'll see Mom again." Emma smiled through glassy eyes and nodded her head. Katie smiled. As we drove out of the neighborhood, I think all of us were thinking about this place and our move back here and what a year it had been. As we pulled up to Dad's and I parked, Emma squeezed my hand.

"You go on in; we'll wait here," she smiled. As I walked up the sidewalk, a now familiar fear came over me. How would Dad be today? How was he going to get through this? Would he be crying or unable to move or, even worse, just plain broken down? I knocked on the door. He took a long time to answer, but he eventually opened the door. He looked OK; he was dressed and rested, and ready to go.

"Hello, son." He smiled as he looked at me, trying to ease my concerns.

"Hi, Dad. How are you?" He paused a bit, drawing as much energy as he could.

"I'm doing well, son. We'll get through this," he said with all the strength and energy he could muster. Then he paused again and looked me right in the eye. "Thank you for all you've done here. For how you helped George and Brit, and were so good to . . ." he paused, gathered himself, and continued, "for how you blessed your mother . . . and me. And we could not have gotten through all this without you."

I smiled at Dad, and we hugged for a while. Then he looked at me again. "I'll drive myself today." Thinking he should still take things easy, I was ready to say no, but something inside me said he was ready, even on this day, to begin life on his own.

Trying to be as encouraging as I could, I smiled back and said, "OK, Dad, we'll meet you there." I walked back to the car, with both Emma and Katie giving me puzzled looks. Getting in the car, I explained what had happened, and we drove off.

As we drove up into the church parking lot, I asked God to please help me and all of us through this. I wanted to honor God and make him known while honoring Mom . . . and taking care of the whole group. It all scared me a bit. As we got out of the car, we slowly and quietly walked to the back door of the church. I opened the door, not really sure what to expect. There were already a lot of people there, and as they saw us, those who were standing around made an effort to make eye contact and smile as we passed by. As we made our way up to the front of the church, Jim, the funeral director, saw me and began to make his way over. I sighed and took a deep breath.

He smiled and shook my hand, and asked me how I was doing. "Fine, I think we're all fine, Jim. Thanks. And are you doing OK today?"

He paused and looked surprised. I'm not sure that was in his script . . . me caring about him. "I . . . I'm doing fine." He stood and paused, computing what just happened; then, he snapped out of it and was back in character. "Where's Alexander?" he asked with some concern.

Convenience

"He's driving over in his own car." That, I believe, scared him a bit, but he didn't inquire further.

"OK, well . . . when he gets here, we'll get him up to the front seat and probably get started shortly after that. Is the rest of the family here?"

I looked around and saw George and Brit and my sisters already seated.

"Think everyone else is here."

"OK," he responded, as he was already looking elsewhere and thinking of something else. He turned and made off to talk to the pastor and song leader. We went to the front row and took our seats next to the rest of the family. I carried Katie, and she sat on my lap. She was a little scared by all the commotion and not used to the surroundings.

As we sat, I turned to the back of the church and looked at the place filling up. There were a lot of people attending. I didn't think Mom knew so many people, but I think she made such a positive impression on so many that it probably only took one meeting, and people didn't forget her. As I was looking back at the crowd, I noticed Jim parting the waters of people to get Dad through and up to the front. Knowing we were almost late to start, as soon as Dad was seated, like a symphony conductor, Jim signaled to the pastor and organist to start. I didn't even have time to say hello to Dad before the organist started. The organist was talented, and the music was beautiful. It almost made me forget my grief for a moment.

As we had asked, the pastor gave a compelling message of a life well-lived and one in which Jesus was the center. As he spoke, I thought of how this was the third funeral I had attended this year: Brock, then Ed, and now Mom. But I also thought of how each had come to know Christ, and all were certainly in heaven. I thanked God once again for His goodness. We all maintained through the message, and even Dad did well through it.

Then came my turn to speak on things we kids remembered about our mother. I spoke through tears as I explained a few precious moments each of us kids remembered. Emma smiled at me periodically, reenergizing me to continue. I ended with my memory of Mom a few days earlier, when she reminded me of how she had trusted God and accepted Jesus as Lord and Savior. We had such precious few moments together. Dad seemed to look down though most of my speaking. I was sure he didn't want to make eye contact with me and cause us both to lose it. George also didn't make eye contact and looked straight ahead, trying his best to keep it together; Brit was squeezing his hand tightly. My sisters were the same, holding back any real focus on what was happening and the tears that would surely flow.

As I finished and took my seat, Dad stood up and shook my hand. Now looking me right in the eye, he smiled but still seemed to be kind of numb, not thinking or focusing on anything too hard. Somehow, we made it through the ceremony and did our best to honor Mom and God. As the surreal funeral concluded, we found ourselves shaking a lot of hands and getting a lot of hugs. I hadn't realized how draining this would be for all of us. Dad was a trooper through all of it, maintaining his composure. We made our way to the cars that Jim had lined up outside, and the group sped off to the cemetery for the last portion and last time to have Mom's body with us.

Jim had everything perfectly lined up and ready at the cemetery. We were dropped off right near the tent area, that telltale symbol of funerals and loneliness and dark clothes and quiet sadness. Jim had chairs set up with our place reserved in front, very close to the casket, which had already been placed over the opening in the ground that would soon swallow up my mom's body. Again, there was a surprising number of people already there seated behind us. As we took our place in the front row, with Dad in the center, Jim began to get things moving. As the first song began, I noticed that Dad was not so stable on his feet and wondered if it might just be the unlevel ground around the gravesite or if Dad was beginning to break down. I reached over and held his hand for a moment to help him settle down.

As the song concluded, the pastor said a few words, and the casket began to be lowered into the ground. Dad was given a hand full of dirt, which he was supposed to throw onto the casket as it was lowered. He looked at me and then at the dirt in his hand. Then he threw the dirt to the side; Jim was going into shock at this action. Dad went over to a flower arrangement and pulled a yellowish rose out of the arrangement. Then he walked over and threw the rose onto the lowering casket. Jim finally took a breath and smiled at Dad, and nodded his head. Dad returned to his seat next to me. As the casket was lowered out of our sight, I could feel Dad start shaking. Tears began to roll down his face. I grabbed his hand tight. But . . . then I started to lose it as well. Emma grabbed my other hand to help keep me from losing it. Then, George began to quiver . . . and Brit grabbed his hand. My sisters, seeing all this reached for each other and held hands and grabbled Brit's hand. As the casket reached its stopping point, we had all formed a bit of a semicircle and were holding hands.

Unprompted by Jim, Dad started to sing the last verse of "Amazing Grace"—exactly like we did as we stood around Mom when she passed at the hospital. We finished the song, and there was a moment of awkward silence. Jim was unable to react as we had altered his schedule.

Clearing his throat, the pastor spoke up. "I had planned a final song, but that was such a beautiful and wonderful moment. Why don't we end with that as our final memory? Thank you all for coming, and I hope you all have a good day."

The group began to shuffle around and shake our hands one more time and quietly departed, leaving us, the family, to stand around and look at each other again, wondering where we go from here as we did at the hospital. Jim came to the rescue, though, and began directing us back into the cars. Dad broke ranks and went, one more time, over to the casket area. He looked down into the dark hole, blew a kiss, and smiled through tears. Then he turned and made his way to the car. We drove off quietly, no one saying a word.

Chapter Thirty-Nine

When we were dropped off at the church parking lot, we again struggled with what to do next. Dad led this time by telling everyone how proud he was of all of us and that we all needed to get back to our lives and press on. Wow, I thought to myself, *Where did he get that kind of strength?* We all chatted for a few minutes, and then we went our separate ways. As Dad turned toward his car, I caught up with him.

"Are you gonna be OK, Dad?" He turned to me, lifting his head a little from its droopy state, smiled, and paused for a moment. "Son, I'll be just fine, I think. This isn't going to be easy for a while, but as you told me, time will help heal my pain." He smiled again, more convincingly this time. Then he turned and continued to his car without a word more. So, I turned back to my car, where Emma and Katie were standing, waiting for me. I smiled at them and picked up my pace to get back to the car quickly.

"Sorry, guys. Didn't mean to keep you waiting out here."

"It's all right, honey. Is Alex OK?"

"Yeah," I responded, with a bit of a puzzled tone. He said he's gonna be fine and turned and walked to his car. Ya know, I think he's right. He's gonna be OK." Realizing that both Emma and Katie needed me, I reached down and picked up my little girl and put an arm around

Emma. "I love you guys so much . . . sorry that I haven't spent much time with you today. Are you guys OK?"

"Yes, Daddy," Katie piped up right away as she smiled. It warmed my heart to see her, and I squeezed her tighter. Emma didn't answer but smiled back at me as well. We all got into the car and made our way home. We didn't talk much on the drive home, and I chalked it up to all of us being exhausted—spent physically and mentally. Katie was asleep by the time we pulled into the driveway. So, we quietly carried her into the house, and I lay her on the couch. Emma still didn't say much but smiled at me as she went into the kitchen. I didn't follow her in but stayed with Katie and got her coat off, and made her comfy without waking her. After that, I sat looking out the window for a minute or so, thinking about Dad and whether he really was OK.

Finally, I decided I would run by really quick to make sure he was OK. I got up off the couch and made my way to the kitchen. Emma was making coffee. I reached my arms around her from behind and gave her a squeeze. "Baby, I think I need to check on Dad one more time. He just didn't seem normal to me—no grieving, just smiling quietly. Gonna drive over really quick. I'll be right back, and we can have a coffee, OK?"

Emma just looked at me. She smiled and nodded her head. "OK, Levi, I'll wait for you." I smiled back and made my way out the door and into the car again.

As I drove up to Dad's house, I saw his light was still on in the living room—just as I left him. I parked quickly and knocked on the door. After what seemed to be a long wait, he finally answered the door. When he saw it was me, a smile came across his face, and he opened the door.

"Hi, Dad. How are you?"

He smiled and paused, almost chuckling. "Why, I'm as good as the last time you asked me thirty minutes ago."

I chuckled myself, taking a deep breath and answering, "OK, OK, maybe I'm a little paranoid. But I just want to make sure you're really OK." We sat down together on the couch for a moment. I could tell he wanted to try to be on his own, so I didn't probe much into how he really was inside. We engaged in a little small talk, and just as I was about to wrap things up and make my way home, Dad looked at me directly. Through a forced smile, tears began to well up, and his face turned red . . . he was trying so hard not to crack while I was there. Finally, I reached over and hugged him. He finally broke down and let out another groan . . . from deep in his soul; it was a scary sound, not like any normal sound coming from a human being. I just held him for a moment.

Then, as quickly as it came on, it subsided. Dad took a deep breath and looked at me again. He smiled, but this time it was for real. He said, "I'll be OK now . . . really." I believed him this time. Then he got a more serious look on his face.

"Where is Emma?" he asked.

"She's at the house," I responded. Dad looked me right in the eye this time.

"Son, you need to think of Emma now. She loved your mom too, and she is probably in need of a good cry herself. She is strong," he smiled again . . . "but not too strong." I looked at Dad and realized he was right. I had assumed she was strong and OK through all this. I had thought of everyone accepting her all day. I smiled again at Dad.

"OK, you're right, as usual. I'll head home now." I stood and hugged Dad one more time.

"Bye, Daddy. I love you."

"Love you too," Dad responded with still-drying tears in his eyes. I turned and made my way out again and got in the car, and drove home.

As I drove up the driveway, it was nearly dark outside. I could see that one light was on in the living room, and the porch light was on for me. I didn't see Emma come to the window and wave and smile like she usually did when I pulled in. I walked up the sidewalk and onto the porch. *I hope Emma is OK*, I thought to myself. As I approached the door, I still didn't see Emma. My heart sank a bit, and I began to worry more about her. I opened the door and peeked in quietly in case she was asleep.

Relieved, I saw Emma sitting on the couch with Katie asleep on her lap. Emma looked up at me. She mustered a tired, no, exhausted smile. I could feel her stress or sadness behind the smile. Without breaking eye contact, I threw my coat off and quickly sat down beside her. Still looking at her, I grabbed her hand tight and paused for a moment. We didn't say another word for a moment. Tears welled up in her eyes and then in mine.

I spoke through a cracking voice, "Oh, love," I paused again. "I'm so sorry." Her eyebrows rose slightly. "I've been so worried about Dad and the others—so busy taking care of all of them that I forgot about the most important person in my life." I stopped and looked down. A tear rolled off my face and onto Emma's pants.

Emma squeezed my hand, and I looked up at her. She didn't say a word but continued to force a smile as she looked at me. Then she began to quiver, and huge tears overflowed and ran down her precious, still-smiling face. Almost simultaneously, we let go of our hands and leaned toward each other, and hugged. Emma's body was now shaking as she let out her emotions—emotions she had held back all this time so as not to "disturb" me, I guess.

"I'm so sorry, love," I managed to say while we held each other. After a while, I could feel Emma take a few deep breaths. She looked at me again. This time with a real smile.

"How about I make us some decaf coffee?" she suggested through her smile.

I smiled back. "I'd love it, dear." So, she made her way to the kitchen, and we sat for another hour and talked about all sorts of things. We finally got Katie to her bed, and we both dropped into bed, exhausted.

Tomorrow was Saturday. I thought we'd sleep in and then go to the park and enjoy the bright spring weather. Dad and the whole family decided we would go out to dinner Saturday night before my sisters returned to their homes. But I'd make tomorrow, all day anyway, about my family—Emma and Katie. Emma fell asleep in a moment, and I held my dear wife closely all night long.

Chapter Forty

I woke up to sunshine on my face. Emma was already up, and I could hear the coffee pot chirping out that familiar delightful brewing noise. Wonderful, I thought as I scooted to the edge of the bed and made my way downstairs. As I got closer to the kitchen, I could also smell bacon and hear the busy sizzle of it and other food on the stove. As I entered, I saw not one but two master chefs, matching aprons, busily working this grand effort.

"Hi, guys," I yelled, maybe a little too loud, startling both as they turned. Katie smiled, and I scooped her up into my arms.

"How's your work coming along?" She smiled bigger and responded.

"Wanted to surprise you, Daddy."

I looked at Emma as she turned to us and smiled. Smiling back, I responded. "This is one of the best surprises—a delicious surprise!" I dug my nose under Katie's chin as she laughed. She looked at me after recovering from the tickle attack, serious again.

"I better get back to helping Mom."

"OK," I responded, equally serious as I set her back on the floor. We had a delightful breakfast together and got dressed, and made our way to the local park a few blocks from our house. It was an old park, like our neighborhood, with massive trees and well-traveled gravel pathways, now lush with its new spring attire. We played together, laughing and running around being silly. It was medicine for all of us after the last few days.

That evening, somewhat exhausted from our day together, we piled into the car and headed to one of the nicer restaurants in town to meet with the rest of the family. It was the first time we all piled into our car since the funeral. I could tell all three of us were thinking just that as we got in and were reminded of that event. Emma quickly changed the focus to our day at the park.

"Katie, did you see Daddy go down the slide and fall on his backside?" Katie immediately giggled, joined by Emma. I tried to hide a smile and have an expression of pain as I rubbed my bottom . . . but failed and cracked up laughing with the rest. Emma was always there to help everyone she came in contact with to brighten their day and make them feel good.

"Thank you, Lord," I thought, *"for Emma and how kind and thoughtful she is . . . and for her pulling me back up from sliding into the sorrowful pit again."* We drove off, still giggling about my "backside."

As we got to the parking lot, I looked through the window and saw that George and Brit were already there, and my sisters had just pulled up as well. Still feeling a little lighthearted, I smiled and waved at George through the window. I could tell he was hurting, but he smiled back and waved. I greeted my sisters with a smile.

What Emma started with us in the car spread to the whole group as we greeted each other in the restaurant and even joked around a little. Dad still hadn't shown up. But as George was dialing his number on his cell phone, we could see him pull up. There was a little sigh of relief from us all as he pulled up and parked. We all waved at him through the window, and he smiled in return. Dad was still gravely wounded, but he walked through the door and joined us, and I could sense he was a little more recharged than he had been over the past week. Getting through the funeral and all that went into it was a real challenge, and I think Dad finally got a little rest afterward. Getting together was probably really useful for all of us. This was how life was going to be now, and I guess we had to get used to it. We did the best we could to talk and try to be normal again. It was tough, and we weren't all that successful. But we were trying. I did get a chance to talk to my sisters, who were leaving the next morning for their homes

Convenience

and got caught up in their lives. We didn't usually talk that much, not because we didn't like each other, but because we each had our own busy lives.

As we wrapped up and headed for our cars, we bid each other goodbye, hugged, cried one more time together, and made our way into the darkness. Everyone had someone except Dad. But somehow, I felt at peace that he would be OK.

The weekend went by quickly, and I soon found myself preparing for work and trying to clear my head a bit and remember my schedule for my students' last few weeks of school. Our little family had a great, restful weekend, heard a great message in church, and regenerated a bit. It was what we all needed.

Monday morning came all too quickly. So much had transpired over the last few weeks. It had been so long since I had gone to work. As I drove out of our neighborhood and into Dad's, all the memories replayed in my head. As I passed Dad's house, a deep pain hit my lower gut. I remembered how I used to stop by and have a cup of coffee with my sweet mother. I quickly moved on in my thoughts, back to school and what I had originally planned for the last three weeks of school before the summer break. Being early, I found a great parking spot right on the first row of the school parking lot. I would have killed for this spot when it was freezing outside. Now it was pleasant in the mornings, warm and clear.

Not sure why but as I parked, Ed came to mind. I remembered how he traipsed through the crackling snow in clouds of car exhaust and how he appeared through the fog with his big smile to talk to me without noticing all the cars racing around and scrambling to leave the icy parking lot. The rush of happy students in the parking lot on this bright sunny, warm spring morning was quite a contrast from what I saw this winter. I quickly parked and joined the flow of kids walking toward the main entrance. As I entered the building, I thought I should stop by the principal's office and thank him for the time off. In the hallway, I was met by a few fellow teachers who all expressed their condolences for my family's loss. It was nice to know they were thinking of the family and me. I saw that the principal was in his office. He looked a little busy, but that was the way he usually looked, so I took a chance and knocked on his door.

He blurted out a rushed sounding, "Come in." I entered, and he spun quickly around from his desk to see who was pestering him on an early Monday morning. As he turned, his demeanor changed from that stone-faced, all-business school leader, to a bright, respectful, and concerned smile directed at me.

"Levi, how are you, and how is your family?"

"We're doing OK, Jim," I responded with what I had hoped was an encouraging smile.

"Sit down for a minute," Jim said, and I quickly grabbed a seat and started in.

"Well, sir, I don't want to take up a lot of your time. I know you're busy." Smiling, I continued, "especially on Monday mornings." He responded with a smile. "But I wanted to thank you for the time off and to thank those who stepped up to fill in. I know the end of the year is a busy time, and I really appreciate you and the others filling in for me."

Jim responded quickly, "Of course, we're all happy to help. I remember earlier this year, when we lost Ed, and how you stepped in to fill the gap—really through the rest of the year." He paused for a moment, deep in thought. Then he looked at me again and continued, "I was at your mom's funeral."

Surprised, I said, "I didn't know that." Jim smiled and interrupted, "I wouldn't have expected that you'd notice everyone there at a time like that. I was way in the back and would have said hello, but I didn't want to disturb you and your family." He paused again, breaking eye contact and looking out the window.

"Levi, that last song at the cemetery where you all held hands and sang. That was one of the most touching things I've ever seen. Everyone seemed so . . . so hopeful and truly genuine." He turned and was now looking squarely into my eyes. A bit of an awkward moment.

I responded, "Well, thank you, Jim, and thank you for coming. I'm really sorry I missed you and would have enjoyed saying hello and introducing you to the rest of my family. Hopefully, sometime I can do that." I smiled and moved to the edge of my chair, motioning that I needed to wrap up and get on to class.

"Yes," Jim replied, snapping out of his paused state. "I'd like to meet them sometime."

I smiled again and moved further to the edge of my chair. "Well, I need to get to class." I stood up and began to move toward the door.

Then Jim called out to me, "Levi." I stopped and turned around again, and he continued. "I . . . well . . . some time, when you have a moment, I . . . I'd like to talk more about . . . well . . . about your faith." He smiled.

I turned and smiled back, answering, "Of course." As I walked out and closed the door behind me, I was calm on the outside but doing cartwheels on the inside. As I left the office and headed down the hallway, I was encouraged . . . a little lighter in my step and amazed at how God works, even in my grief.

Chapter Forty-One

Three weeks later. It was hot and noisy as we entered the gym through one of the floor-level entrances. People were scurrying around, talking, laughing, and shaking hands. The sound of everyone's chatter and the scooting of metal chairs on the gym floor was deafening as it echoed loudly through the place. Everyone was happy, joking, and laughing with one another. After all, it was graduation day—a victory in many ways for many people. The bright sun shone outside, and many people were celebrating the victory of getting through the cold dark winter, getting through the challenges of the year, and getting to this point.

We looked for Dad as we entered. "There he is, waving his hands frantically, way up near the front behind the reserved seats." I pointed as I spoke to Emma and Katie. I laughed. "He reminds me of a lone survivor on an island waving to be rescued." I waved back, and we began making our way toward him. Nearly every few steps, I'd run into a proud parent whose son I'd had in PE or math class or who had met me at one time or another. Emma and Katie held my hands as we pushed through the waves of people.

About halfway to Dad, I stopped and put Katie on my shoulders, so she could see all the commotion from a higher vantage point and enjoy the moment.

"Son, you finally made it. I wasn't sure if I could hold these seats much longer." Dad was thrilled and doubly proud of George, but he was not quite as animated as some of the parents. He smiled as we got closer to the spot. It was in the furthest row forward, directly behind the graduates' seating. He had saved us three places there. He must have gotten there pretty early to get that spot. He smiled again as we got to the seat.

As we finally got settled, Dad smiled as he whispered to Emma and me, "People were giving me some funny looks as I tried to lay something on each chair to show it was taken."

Dad hugged me and grabbed Katie from my shoulders, and gave her a big hug too. Then he reached across us to greet Emma, grabbing her hand for a moment. Emma responded in kind but seemed a bit out of breath, and her face was flushed.

"Are you OK?" I asked her as she released Dad's hand.

"Yeah," she smiled as she responded, "it's just a little hot in here with all these people. Think I'll go grab some water in the lobby." She smiled again and turned, and began to make her way back through the crowd. I was a little worried about her but let her brave the crowd again.

As I turned back to the front of the gym, I tried to get a glimpse of George and Brit. I happened to catch George as he was scanning around the room, probably looking for us. I waved, and he finally saw me. A smile grew on his face as he looked at me, and he yelled and raised one fist into the air. I laughed and raised a fist back at him. He nudged Brit, who was next to him, and she turned and saw me and waved. I had never seen her so happy.

George and Brit were seated way up front and not in their normal alphabetical order. The principal had broken protocol this year and was going to allow Brit to go up to get her diploma right after the honor students since she was ready to have that baby any moment, it seemed, and so she would not have to stand and wait too long. He also let George accompany her to help her up and down the stairs to the platform. So, they would both receive their diplomas, kind of together, and then would proceed right out the side door. Jim, the principal, although generally a bit of a hard man and stickler for rules and propriety, seemed really impressed with Brit for her choice to have the baby and stick out

Convenience

the rest of the year—and graduate. He was also impressed with George, who chose to stick with Brit through it all. And actually, they both had become a sort of an item with all the students. They had become, well, a source of hope, a good news story. They reminded everyone of a day when people were less focused on just themselves.

Emma finally made her way back to her seat. Her face was still unusually red, but she reaffirmed that she was OK. As I looked down the row when Emma came back, I noticed Brit's Mom, who must have also gotten here really early. She was in the same row. I waved at her, and she waved back. She was beaming with joy and pride. I wondered at times if she thought she'd ever see this day.

Things got quiet as the principal made his way to the stage. Soon everyone was seated, and the ceremony began. The student leader made his way first to the podium, welcoming everyone and offering a short speech. I wasn't sure if I heard one word of what he said as my mind wandered off, studying the crowd and thinking of the events of the day and year. After the student finished, it was Jim, the principal's turn to speak. Again, even as cognizant as Jim was of keeping things short and moving along, he couldn't help but expound on a "short" review of the year. I drifted off again, but Jim brought me back as I heard him mention George and Brit.

"As many of you know," Jim said, giggling, "I'm quite a stickler for protocol and, well, doing things right and orderly and professional. Well, I guess I've grown a bit soft in my old age. Although not in normal order, I'm going to let Ms. Brit Johnson and Mr. George Bell come up to receive their diplomas right after the honor students. Brit is due to have her baby any time now, and I don't want to keep her in line any longer than we need to. George will accompany Brit to the stage directly after the honor students." He paused for a moment and looked out over the crowd, and cleared his throat. "As I said, I know I'm breaking protocol a bit, but this young couple so inspired me this year that I had to point them out and make an exception to our normal rules."

He seemed like he was going to move on to the next topic, but he paused for a second, took a deep breath, and looked out over the gym floor. Then he smiled and began to speak. "We all have our trials, and it just seems to me that, well, we've gotten busier and busier in life—I mean . . . me included. I feel like . . . well, we've gotten a bit out of focus in society." He got a puzzled look on his face and leaned into the podium, looking at us more intently as if he was speaking to each of us individually. "It's not like I remember when I was younger. I think we are losing our focus on community and on our fellow citizens. Anyway, I know I'll embarrass Brit, and for that, I apologize." He smiled again as he looked at Brit. "But I have to say this: thank you. Thank you for inspiring me this year."

He turned back to the full audience. "As I mentioned, Brit is pregnant." He paused again to gather his thoughts. "She could have taken the easy, more convenient way out and opted not to have this baby. She was doing well this year in all her subjects—even math." Jim smiled as he looked at Brit again, who was now turning many shades of red. "She really took a risk that she might fall behind in probably her best academic year and in her future. For that matter, George could have pursued the same, more convenient path. But he has stuck by Brit." He smiled at them. "Again, thank you both for inspiring me and all of us. You've been a bright spot for me and many others this year and a source of hope, commitment, and love."

He began to clap, and the whole place erupted into clapping and cheering. Feeling like he was losing control a bit, Jim quickly quieted the crowd and continued with his closure. "And so, now I'd like to start the final portion of our ceremony by calling each graduate to the podium to receive their diploma."

That was the honor students' cue to stand up and be ready to move when their names were called. I watched them stand and watched Brit and George stand too. It was so unreal and so awesome. As each made their way to the stage and up the stairs and then backed down, it seemed like Brit and George got more and more excited. Then, it was time for them to climb the stairs together. Jim called their names, and as they reached the top of the stage, I saw their beaming faces. The crowd cheered again as they walked across the stage. Jim shook their hands and wished them well with a big smile. As they moved across the stage, they stopped and faced the crowd—I have never seen happier faces. The

Convenience

crowd cheered louder as Brit raised her hand in victory. She smiled at her mother, who had tears streaming down her face. Then they turned and gently proceeded down the stairs and straight out the side door.

As they proceeded to the door, Emma leaned into me and told me she would go home with them and meet me there. She still wasn't feeling her best for some reason. I told her I'd stay and see her soon. So, they departed out the side door, and that was that. Dad and Katie, and I sat patiently through the rest of the students' ceremony. I couldn't help but thank God every few minutes for how awesome this all had turned out. I also wondered if Mom could see all this somehow. And I wondered if Dad thought the same. He was so proud of George and Brit.

Chapter Forty-Two

After the ceremony was finished, the noise of happy people and the shuffling of chairs broke out in a symphony of joy. I looked over at Brit's mom as she was standing by herself. Dad had an eye on Katie, so I walked over to Brit's mom.

"Hello, what a day, huh!" She looked at me and smiled.

"Yes, quite a day." She seemed to struggle to speak as though nearly all she had in her was drained from the rush of emotions. She quickly gathered herself though and looked at me. "Levi . . . I . . . I just want to say thank you again."

I stopped her mid-sentence. "Oh no," I said jokingly, with a smile. "Now I've heard enough of that, and it's my turn to say thanks. I want to thank you. You are the one who sacrificed all these years. You could have walked away from your pregnancy eighteen years ago and pursued your own desires. But you didn't. You raised a wonderful young lady. And I am sure it wasn't easy—not ever. So, I thank you for giving our family and us a wonderful—hopefully soon, wife for George. She has changed him into a great young man with unlimited potential instead of an angry, unsure, and unstable teen."

I continued to smile at her. But she just stared at me, keeping her expressionless face intact. *Did I say something wrong*, I wondered? Her half-smile faded a bit, and she began to quiver, which turned into tears rolling down her face. She reached out and hugged me and began to sob.

Again, was it something I said? I thought to myself. But then I realized it was actually just the outpouring of emotions and joy that she had to let loose.

I guess this was as good a time as any to ask her if she wanted to come over. "Would you like to come over for lunch today? We were gonna cook some burgers on the grill and make a salad and celebrate the graduation. You can ride with us."

She paused for a moment and responded. "Well, I'd like to, but I have to work today at four thirty."

"Oh, that's no problem," I responded. We can bring you back to your place by about three thirty or so if that works."

She smiled again, getting somewhat over her emotional release. "OK. I think I can do that, yes."

"All right then," I said.

Dad and Katie were catching up to me, and we all turned and joined the crowd, being herded out the exits. We had a great chat on the way home, and Brit's mom told us that she actually had Jim as an English teacher when she was in high school. "He didn't think much of me then, for sure. Guess I just didn't come from a great family. And now to have him honor Brit that way . . . well, it was such a great thing . . . a real thrill."

We made our way to the house, and as I parked the car in the driveway, I suggested we all surprise them with a shout as we entered, honoring the grads. We barged in the front door with big smiles, especially Katie, yelling and clapping. But all we saw was George standing in the hallway. He had a big grin on his face and began to chuckle as we got close to him.

"Brother, have you forgotten who you're dealing with here? My very pregnant Brit is lying down in Katie's room, taking a nap. And your wife, well, she went into her room to check on something, sat in your recliner . . . and fell asleep."

I looked at my fellow partiers, and we all had a good chuckle. I then offered, "I'll start the grill then and get some burgers on, and we can wake up the sleepy heads when the food is ready."

Brit's mom began making her way to the kitchen with Dad and Katie in tow. "I'll do the salad if that's OK," she said as she proceeded.

Convenience

"And I'll peel potatoes," Dad chimed in with a smile. They disappeared into the kitchen.

I looked at George and smiled. "Proud of you, brother." He didn't say anything and just smiled.

I got the grill going and smashed some hamburger meat, seasoned each patty, and put them on the grill. I could hear Dad, Katie, and Brit's mom talking in the kitchen. They seemed happy. George was talking to me but snuck off to check on Brit. I sat for a moment, thinking about the day and the year. Despite losing Mom and the others, I still thought about how good the Lord was and how far we all had come over the past year. Giving the burgers one final flip, I shut the grill off and stepped inside for a moment.

Seeing all was well, I snuck off to see Emma. She was still sound asleep. I hadn't seen her so tired before, but I guess the events of the day and the last few days had really worn on her. I decided to let her sleep a little more, covered her up with a blanket, and went back out to check on the food. As I was putting the burgers on a plate, two fingers poked at my ribs and almost made me drop the whole plate!

Emma cracked up behind me. "Whoops," she chuckled, "that would have been a bit of a disaster." I turned and laughed. As I put the plate down, I grabbed my beautiful wife.

"You shouldn't sneak up on a guy like that. He might drop everything and retaliate." We looked into each other's eyes for a moment.

Just then, George popped outside. "Hey, you two love birds gonna just stand there until the meat gets cold?"

We broke from our trance, giggling a bit, and looked at George. I yelled back, "Just getting the food that I worked so hard to prepare for you, brother." We headed toward the door with the goods.

As we entered, we were met with smiles from the kitchen and Brit's mom setting the table. It was so nice to see us happy and together . . . and celebrating George and Brit's accomplishments. Even with all the challenges of the year and all that seemed to have been working against them, they won. Despite all the losses this year, especially the loss of precious life, we were celebrating new life. Brit had been told only this last week that she was carrying a little boy.

As I was lost in my own little world for a moment, Brit came around the corner, all smiles and beaming with joy. She had been cheered in the gym with the most sincere, supportive, and respectful cheers—something she had likely never experienced before. I remembered for a second her mother, in the gym watching all that, tears running down her face, so happy that her daughter was being honored. Back to reality, I looked around the room and just took in the moment, all smiles—something I hadn't seen for a while, especially since Mom's passing. I thought to myself, *"Thank you, Lord; you are so good."*

"Hey, love," George spoke out as he grabbed Brit and gave her a hug. "Missed you." Smiling, he continued. "I had to make sure everyone out here was behaving. Emma was trying to make Levi drop the burgers, and your mom was tossing salad all over the place.

Brit just looked at George with a grin. "You saved us . . . I guess . . ."

We all got a good laugh as we finished setting the table and sat down to eat. As we sat down and looked around at each other, things got quiet for a moment. I didn't like when that happened because we all would get a moment to think about the one who was missing from our ranks. That still hurt all of us a bit.

But I knew they were waiting for me to pray. So, I didn't hesitate; grabbing Emma and Katie's hands, I prayed: "Dear Lord, so much has happened over this year. And as I look around at your wonderful springtime day, I can't help but feel how much you love each of us. Thank you for all you've blessed us with and for your strong and mighty arm that stretches out around us . . . we feel it. Amen."

We all dug in but were still quiet; George broke in with a comment as he bit into a hot dog. "Hey brother, are you sure you didn't drop this?" Everyone laughed as we enjoyed our time together with lots of small talk and a review of the graduation and plans for the future.

After we finished our late lunch, a bit of exhaustion set in. It had been a long day, and even with Emma and Brit napping a little earlier, we all were ready to rest a while. Emma made Dad some take-home leftovers as he looked for his car keys. I could see on his face how he enjoyed his day with his family, but at the same time, I could see his more somber focus now on returning to his empty house. He smiled and thanked everyone,

Convenience

hugging Brit and George and congratulating them one more time as he departed. Brit and her mom also began to gather their things as George prepared to take them back to their house. They made a quick exit since Brit's mom had to get ready for work, and Brit needed an evening of rest.

As we watched them drive off, Katie grabbed my hand and smiled at me. I reached down and picked her up in my arms. I swung her around the living room as if we were dancing and sang about the great day we had. Emma stopped us for a second.

"May I cut in?" she asked with a smile. "Well . . . no," I responded, "but you can join us!" The three of us did a few more rounds around the living room. What a great day it was . . . what an amazing year it had been . . . and what a great start to our summer.

Chapter Forty-Three

"Hey, little guy." I tapped on the glass. "Hey, Levi . . . or . . . Levi Junior, that is. Do you think he can see me? I mean, you know, do you think he can tell I'm family?"

Emma giggled and responded. "Levi, you know how people say they weren't born yesterday?" Emma giggled again. "Well," she looked at her watch, "actually, yeah, 12:05 a.m., little Levi *was* born yesterday." She laughed again, and I laughed with her.

"OK, OK, so I'm a getting a little silly here; but it's been a long, long day, and he is, after all, my first nephew . . . and . . . George and Brit did name him after me. How cool is that!"

I looked at Emma as I spoke and noticed that she had a funny smile on her face—one that made me wonder what she was thinking. I lowered my eyebrows as I returned the gaze.

After I finished staring at Emma, I continued. "So glad that Brit and George are finally getting some sleep." I turned back to the glass partition and began to tap on it again. "Hey guy . . . really, Emma, don't you think he knows I'm family?" I glanced at Emma and did a double-take.

She still had that weird grin on her face. She finally broke the silence and spoke to me with that funny smile still there. "Well, soon you'll get to know more about how babies react to you up close." She smiled even bigger.

Still oblivious, I responded, "Yeah, if they ever let me hold Levi Junior."

I looked back at Emma again. She was still smiling and staring at me. She finally spoke up again. "No, I mean, soon *you'll* get to know *again* how babies act firsthand!" She chuckled a little through her smile.

Finally making the connection, I looked back at her. My eyes got as big as silver dollars, and my mouth dropped open. "What . . . you . . . me?"

Emma nodded and smiled again in confirmation and touched her stomach. "Yep!!"

I forgot where I was for a second and yelled out loud, "Oh, oh, whoo-hoo!"

"Shhh," Emma responded with a smile. "You're gonna get us kicked out of here. It's midnight, you know."

"Oh, sorry." I looked away . . . and then back at Emma: "You . . . me . . . us?"

Emma giggled, "You said that already."

I just smiled back at her and raised my voice again, "Whoo-hoo!"

Just then, the older night shift nurse, with furrowed brow, looked around from her desk and gave me the stare of death. I looked back at her and responded in a whispering kind of yell, "Whoops, sorry. But I just found out we're gonna have a baby too!" The nurse's furrowed brow turned to a big smile. We all laughed, probably all now a bit too loudly.

Emma and I finally made our way to Dad's, where he and Katie had been for the evening. He was asleep, and Katie was long since asleep on the couch. We gently woke Dad, thanked him, and quickly left for home.

As I drove between those four tall cottonwood trees that always welcomed us into the neighborhood, it reminded me of the first time I drove up to the house a year ago when we first arrived. The events of the year quickly passed through my mind. I thought, how good and precious God is, how precious life that he created is! *"Thank you, Lord,"* I thought to myself. *"Bless you, Lord!"*

As I pulled up to the house, I guess it would have been more convenient to park along the curb facing the wrong direction . . . but I decided to take the less convenient option. I turned around in the street and parked facing the right way.

Final Thoughts

The impetus for *Convenience* was born years ago out of a Sunday School discussion about abortion as I listened to a young couple's opinion. They said ideally, couples should finish their higher education and get financially established before they have children. My first reaction was, "That makes sense to me." Then they shocked me. They gave an example of a married friend of theirs who was pregnant. They argued that an abortion might be OK since the couple was just starting out and would find it terribly inconvenient to have a baby at that point in their lives. They reasoned that the couple could do more justice for a future child once they had their education and finances where they wanted. I thank God for allowing me to hear that young couple's rationale and for putting the thought for this book in my heart.

The couple in my Sunday School class echoed the thinking of many in our society whose thoughts about abortion evolve with their ever-changing views on what is convenient. In earlier drafts of this book, I included a scene about a fictional situation in which society had deemed it acceptable to do day-of-birth abortions, thinking that was the most extreme position we would accept. At the time, I wondered if that was a little too far-fetched to include in the book. Yet today, there are some who have adjusted their thinking to the point that abortion that late in a pregnancy has become a goal and, in some areas, nearly a reality. How convenient! So, I had to adjust that scene to portray something even more extreme. I can only hope that such an extreme never becomes a reality, but there are some who might think that to be OK—for the sake of convenience, of course.

About the Author

The author was born in a small town in the Northwestern United States. He and his family have traveled the world and lived in Asia, Scandinavia, the Middle East, and various parts of the United States. He earned a bachelor's degree in political science and a master's degree in adult education. The author and his wife have served their country in the military and other venues for over forty years. Everywhere they lived, they worked in churches and helped with Christian projects, and they were blessed to meet many fascinating and wonderful people. They have four amazing children and eight equally amazing grandchildren. The author lives in Virginia with his wife and their youngest daughter where they enjoy access to the foundational history and heritage of America and the beautiful seasons God paints on the hills and valleys and shores.

www.ingramcontent.com/pod-product-compliance
Lightning Source LLC
Chambersburg PA
CBHW050519170426
43201CB00013B/2009